TOURISM MARKETING

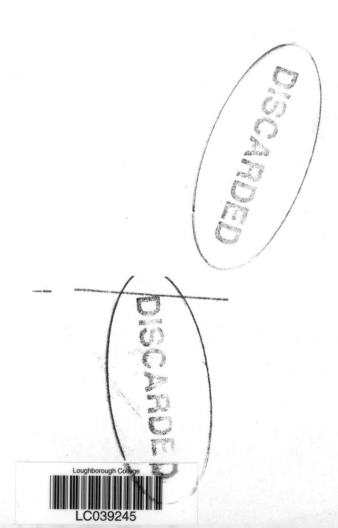

Tourism Marketing

Quality and Service Management Perspectives

Eric Laws

continuum
LONDON • NEW YORK

Loughborough
College

Continuum

The Tower Building   370 Lexington Avenue
11 York Road   New York
London SE1 7NX   NY 10017-65503
www.continuumbooks.com

First published 2002

British Library Cataloguing-in-Publication Data
A catalogue record for this book is available from the British Library.

ISBN: 0-8264-5335-X (hardback) 0-8264-5336-8 (paperback)

Typeset by YHT Ltd, London

Printed and bound in Great Britain by MPG Books Ltd, Bodmin

Contents

Author profiles

Eric Laws is Professor of Hospitality and Tourism Management at The Robert Gordon University, Aberdeen, Scotland. He is the author of some forty articles and five books, and he has edited four other books on tourism management. His research interests are in the meaning and management of tourism services quality, the impacts of tourism on destination areas and communities, and structural relations in the tourism industry. Eric regularly presents papers on these topics at international conferences and in seminars at universities in Europe, Asia and Austalia.

Ronnie Ballantyne is lecturer in Marketing within the Leisure and Tourism Management department at the Scottish Agricultural College, Ayr campus, and guest lecturer in Marketing to the Department of Business and Management at the University of Glasgow Business School. His specialist area of research is consumer brand choice and he is currently writing up his PhD in this area. He has presented papers on this research topic at international conferences in both Canada and the UK. Ronnie has also been a guest speaker on the use of brand image and brand personality within advertising campaigns at the Leo Burnett advertising company in Chicago, Illinois.

Agnes L. DeFranco is Associate Dean and Associate Professor at the Conrad N. Hilton College of Hotel and Restaurant Management at the University of Houston. Her interests in teaching excellence and improvements are evident in her early research work and her teaching awards. She has authored over 50 articles and a text on cost controls. Her research areas are hospitality education, finance, cost control, accounting and cultural issues.

Michele Grant is Consultancy Director for L&R Consulting, a tourism and leisure practice. She has worked in the tourism industry for over 13 years both as a consultant and with the English Tourist Board. Over the years she has developed specialist knowledge in visitor and destination management, in particular in historic towns. She has written numerous articles for various publications including the BTA Market Intelligence Publication *Insights*.

John Gountas lectures in Consumer Behaviour and Marketing Strategy at Deakin

University in Victoria, Australia. His research interests are in Consumer Behaviour, Market Segmentation and Marketing Strategy. The author wishes to thank Glenda Lamont and Helen Archibald from Air 2000, for all the assistance provided for the case study, which is the result of working together on various projects during the past two years.

Brian Human is Head of Policy and Projects in the Environment and Planning Department at Cambridge City Council. He has 30 years experience of work in the public sector in forward planning and tourism, paying particular attention to the need for integration between a wide range of activities. Particular interests are the relationship between tourism and place and the incorporation of tourism into the mainstream planning process. He is Chair of the English Historic Towns Forum Tourism Group, contributes to conferences on tourism issues and has written articles, including contributions to the BTA Market Intelligence Publication *Insights*.

Connie Mok was Associate Professor at the Conrad N. Hilton College of Hotel and Restaurant Management at the University of Houston. Dr Mok has extensive teaching, industrial, and consulting experience in the hospitality and tourism fields. She is the author or co-author of over 70 published articles in academic journals, conference proceedings, books, and trade journals.

Gianna Moscardo is a Principal Research Fellow at James Cook University. She leads a team of researchers in a series of projects focused on understanding nature-based tourism in general, with a particular focus on visitors to Australia's reef and rainforest world heritage areas. These projects investigate visitor expectations and motivations, decisions, satisfaction, and changes in their attitudes towards, and understanding of, conservation and minimal impact behaviours. Her disciplinary background is a combination of psychology and sociology and she has published more than 50 refereed academic publications. The research referred to in this case study was funded by the Cooperative Research Centre for the Great Barrier Reef World Heritage Area (CRC REEF) based at James Cook University.

Dr Francis P. Noe was an adjunct professor and continues to work with colleagues in the department of Hospitality and Tourism Management at Virginia Polytechnic Institute and State University, where customer satisfaction consumes his interest.

Barbara Le Pelley is a Principal Forward Planning Officer with the States of Guernsey. She has 27 years experience of working in the public sector in forward planning, economic development and tourism. Barbara has considerable practical experience in developing regeneration techniques through her work in East Kent. She regularly presents papers to tourism conferences and her contributions to books and articles include the BTA Market Intelligence Publication *Insights*.

Dr Harald Pechlaner currently holds the position of assistant professor at the Department of General and Tourism Management at the University of Innsbruck. Having worked as the managing director of South Tyrolean Tourism Board/Italy he is specializing in the field of tourism destination management.

Bruce Prideaux lectures in tourism at the University of Queensland, Australia. His teaching centres on tourism transport and distribution, tourism policy and Asian tourism issues. His principle research interests are issues pertaining to resort/destination development, tourism transport and distribution, issues in Asian tourism particularly in Korea, East Timor and Indonesia, regional tourism development and the future of tourism. He is a Fellow of the Chartered Institute of Transport in Australia, a member of the Queensland Korea Chamber of Commerce, Member of the Asia Pacific Tourism Association and Member of the Ecotourism Society of Australia. Prior to accepting the lecturing position, Bruce worked in various capacities in the Queensland Department of Transport.

Elmar Sauerwein currently holds the position of assistant professor at the Department of General and Tourism Management at the University of Innsbruck. He specializes in the field of customer satisfaction, doing research on methods for distinguishing product and service requirements in their impact on satisfaction. From January 2002 he has been Managing Consultant for Horváth and Partner in Munich taking responsibility for Customer Relationship Management.

Noel Scott was the Research and Strategic Services Manager for over five years at Tourism Queensland, the State Tourism Office for Queensland, Australia. He has extensive experience in strategic marketing, market research and consumer behaviour. He is currently studying for a PhD in Tourism and is the inaugural 'Martin Oppermann Memorial Scholarship' holder. His topic is 'Trends in Tourism'. He also holds a Masters of Business Administration and a Masters of Business (Marketing).

David Telfer is Associate Professor in the Department of Recreation and Leisure Studies at Brock University, Canada, where he is also the Co-ordinator of the Bachelor of Tourism Studies Degree. He teaches in the areas of tourism planning and heritage tourism. His research interests include linkages between tourism and development theories, economic linkages of tourism with host communities, strategic alliances and rural tourism.

John Tribe is Professor of Tourism and Head of Research in the Faculty of Leisure and Tourism at Buckinghamshire Chilterns University College, UK. He has authored books on strategy, economics and environmental management and research articles on service quality, epistemology and education in tourism. He has also led two major EU-funded projects in tourism.

Muzaffer Uysal is a professor of tourism in the department of Hospitality and Tourism Management at Virginia Polytechnic Institute and State University. His research interests centre on demand/supply interaction, international tourism and marketing.

Grace Wen Pan is a PhD candidate in tourism marketing at Griffith University, Australia. Her current PhD research project is mainly on business networks and the relationships associated with the Chinese inbound tourism market to Australia. In addition, her other areas of research interest are services marketing, international business, cross-cultural studies and tourism marketing.

Figures

Tables

Preface

This book argues that the main challenges facing providors of tourism services are to recognize and respond to their customers' service expectations. In part, expectations are built by marketing practices, particularly those related to the product's image, availability and pricing. For a business to get these right, it has to understand its own position vis-à-vis competitors and its customers' perceptions and behaviour. But customers are influenced by many factors which are beyond managers' control, such as their past experiences and their mood. The result is that each customer has a unique set of expectations regarding what he or she expects from a tourism service, and also evaluates their service experiences individually. Service that delights one customer may not impress a second and that same service could be considered unsatisfactory by a third client.

Another complicating factor for tourism managers and researchers is caused by the complexity of the industry. Typically, a holiday is purchased from a travel retailer, often after consulting many brochures and other sources of information. There is then an interval of weeks or even months before departure to the airport. There, the traveller has to deal with a bewildering variety of activities including checking in, passport control, security, gate controllers and so on before boarding the aircraft. During the flight, cabin crew perform a number of roles, and often it is only after collecting luggage on arrival that the client actually meets a member of the holiday company's staff (although often the transfer is conducted by a representative or handling agency). It is only then that the core of the holiday, the destination experiences and activities, begin. Hotel services, excursions and other activities are also provided by other companies, yet the client (and the law) considers that the travel retailer and tour operator are responsible for the quality of virtually all aspects of a holiday.

The discussion in this book ranges quite widely through the main components of the tourism industry, but concentrates attention on leisure tourism. Leisure tourism is discretionary on the part of the purchaser, it is quite complicated to purchase, the production and logistics of all arrangements and facilities needed by travellers are prone to disruption, and the effects of tourists' activities at their destinations have a variety of consequences for those areas; all these factors impinge on tourists' enjoyment of their holidays and are therefore aspects of tourism service quality.

In order to understand the mosaic of tourism service systems this book focuses on the customer's experiences and examines how some key decisions taken by tourism suppliers affect the customer's satisfaction through influencing his or her expectations or experiences. The book also considers some of the ways in which suppliers work together to provide cohesive images through which to promote their products, and to achieve consistent service standards. The book is organized in two sections, the first provides a selective introduction to quality and service management theory particularly as it applies to the marketing of tourism. The second section consists of twelve case studies illustrating how managers actually deal with some of the situations highlighted in the theoretical discussion. The case studies draw on current practice in the USA, Australia, Asia and Europe, and have been written for this book by experts in the topics they deal with. The case studies provide not only illustrations of a dozen interesting contemporary tourism situations from China, Korea, Australia, the USA and Europe, but also demonstrate the application of a range of analytical techniques to analyse the complex situations described. This is a dynamic field of study, factors such as developments in technology, competitors' improvements to their services and customers' expressed preferences for different styles of service produce a climate in which managers frequently adapt their ways of doing business, and within which they exercise their creative flair to meet new market opportunities.

As this book was nearing completion the New York World Trade Centre was destroyed by terrorists. The full ramifications of this event are not apparent at the time of writing, but the status of international tourism as a major world industry has been threatened, as it was by the Gulf War a decade earlier. Then, global tourism declined by 5 per cent, with US visitors to Europe down by 22 per cent, and the industry did not recover for three years. In 1997, some 58 tourists were killed during a coach tour to the Temple of Hatshepsut in Luxor, and as a result of the ensuing publicity, visits to Egypt declined by 14 per cent and tourist receipts dropped 45 per cent in 1998.

Against this background, the issues of service quality and customer satisfaction which are the themes of this book may appear to be quite trivial, but tourism is a resilient industry with the unique characteristic of moving people away from their homes for purposes of relaxation and enjoyment on a temporary basis. During their travels people from many cultures meet and through this, it is to be hoped, new friendships may be formed. Given time, this close contact may assist in weakening the grip over peoples' minds exercised by fundamentalist religious beliefs and simplistic appeals to nationalism that have led, throughout recorded history, to war. War, as I have pointed out in a previous book, is the antithesis of tourism, and hatred and distrust between races is less likely when direct relationships are established between people of different backgrounds in the friendly business context of tourism.

1 Tourism marketing, quality and service management theory

1 Marketing Tourism Services

Eric Laws

Introduction

A desire to understand quality in tourism service systems underlies this book. Interest in travel is as old as recorded history, but only recently has it become possible for large numbers of ordinary people to visit distant places for enjoyment. WTO (World Tourism Organisation) data documents the phenomenal growth of the new industry of tourism during the second half of the twentieth century. The rapid expansion of international leisure travel would not have been possible without a number of key enabling factors, particularly the availability of cheap aircraft at the end of the Second World War, the increasing prosperity of many people, and paid holidays. Modern mass tourism has its origins in Western Europe (see Bray and Raitz, 2001 for a personal account by Raitz, the man credited with originating the inclusive holiday package). Case study D provides an interesting contrast in documenting the rapid development now occurring in the latest and potentially greatest tourism market, China.

The establishment and development of a new industry require entrepreneurial vision and skills to identify innovative business opportunities and to stimulate demand for them. Three factors distinguish tourism from other major industries. The two considered in this book are the discretionary nature of tourism purchases and its characteristics as a service industry; together these present special challenges in marketing tourism. The third factor is the impacts of tourism on destination areas and communities, these are mentioned briefly. Readers interested in this important topic are referred to Laws (1995) and other specialist titles.

Tourism marketing

Marketing is widely regarded as the core business function concerned with matching the organisation's skills with market demand. 'The organisation's task is to determine the needs, wants and interests of target markets and to deliver the desired satisfactions more effectively and efficiently than competitors in a way that preserves or enhances the customers' and the society's well being' (Kotler, Haider and Rein, 1994:26).

4

In a very competitive and fast-changing market such as leisure tourism, deployment of the basic four marketing tools which feature in most introductory marketing courses (price, promotion, place or distribution, and product) is not sufficient. This is not to deny their importance. McDonald (1995) provides an excellent discussion of how each of the four Ps makes a significant contribution, both individually and in combination with others, to marketing strategy.

At a strategic level, marketing is about matching a company's abilities to the needs and interests of its customers, both existing and potential. Flair is required to present the product as different from its competitors in ways that appeal to customers, and most importantly a range of managerial skills is needed to ensure that customers' expectations of satisfying experiences are actually met, and quality services are provided.

Tourism promotion

Marketing promotions are intended to convey, in text and image form, information on which the potential consumer can choose between available products. But effective promotions are persuasive in their purpose and are intended to obtain the custom of selected client groups. This is achieved through positive influences on their perception. Perception is the basis for personal interpretation of the world. Given the wide range of stimuli we are exposed to, it has been argued that 'people tend to select from the myriad stimuli to which they are exposed those which appear to be relevant to their needs. Information, for example, will be filtered through the mesh of personal interests, attitudes, motivational structure, social background, and cultural influences. Existing personal cognitive structures will also affect … the individual' (Chisnall, 1985). By extension, perception is also important in the judgement consumers make of the quality of a product or service. Wilkie (1986) argued that two key factors determine how something is perceived: its stimulus characteristics and the characteristics of the consumer. He continues by indicating, 'The issue of which stimuli consumers choose to perceive becomes a key question.' The question of individually perceived service standards underlines the problem for managers seeking to design and deliver services satisfying the expectations of many clients. Others have discussed the significance of the point, and the difficulties which result. 'Customer perceived quality is rather a blend of objective facts and subjective judgements, of knowledge as well as ignorance. . . . Nor can manufacturers consider themselves experts . . . Quality has become an integrating concept between production orientation and marketing orientation' (Gummesson, 1988). Syzbillo and Jacoby (1974) have distinguished between internal cues, the specific characteristics of the product, and external cues including the price, brand images and promotional messages employed in its marketing. 'Either singly or in composite, such cues provide the basis for perceptions concerning product quality.'

Moving even further from the 'hard' and measurable concerns of much of the literature dealing with the management of quality, Campbell (1987) argued that day-dreaming and anticipation are central to the process of consumption in modern society. Satisfaction is not derived so much from the purchase and use or consumption of products, as from anticipation of pleasure. The basic motivation for consumption is to experience pleasure, but since reality is imperfect, each purchase leads (or has the potential to lead) to disillusionment. The significance of this for the consumerist gap study can be understood from arguments such as Urry's that most tourism purchases present a particular characteristic which make them prone to result in dissatisfaction for the client. They are

> constructed in our imagination through advertising and the media, and through the conscious competition between different social groups . . . Tourism daydreams are not autonomous, they involve working over advertising and other media generated sets of signs. Almost all the services provided to tourists have to be delivered at the time and place at which they are produced. As a consequence, the quality of the social interaction between the provider of the service, such as the waiter, flight attendant or hotel receptionist, and the consumers, is part of the product being purchased by tourists. If aspects of the social interaction are unsatisfactory . . . then what is purchased is in effect a different service. The problem results from the fact that the production of such consumer services cannot be entirely carried out backstage, away from the gaze of the tourist. (Urry, 1990)

The promotion of tourism products is undertaken by both private and public sector organizations (with increasing involvement of not-for-profit operators such as museums). Various aspects of the dynamic relationships between these is examined in case studies E, F, G, J, K and L.

Travel distribution channels

The term 'distribution channel' describes the formal business structures through which consumers obtain products or services from producers. In a service industry such as tourism the flows are movements of information and finance rather than the items sold, and include the bringing together of the various services which principals provide within the convenient umbrella of a packaged holiday.

Channel management tasks for a tour operator include setting up discount structures to reward and motivate channel members and their staff, organizing the logistical services required to distribute brochures and other sales support through the system so that it is available to potential clients. In tourism retailing, brochures are one of the main bases on which clients make their decisions, and they also include the booking forms that function as a contract between clients and travel organizations. These tasks are continuous, the need to work with their retail partners beginning again for tour operators about the time when the coming season's brochures are finalized. The need arises from the specialized nature of the contributions to tourism distribution made by tour operators in creating the packaged holiday product, and by the travel retailers who stimulate customers' interest, deal with their queries and process their bookings (Buhalis and Laws, 2001).

Table 1.1 Factors constraining travel principals' dealings with consumers and the roles of travel retailers

Factor	Travel agents' functions
Distance	Outlets located in customers' vicinity
Time	Provide facilities for advanced reservations
Information	Provide comprehensive information

Table 1.1 lists some of the factors constraining effective communication between travel principals such as tour operators and their customers, indicating the ways in which travel retailers help bridge these gaps. Tour operators and travel retailers are therefore in a synergistic business relationship.

Retail travel agents

Retail travel agents earn commission from the travel principals whose products they sell. From a consumer's perspective, they provide easy access to information through their high-profile presence in shopping centres, through brochures and advice about a wide range of destinations spanning the globe. The principals can gain a detailed and rapid understanding of consumers' fast-changing holiday preferences through analysis of the requests for information and the bookings which travel agents undertake. Retail travel agents therefore play crucial roles in the tourism distribution system, and are the predominant point of contact between travellers and travel suppliers (Holloway and Robinson, 1995).

Many full service travel agencies evolved into more specialized 'holiday shops' and a further development saw them becoming selective about which tour operators' products to offer. This can be understood at two levels, in the first place they choose which brochures to display on their racks or to feature in window displays. Secondly, many agencies keep additional brochures in their files, from which they sell on request. These are usually from small or specialized tour operators whose sales potential for the agency is quite limited. However, by filing these brochures rather than openly displaying them, the opportunities for customers to consider what they have to offer is reduced.

The primary rationale for any business partnership is mutual benefit. An agency may promote one tour operator in the hope that it can create a high level of sales which will result in better support in terms of staff training, brochure supplies and higher levels of commission or overrides. This arrangement is sometimes linked to an exclusive local deal whereby only one agency racks a particular brochure in the town, or where competing brochures are not racked in that agency. But bad experiences with a particular company can result in the agency's decision not to deal with it any longer. Relevant factors include relatively low commission rates, difficulties in collecting commissions, and consumers' complaints about their holiday experiences.

Integration in travel distribution

During the last two decades of the twentieth century, vertical and horizontal integration has occurred in travel distribution to rationalize the ownership of retail travel outlets so that they are more effective in selling the services of the major tour operators. Some of the most well-known travel retailers are in fact owned by large tour operators, forming integrated travel companies (see Bywater 2001 for an analysis of the European tourism industry). This provides their owners with several advantages, including the maximum retention of profits within the group, enhanced selling strength for the holiday brands which results from inhouse retailing, reduced outlets available for competitors' brands, and opportunities for improvements in retail staff training in the tour operator's own brands, products and business systems. The integrated travel companies have more rapid access to information on constantly changing market conditions, and can therefore make informed decisions about when, and by how much, to adjust prices or which resorts or departures to promote at particular times. Buhalis and Laws (2001) note the concerns which have been expressed by consumer groups and regulatory bodies that the overall effect is to reduce the choice available to consumers. Trade bodies are concerned about the future prospects for smaller companies, both retailers and tour operators, in a market dominated by the continuing growth in power of integrated, and increasingly multinational, organizations. This point is significant in the discussion of tourist service quality as many complaints appear to stem from mis-sold package holidays in the sense that customers' expectations were unduly raised.

Buying decisions

The key functions of tourism distribution are to provide consumers with information and to influence their choice of holiday product by making them more aware of the particular holiday, destination, activity or attraction (Woodside and Sherrell, 1977). Understanding consumers' information-search behaviour is crucial to strategic decision-making (Uyssal and Fesenmaier, 1993). Consumer preferences are about choice between what is available in the market, but also reflect what consumers consider to be 'ideal' products, a concept combining image and expectation which is discussed later. There is a potential risk that the holiday experience may not match what the consumer had anticipated. The general marketing services literature indicates that more intensive search activity for decision-making information occurs when risk rises (Murray, 1991).

Travel decision-making processes have been the subject of considerable research, but there is little consensus beyond the broad elements which influence most holiday-makers. The field of literature has been well summarized in several recent papers including Moorthy, Ratchford and Talukdar, (1997) and Fodness and Murray (1997). There is still debate over the ordering of the choice of elements in a holiday (where to go, where to stay and how to travel); the relative influence of decision-makers in a family or a group of friends, and the trade-off between the effort invested in searching for information compared to the relief that a decision has been made, often followed by searches for more specific information regarding what to do during the destination stay. See case chapters E, G, I, J, L, and Chapter 4 for discussion of further issues relating to destination choice.

Pricing tourism services

Price is one of the major marketing tools used in tourism, but its implications for tourism service quality are seldom analysed in tourism text books. The price of a product has differing significance to its producer and its consumers. For businesses, the total sum paid in a period by all purchasers of its products is its main source of funds to defray operating expenses, grow the business and return a profit to its owners. From a customer's perspective payment for one item has the effect of reducing the money available for all other purchases. In combination, these two points underlie one of the fundamental models in economic theory, Marshall's explanation of the market clearing mechanism through which supply and demand are brought into equilibrium by aggregate responses to price signals. A higher price stimulates increased output, but it generally restricts the level of demand. Price has further functions in the contemporary varied and dynamic marketplace. Of particular significance is the way in which relative price may act as a signal of quality to consumers and influence their purchasing decisions. Furthermore, most organizations market a range of products at various stages of their life cycle, each facing different levels of competition, so that each may be priced on different criteria. The decisions which an organization adopts to pricing its services are taken in the context of its overall aims as McCarthy and Perreault (1988) have pointed out.

> Managers develop a set of pricing objectives and policies in the context of the company's objectives. The policy explains how flexible prices are to be, the level at which they will be set over the life cycle of the service, and to whom and when discounts will be allowed.

One of the most visible features of the tourism marketplace is the high level of competition between tour operators, airlines, hotel groups and travel retailers based on price, evident in their advertising and in retailers' shop windows. Medlik (1993), noting that price competition features strongly in the travel industry, defined this as a

> [m]arket situation in which firms compete on price rather than quality of product or other factors to influence the buyers' choice ... Price competition is sometimes chosen as a deliberate strategy but often is the result of unforeseen market conditions, in which planned capacity or sales exceed actual demand.

The immediate result of low prices has been to stimulate demand for holidays currently on offer, however there is also evidence of effects with long-term significance for the industry. Low prices have altered the timing of demand, for example by extending the holiday season, and have changed the demographic profile of holiday-makers, to include all age groups and most socioeconomic sectors of society. Low prices have also been the locus of power plays between competing companies and between the various organizations in the holiday industry system. Several major companies including tour operators and charter airlines have failed, and there have been many take-overs and mergers between tour operators, travel retailers and charter airlines. Not all of these events can be ascribed to the results of pricing policy, but by putting the customers' focus at the point of holiday purchase on price comparisons rather than distinctive destination or activity features, they contribute to the commoditization of holiday destinations noted and criticized by many analysts of the industry, notably Krippendorf (1987), Urry (1990) and McCannell (1992). See Chapter 4 for a fuller discussion.

Pricing inclusive holidays

One of the most common ways of setting holiday price differentials is the seasonal banding typical of tour operators' brochures and familiar to all who purchase inclusive holidays, in the form of price and departure-date price matrices. The peak season is when limited discounting is undertaken because many holiday-makers are willing to pay premium prices. This is shown in Figure 1.1 as the broad central column, flanked by two shoulders of unequal width representing the early and late seasons. The more restricted nature of demand during the shoulder seasons limits opportunities to charge premium prices, but offers scope to stimulate market demand through a variety of discounting practices. In contrast to the generalized three-season price banding modelled in Figure 1.1, it should be noted that tour operators' brochures typically band their holidays into up to a dozen seasonal prices.

Middleton (1991) identified eleven influences on the prices of tourism products, including high price elasticity in discretionary segments, fixed capacity, high customer psychological involvement, high fixed costs, long lead times between price decisions and product sales, and short-run crisis management. Duadel and Vialle (1994) distinguished between 'spoilage' – the under-utilization of resources, and 'spill' – selling too cheaply early, with the result that later, higher yielding demand has to be denied. They argued in favour of yield-management techniques, using price to balance the market conditions of supply and demand. The principle of price setting for optimum yield management is based on setting various thresholds to segment customers' varying ability or willingness to pay. The relevant thresholds reflect assumptions about price-related differences in buying behaviour, particularly in respect of seasonal choices, late or early booking habits, and departure airport preferences. These can be modelled by analysis of the company's historic data (Relihan, 1989; Laws, 1998, price).

The complexity of pricing packaged holidays for a tour operator has been highlighted by Holloway and Robinson (1995). Robinson was the Group Marketing Manager of First Choice, one of Britain's leading tour operators, and the authors noted that the company:

> 'produced some 2300 brochure pages for the summer 1995 season. Most featured a price panel with perhaps 100 separate prices, making a total of almost a quarter of a million prices.' First Choice's pricing was based on a straightforward cost-plus approach, but it also reflected a range of objectives for different products, such as to regain market share in specific resorts. Further adjustments were made to achieve an overall price advantage: 'the brochure price is determined, but so too is the proposed policy on early booking discounts, child discounts, late sales reductions, travel agent commission incentives and the like. This is because the overall profitability target of the programme must be set against the actual sales price likely to be achieved.'

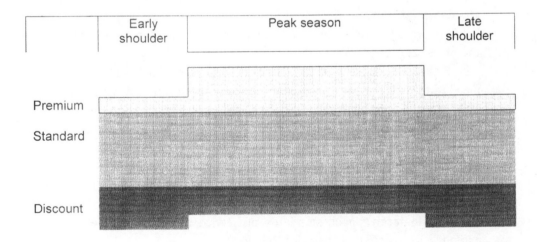

Figure 1.1 A general model of seasonal price banding

Price relativity as a signal of product quality

From the perspective of service quality, price should be seen as a relative measure of the value of a holiday. Garvin (1988) noted that 'it seems to be difficult to determine a generally valid link between price and quality'. Value is generally regarded as meaning the delivery of more of some desired attributes of the service than the customer expected. In the short term this may occur as a result of deliberately underpromising, or it may result from higher than normal performance in the service delivery system. The longer-term significance is that experience of superior service raises customers expectations for future services.

Kimes (1994) has noted that consumers accept yield management in the airline sector, where they receive specific benefits if they accept certain restraints, for example the right to alter flight arrangements after a booking is made. However, she raised the question of how customers react to it in other industries, suggesting that 'a customer who pays more for a similar service and cannot perceive a difference in the service may view the situation as unfair'. Kimes developed her argument on the basis of a reference price, derived from market prices and the customer's previous experience. At a normal (or reference) price, a high standard of service and amenities will please the client, but those same standards will only satisfy clients paying premium rates. Customers enjoying normal or superior standards on a holiday for which they paid low prices will be pleased, or delighted. In contrast, customers receiving normal levels of service in return for high prices will feel at best exploited, and if standards fall further, they are likely to experience (and express) anger. Low levels of service or amenities are likely to provoke negative responses whatever the price paid for them.

Figure 1.2 suggests that customers who receive a level of service commensurate with the price they paid are likely to be satisfied with that service. They expect a 'normal' level of service if paying a 'standard' price, but anticipate better service when paying a premium. If a customer buys a discounted holiday but receives superior service he or she is likely to be delighted, but in contrast someone buying an expensive holiday and getting poor service will probably react angrily. The high incidence of complaints about low standards for discounted holidays can be understood in terms of Figure 1.2 which suggests that clients who receive poor standards of service are likely to feel angry and exploited irrespective of the price they paid.

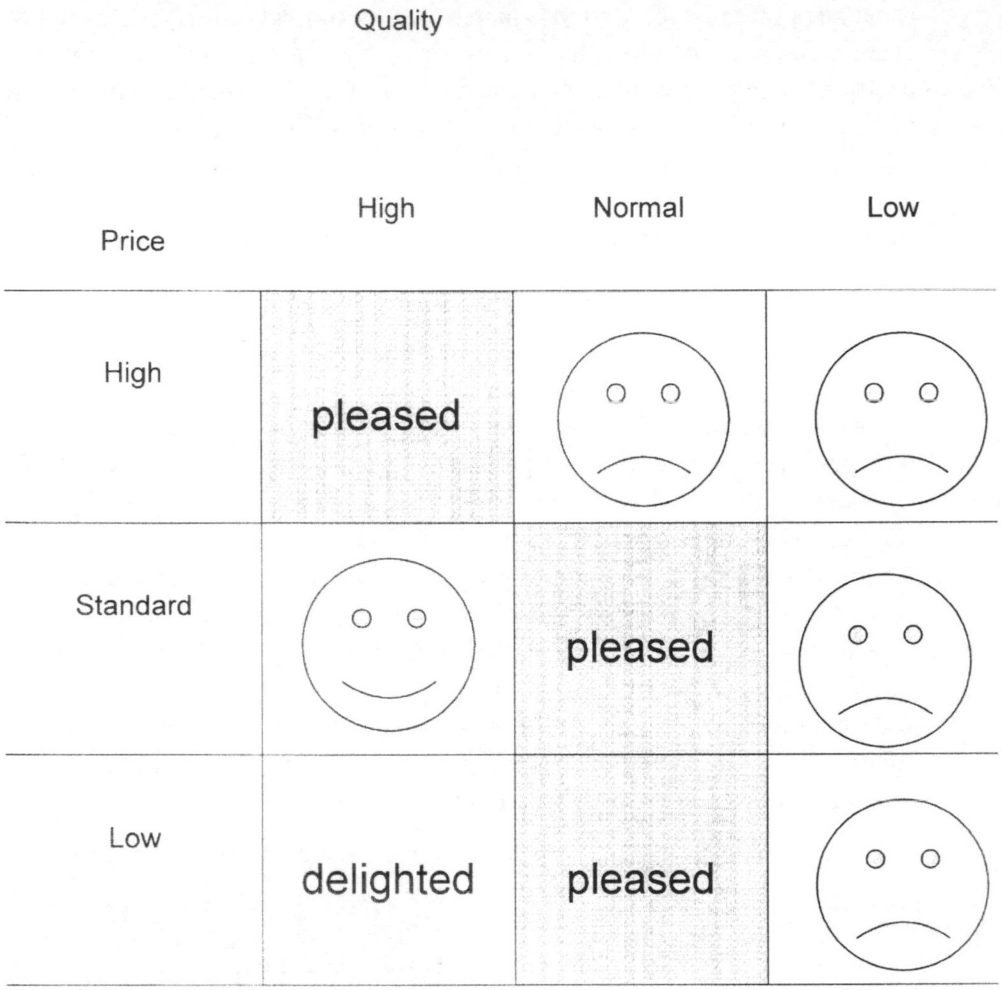

Quality

Price	High	Normal	Low
High	pleased	🙁	🙁
Standard	🙂	pleased	🙁
Low	delighted	pleased	🙁

Figure 1.2 Tourist consequences of differing price/quality combinations

Core and enhanced services

Tourism companies can make their service different from competitors through enhancements to the basic service. Marketing theorists have pointed out that all purchases are made to satisfy needs. Any item purchased must be able to perform the function claimed of it, and for which it was primarily acquired; this is the core of the product. Thus, the core of an airline's market offering is its capability of transporting its clients safely from airport A to airport B at the times agreed. However, all airlines have this capability, and it seems that consumers often have in mind a more complex concept, one which includes a wider range of benefits. It has also been argued that customers buy a total package having the combined characteristics of solving their purchasing problems. It is these additional features of products which are the locus of competition: 'The new competition is not between what companies produce in their factories, but between what they add ... in the form of packaging, services, customer advice, financing ... and other things that people value' (Levitt, 1969).

The core service is the basic market competency of the firm, but it is insufficient as the basis for commercial success. In common with most other businesses, airlines offer more than basic transport in an attempt to succeed against competition, whether from other airlines or alternative modes of transport. The enhanced airline product includes physical comfort to specified standards, inflight entertainment and stylish, appetizing meal or beverage service. Other improvements to the basic transport service include airport facilities, and special attention to passengers' individual needs as each airline seeks to create an image as part of its marketing strategies to distinguish its appeal from other airlines. As Kotler and Armstrong (1987) put it, 'to best satisfy customers, the producer has to offer an augmented product'. For airlines, additional features of their service may include attention to individual wishes, enhanced comfort, varied menus, inflight entertainment, frequent flier schemes or improved procedures at their terminals.

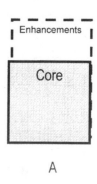

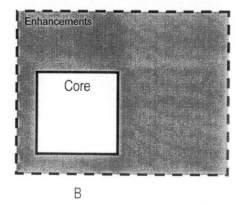

A   B

Figure 1.3 Core and enhanced tourism services

Figure 1.3 shows how one company (A) might develop one dimension of its core service with selected enhancement, while in a contrasting approach all aspects are enhanced by company B. Here, the enhancements are given greater prominence than the (still essential) core service.

Given the purpose of enhancements to the core service, it is important to select features which will attract customers. A variety of formal research techniques such as focus-group work, participant observation and content analysis of customer correspondence can provide realistic and revealing insights into what is significant from the customers' perspectives. Another approach is to identify aspects of the current service which consumers do not enjoy in order to improve them. Service blueprinting and consumerist-gap methods can be used to generate data of this type which can help prioritize those aspects of the service requiring development or attention. These are discussed later.

Differentiating tourism services

The vision of its service enables one organization to present its service with a special style which clearly distinguishes it from the ways in which its competitors operate. Three aspects have to be considered when differentiating a service in tourism, as shown in Table 1.2.

Table 1.2 Differentiating tourism services

Points of differentiation	Tour operator example
Service strategy	Provide good hotels in smaller resorts
Service delivery system	Available through multiple outlets and direct, local departures, convenient journey times
The people who deliver the service	Resort representatives selected for their knowledge of and enthusiasm for the area, as well as for skills and experience.

(Based on Thomas, 1987).

As examples of service-style differentiation, staying in a Sheraton hotel does not give the same experience as staying in a Hilton, and it is not intended to. However, staying in a second Sheraton, even in another country, *is* intended to provide the customer with a similar experience to his or her stay in the first Sheraton. Similarly, a flight between America and Europe on British Airways is not intended to give the same experience as a transatlantic journey on KLM, Olympic, United or Air New Zealand. In both these examples the core of the service provided to customers is very similar, staying in a good hotel is essentially about getting a good night's sleep, crossing the Atlantic is mainly about getting safely and quickly to the opposite shore. Differentiation is therefore a key strategy used by managers to attract clients in a competitive market. The tools available include price, convenience, comfort and brand image, or some combination of these.

Brand management is increasingly recognized as a strategic management tool rather than as an abstract concept (Lawson and Balakrishnan, 1998). Branding is about developing the consumers' attitudes towards the firm. Managers can select one of three approaches to branding consistent with either functional, symbolic or experiential concepts.

Style differences are important in 'positioning' a service. The basis of market positioning is to identify some key performance dimensions which influence customers' purchasing and consumption preferences, such as degree of luxury, or cost. These are used to calibrate the axes of a map (see Figure 1.4), and competitors' services are located according to their perceived performance on each characteristic. Market analysts can then gain a visual impression of where the market is not well served, and adapt or position their services into the most advantageous position, taking into account the strength of demand, degree of competition and the likely profitability of each possible mix of service criteria. The strategy is generally used aggressively against competitors, but it is also becoming seen as a way of forming business partnerships for destination operators, see Case Chapters C and J.

Conclusion

This chapter has provided a summary of marketing practice in relation to tourism service quality. It has shown that decisions about how to promote or what price to sell holidays at are quite fundamental to the management of service quality, and to customer satisfaction. The chapters which follow in Part 1

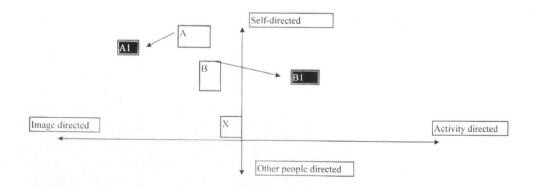

Figure 1.4 Positioning a package-holiday concept (based on Laws, Scotland Parfitt, 2002)

proceed to analyse in more depth the meaning of service quality and to examine some of the tools available for managers (and researchers) wishing to better understand these issues. Part 2 provides a series of case studies illustrating aspects of tourism services marketing practice.

Bibliography

Bray, R. and Raitz, V. (2001) *Flight to the Sun*. Continuum, London.

Buhalis, D. and Laws, E. (eds) (2001) *Tourism Distribution Channels: Practices, Issues and Transformations*, Continuum, London.

Bywater, M. (2001) 'Who owns whom in the European travel distribution industry?' In Buhalis, D. and Laws, E., eds (2001) *Tourism Distribution Channels: Practices, Issues and Transformations*, Continuum, London.

Campbell, C. K. (1967) 'An approach to research in recreational geography', *Occasional Papers no. 7*, Department of Geography, University of British Columbia, Vancouver, pp. 85–90.

Chisnall, P. (1985) *Marketing, a Behavioural Analysis*. London: McGraw Hill.

Duadel, S. and Vialle, G. (1994) *Yield Management: Applications to Air Transport and Other Service Industries*. Paris: Institut du Transport Aerien.

Fodness, D. and Murray, B. (1997) 'Tourist information search', *Annals of Tourism Research* 24 (3), 503–23.

Garvin, D. A. (1988) *Managing Quality, the Strategic and Competitive Edge*. New York: Free Press.

Gummesson, E. (1988) 'Service quality and product quality combined', *Review of Business*, 9 (3).

Holloway, J. C. and Robinson, R. (1995) *Marketing for Tourism*, 3rd edn. Harlow: Longman.

Kimes, S. E. (1994) 'Perceived fairness of yield management', *Cornell H.R.A.* Quarterly, February.

Kotler, P. (1998) *Marketing*. 4th edn. New York and Sydney: Prentice.

Kotler P. and Armstrong, G. (1999) *Principles of Marketing*. International edn. London: Prentice Hall.

Kotler, P., Haider, D. and Rein, I. (1994) *Marketing Places*. New York: Free Press

Krippendorf, J. (1987) *The Holiday Makers*. London: Heinemann.

Laws, E. (1995) *Tourist Destination Management: Issues, Analysis and Policies*. London: Routledge.

— (1998) 'Package holiday pricing – cause of the IT industry's success, or cause for concern?' In Baum, T. and Mundambi, R. (eds), *Tourism Industry Economics*. Chichester: Wiley. pp. 197–214.

Laws, E., Scott, N. and Parfitt, N. (2002) 'Synergies in destination image management: a case study and conceptualisation', *International Journal of Tourism Research*, 4, 39–55.

Lawson, R. and Balakrishnan, W. (1998) 'Developing and managing brand image and brand concept strategies', *American Marketing Association* (Winter), 121–6.

Levitt, T. (1969) *The Marketing Mode*. New York: McGraw Hill.

MacCannell, D. (1992) *Empty Meeting Grounds, the Tourist Papers*. London: Routledge.

McCarthy, E. and Perreault, W. (1988) *Essentials of Marketing*. Homewood, Ill.: Irwin.

McDonald, M. (1995) *Marketing Plans: How to Prepare Them, How to Use Them*. Jordan's Hill, Oxford: Butterworth Heinemann.

Medlik, S. (1993) *Dictionary of Transport, Travel and Hospitality*. Oxford: Butterworth Heinemann.

Middleton, V. T. C. (1991) 'Marketing the margin', *Quarterly Review of Marketing*, Winter, 14–17.

Moorthy, S. Ratchford, B. and Talukdar, D. (1997) 'Consumer information search revisited: theory and empirical analysis', *Journal of Consumer Research*, 23 (March), 263–77.

Murray, K. (1991) 'A test of services marketing theory: consumer information acquisition activities', *Journal of Marketing*, 55 (January), 10–25.

Relihan, III, W. (1989) 'The yield management approach to hotel pricing', *Cornell HRA* 30 (1), May, 40–5.

Syzbillo, G. and Jacoby, J. (1974) 'Intrinsic and extrinsic cues as determinants of perceived product quality, *Journal of Applied Psychology* 59, 74–7.

Thomas, M. (1987) 'Coming to terms with the customer', *Personal Management* (24–28 February).

Urry, J. (1990) *The Tourist Gaze*. London: Sage Publications.

Uyssal, M. and Fesenmaier, D. R. (eds) (1993) *Communication and Channel Systems in Tourism Marketing*. New York: Haworth Press Inc.

Wilkie, W. (1986) *Consumer Behaviour*. Chichester: Wiley and Sons.

Woodside A. and Sherrell, D. (1977) 'Traveller evoked, inept and inert sets of vacation destinations', *Journal of Travel Research*, 16 (1), 14–18.

18

2 Services Marketing and Quality Theory

Eric Laws

Introduction

This chapter introduces service theory, differentiating it from more general management theory and relating it to the need in the tourism industry to manage their clients' expectations and experiences of the services they purchase.

Several concepts are introduced by which managers (and researchers) may understand their customers' perceptions of service events, and better understand the design and delivery issues in providing tourists with satisfying services.

Tourist satisfaction is examined in the framework of both services and quality management theory, with implications being drawn for appropriate ways to manage tourism organizations so that they focus most effectively on providing the customer with satisfying services.

Service theory

The theoretical and managerial marketing literature has come to accept that effective service-sector management requires specialized approaches which are generally thought to be less relevant in the manufactured sectors (Normann, 1991). The term paradigm is defined as 'a set of assumptions about the world which is shared by a community of scientists investigating the world' (Deshpande, 1983). The main paradigm in theories of marketing strategy has traditionally been the managerial requirement to bring potential clients to the point where the action of purchasing a product yields some benefit to the customer and profit to the vendor. More recently, it has been recognized that purchases are made to gain certain benefits from use or ownership, leading to the 'market orientation' paradigm, and it is this which underlies the concern in this book to define the conditions under which clients are more, or less, likely to purchase future tourism services from a particular business.

It has been argued that customers' experiences with any purchase give rise to outcomes for them varying from dissatisfaction to satisfaction. These are emotional responses, reflecting a divergence from expectations, as the following quotations indicate.

> The seeds of consumer satisfaction ... are planted ... during the prepurchase phase of the consumer decision process. (Wilkie, 1986)

> Satisfaction is defined ... as a postconsumption evaluation that the chosen alternative is consistent with prior beliefs and expectations (with respect to it) ... Dissatisfaction, of course, is that outcome when this confirmation does not take place. (Engel, Blackwell and Miniard, 1986)

Formal study of the services sector is relatively new. Several factors distinguish services from manufactured products, these are summarized in Table 2.1.

Table 2.1 Distinguishing services from manufactured products

Service characteristic	Service feature
Intangibility	The customer cannot sample a service before purchasing it
Inseparability	The customer is part of the service and interacts directly with the organization and its staff during the service
Heterogeneity	A particular service may be experienced differently by each client
Perishability	The organization cannot put an unsold service into storage

Cowell (1986) wrote of *heterogeneity* 'even though standard systems may be used, for example to handle a flight reservation ... each unit of service may differ from other units'.

Everyone experiences a given service differently due to their differing personalities, any previous experience of the type of service, its importance or urgency to them on the present occasion, their moods and so on. The general notion of heterogeneity is illustrated by the two faces in Figure 2.1. One customer is pleased with the service, while another is disappointed with his or her experience of the same service design and delivery system.

Perishability is a significant managerial problem, its meaning is that a service such as an unsold airline seat on a specific departure cannot be stockpiled for sale at a later date. Most service sectors, including hotels, restaurants

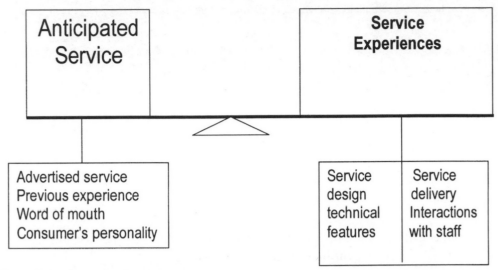

Figure 2.1 Enjoyment of services

and tourist attractions, experience the problem of perishability but also have to deal with the converse difficulties resulting from peak-period demand and congestion. The typical response is to discount prices as departure dates approach, or to charge a premium for peak-season travel. These policies have been very successful in stimulating sales and evening out the peak, but there are also some detrimental consequences which are discussed later.

Some authors have proposed a fifth factor distinguishing services from manufactures, *ownership*, but it has limited relevance to the issues examined here. Its meaning is that the customer does not obtain a legal title as a result of purchasing access to service facilities. Cowell (1986) points out that people attending a theatre don't purchase their seats in the sense that they could take them away with them after the performance. Similarly, hotel guests have access to their room only during the period they have paid for, and don't legally have the right to take towels or other room furnishings home with them!

The challenge of managing services

The distinctions noted above were important in helping the development of a separate field of study for services, and helped identify several general challenges facing service managers summarized in Table 2.2.

In summary, it had become clear by the 1980s that services were more complex, more variable and less easy to control than manufacturing due to two key differences, the ability to reduce (or even eliminate) production-staff

Table 2.2 Management challenges in manufacturing and services

	Manufacturing	Services
Consistent performance	Variances between models are minimized during manufacturing	Customer interaction with staff during service delivery makes it hard to achieve precise standards
Conformance to specification	Can be achieved through monitoring and sampling	Responsiveness to individual preferences are a feature of many services
Variegated product lines	Easy for manufacturers to segment their markets by offering different performance characteristics	Different levels of service are offered to each class of client at one time
Communicating performance features	Easy for manufacturers to specify performance or luxury features	Imagery and life-style appeals do not distinguish service features

judgements in manufacturing-production processes, and the absence of direct customer involvement in manufacturing production.

Another important difference is services' dependence on direct contact between staff and clients in the delivery of the service. In contrast, the manufacturing of most products occurs 'off-stage', remote from the view of customers. Although managers may wish to specify precise standards for their services, just as a production manager in a factory setting would be expected to, in reality each service transaction is itself a variable, and the quality of the service is dependent on the interaction between staff and client in the context of the physical setting and the technical features of the service delivery system designed by its managers. Furthermore, the quality is judged by each client while the service is occurring.

Experts including Shostack, Gronroos and others regard strategic service management as doing the right job, based on correctly evaluating what the customer expects, and creating service packages which reflect those expectations. The tactical requirements of operational service management are about doing the job right. 'Customer expectations must not only be met in service design, but also in service delivery, ensuring that the service package is provided without fault' (Horovitz and Panak, 1992). Garvin (1988) emphasized the need for market research if products are to offer the dimensions of quality that are of greatest interest to consumers and if they are to target a defensible quality niche. Similarly, Band (1991), arguing that organizations should create more value for their customers in order to remain competitive, has advocated the systematic examination of all facets of a company's operation to identify their contribution (active and potential, positive and negative) to customer satisfaction.

Performance criteria

It is common practice for managers to specify the technical performance goals for the main events in a service delivery system. A familiar example is the target of answering the office telephone before it has rung more than a given number of times, or of delivering a burger within a stated number of minutes of ordering it. Transport companies publicize the proportion of their 'on-time' arrivals, and airlines aim to open the plane's doors within two minutes of 'engines-off'. Many goals of this type are actually dependent on the way staff perform their roles; Locke and Schweiger (1979) identified eight characteristics of effective programmes dependent on staff, summarized in Table 2.3.

Table 2.3 Effective service staff performance targets

* specific
* accepted
* cover important job dimensions
* be reviewed
* with appropriate feedback
* be measurable
* and challenging
* attainable.

(Based on Locke and Schweiger, 1979)

An additional factor in many services is that the variety of tasks involved calls for the organization to adopt a team-based approach. Consequently, it has been pointed out that 'team work is the focus of service quality programmes in several firms known for their outstanding customer service' (Garvin, 1988). As will be shown below, for tourism there is an added complication, that of managing the service standards of the many organizations which contribute to the supply chain.

Shostack (1985) has shown that in the best service firms there is a 'pronounced emphasis on controllable details, continuous investment in training, a concern with the customer's view and reward systems that place value on service quality. In poor service firms, however, one sees an internal rather than external orientation, a production orientation, a view of the customer as a transactions generator, a lack of attention to details affecting the customer, and a low priority placed on "soft" service quality values.' 'Soft' refers to the human as opposed to the 'hard' technical aspects of service delivery.

The consumerist-gap model

The consumerist-gap concept was developed to analyse mismanaged passenger experiences following a technical failure in an airline service (Laws, 1986). The consumerist-gap concept represents a concern to gain an understanding of the customers' perceptions of the factors which are significant in their evaluation of service quality, and it will be contrasted to other approaches which tend to focus on technical and managerial perspectives such as those expounded in a series of papers by Parasuraman, Zeithmal and Berry (notably in 1985, 1988 and 1990).

The consumerist gap conceptualizes a service episode as consisting of a series of events. Each event has an outcome for the client in terms of varying satisfaction levels compared by that person to his anticipated satisfaction. Clients' experiences during each event of a service episode may therefore be measured along a continuum ranging from 'very satisfied' to 'very dissatisfied'. This continuum forms the vertical axis of the consumerist-gap diagram shown in Figure 2.2.

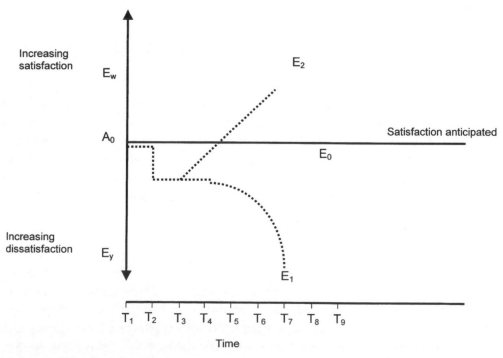

Figure 2.2 The consumerist gap

In the consumerist-gap model, A_0 represents the level of service which clients anticipated at the time of purchase; the satisfaction they experience during the delivery of a service is tracked by the paths E_0, E_1 and E_2 and can be higher or lower than anticipated as the various events in the service unfold. The assumption is that the company passes its acid test of consumer satisfaction when an individual's anticipated level of service as measured by E is indeed experienced, and $E = A_0$. By definition, this occurs at the outset of a service, and it is a measure of managerial success (the acid test) to return satisfaction to this level after any problems.

When service standards are higher than anticipated, consumers are very satisfied, and at level E_w positive outcomes include compliments to staff and favourable personal recommendations of the company to friends or colleagues by clients. The opposite extreme, when the service standards fail to meet the clients' expectations, is characterized by their increasing discomfort, frustration and ill will. This situation can result from unscheduled interruptions to a journey, or from unsatisfactory performance of service events. Such problems are recorded at E_y where individual clients experience so much discomfort that they complain.

The horizontal axis of the model is calibrated in time units $(T_1 \ldots T_n)$ during which the service episode evolves. Initially, satisfaction is at the level anticipated, and the service proceeds smoothly. But if an interruption or other failure occurs, satisfaction falls below the anticipated level and the company responds by seeking technical solutions to restore normal service. In the model this occurs at time T_2, when a gap in consumer satisfaction is opened. The depth of the gap below A_0 reflects the degree of dissatisfaction which the consumer has experienced.

The sequence and intensity of the company's responses to any technical (type A) problems during a service affect clients' satisfaction and are a particular concern of this analysis. It takes some time to marshal the resources needed to overcome failure, and this takes the model to T_3, when the company begins to correct the problem. At the same time service responses (type B) are needed to restore customers' confidence or overcome their anxieties and discomfort. If these responses are inappropriate, by T_4 their dissatisfaction will have deepened. However, with effective action the model shows that technical (type A) problems have been overcome and the normal service is resumed by time T_5. The final level of satisfaction depends on how clients' needs were met by type B responses during the interruption episode. Appropriate type B responses can bridge the consumerist gap, even building greater customer satisfaction than had been anticipated. These are shown in path E_2. In contrast, path E_1 tracks the result of inappropriate actions which deepen the dissatisfaction experienced by clients. The conceptual model charts the ensuing fluctuations in their satisfaction levels.

The outcome of each event may boost or depress customer satisfaction, but the intangible nature of services makes it hard for the client to judge what to expect, or to know how to assess what was received.

> In most service encounters, there are few or no natural clues to utility, either before the service occurs or after it is accomplished. Often, the customer does not know how to tell when she or he would be satisfied, and managers do not know how to structure the service process to satisfy customers. Yet this satisfaction is crucial to both customers and service providers. (Blackman, 1985: 291)

A synthesis of service experiences and service design

The implication of the consumerist-gap approach and research by other authorities, notably Shostack, is that customer satisfaction can be managed. This is illustrated in Figure 2.3 where technical and service-design aspects form the two poles on the horizontal axis. Another foundation of the consumerist-gap concept is a recognition that the outcome of service events and interactions varies along a continuum ranging from extreme satisfaction to extreme dis-

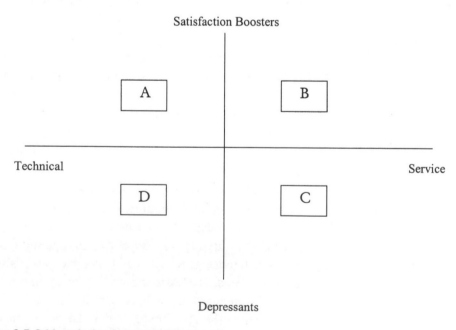

Figure 2.3 Grid analysis of consumerist-gap outcomes

satisfaction; this forms the vertical axis of the consumerist-gap outcomes model.

Figure 2.3, quadrant A encompasses the conditions when a flight is operated efficiently at a technical level, proving comfortable, arriving on time and offering the passenger satisfying entertainment and meals as well as a pleasing standard of service from the staff.

Quadrant B describes a flight where any technical shortcomings such as a delay or the non-delivery of a special meal request have been overcome by the effective responses of staff, or one where there were no difficulties, but service was particularly pleasing.

Quadrant C shows that it is not sufficient to restore the technical conditions of a service after a failure. If the response offends or provokes the passenger the result is seen in quadrant C, where the acid test has been failed, and the passenger is unwilling to return to that company.

Quadrant D results when technical factors do not match what the passenger had anticipated. As examples, the control of cabin pressure or temperature affects the way a passenger experiences a flight. Uncomfortable, broken or dirty seats are another example.

Quality in tourism services

On several occasions so far the phrases 'quality', 'service quality', and 'customer satisfaction' have been used without formal definition. This chapter explores the meanings of these terms and brings together a number of key issues which need to be clarified before further analysis of tourism service design and delivery systems can be developed.

Consumer satisfaction modelling is based on the gaps which may be perceived by customers between what they had anticipated, and their experiences as the various events in a service unfold (Parasuraman, Zeithmal and Berry, 1985; Laws, 1986). Zeithmal, Parasuraman and Berry (1988) argued that the customer reaches a judgement about the quality of service actually experienced when measured against the perceived service. The degree of quality experienced in a service transaction can be considered to give rise to a level of satisfaction which may vary between customers, as is illustrated in Case Chapter A. Nyquist, Bitner and Booms (1985) identified the following factors as significant in understanding this variability in the enjoyment of services:

- Service quality is more difficult for the consumer to evaluate than the quality of goods.

- Service quality perceptions result from a comparison of consumer expectations with actual service performance.
- Quality evaluations are not made solely on the outcome of a service; they also involve evaluations of the process of service delivery.

The difficulty revolves around the fact that there are two roots to services, termed 'type A' and 'type B' (Laws, 1986). The 'hard' technical aspects of managing equipment and materials (type A management) require different skills from managing the interactions between staff and clients ('soft' or type B service management). It is important to note that both types of skill are needed to deliver quality services. Differing, though connected, implications flow from distinguishing between hard and soft, two factors in service management and service consumption. While type A factors are generally under the direct control of managers, the type B factors are more complex and less amenable to precise control. Type B factors include the role specifications, skills and motivations of staff, including their personal ability to interact effectively with clients, but a high degree of unpredictability results from the variable expectations and behaviour which different clients bring to the service episode and its constituent elements.

Gronroos (1990) argues that service quality comprises two fundamental components: technical quality ('what' is delivered) and functional quality ('how' the service is delivered), with an important third component, the organization's image. If the quality of tourism services could be determined by managerial decisions, then all clients participating in one service episode should experience it in similar ways. The fact that this often does not happen can be illustrated from analysis of customer correspondence, through focus-group methods and from our individual experiences. Assuming that all participants in one package holiday were in fact offered identical service, any remaining differences they report in the satisfaction which they experienced could be ascribed to any or all of three major variables. These are their individual attitude at the time, their involvement with (enthusiasm for) the holiday and destination, and differences in their prior experience of similar services. The concept of involvement is discussed more fully in Chapter 4.

Definitions of quality

In the manufacturing sector the concept of quality is well understood and widely accepted by both industry and consumers. The basis is technical specifications for components, dimensions and performance. Feigenbaum (1956) developed the notion of total quality control starting with the design of the product and ending only when the product has been placed in the hands of a customer who remains satisfied. He also stressed the need to recognize that quality is everybody's job, thus initiating the strategic approach to quality management outlined in this book and analysed in Laws (2001).

Garvin has remarked that 'despite the interest of managers, quality remains a term that is easily misunderstood ... Scholars in four disciplines – philosophy, economics, marketing and operations management have ... each viewed it from a different vantage point.' Thus, even in the case of manufactured goods, the management of quality is problematic. Part of the problem arises from the differing views of its meaning and significance taken between the various functions of one company as a consequence of their task cultures and traditions. 'But all share a common problem, each is vague and imprecise when it comes to describing the basic elements of product quality' (Garvin, 1988). His concern led him to make a comprehensive study of quality in products and services, from which he was able to classify quality in five ways.

Transcendent quality varies between individuals and over time, and is summed up by the common phrase 'I know quality when I see it.' An approach relying on the measurable features of the product, an *expert view of quality* leads to design specification and technical drawings. *User-based quality*, while in part based on individual judgement, is also the basis of consumer legislation which introduced the test of merchantability, requiring goods sold commercially to be fit for their purpose: the classic test was that a bucket should not leak. *Manufacturing quality* is focused on minimizing deviations from the standards set in technical specifications. Goods meeting internal specifications therefore conform to the manufacturer's requirements, whether or not customers are satisfied. The fifth classification is *value-based quality*, which was discussed in Chapter 1.

Issues in service quality

Harington and Akehurst (1996) undertook a detailed review of twenty-one leading articles on the topic of service quality, and from this identified some sixty terms used by various authors to define the dimensions of quality. Examination of their data indicates that the most frequently discussed general factors were service delivery and interactions (14 mentions), standards of performance (12), technical factors (10) and image (7). Gronroos (1990) noted that the two fundamental aspects to quality are the technical quality provided by the company and functional quality – how it is perceived by the client. Elaborating on this, he wrote:

> what customers receive in their interactions with the firm is clearly important to them and to their quality evaluation. Internally this is very often thought of as the quality of the product delivered. However, this is not the whole truth. It is merely one quality dimension, called the technical quality of the outcome of the service production process ... However, as there are a number of interactions between the provider and the customer, including more or less successfully handled moments of truth, the technical quality dimension will not count for the total quality which the customer perceives has already been received. The customer will obviously also be influenced by the way in which the technical quality, the outcome or end result of the process is transferred to him or her ... This is the functional quality of the process. (Gronroos, 1990)

A constant underlying theme in the literature on service quality is concerned with customers' perceptions of a service. Perception is the basis for personal interpretation of the world. Given the wide range of stimuli we are exposed to, it has been argued that

> people tend to select from the myriad stimuli to which they are exposed those which appear to be relevant to their needs. Information, for example, will be filtered through the mesh of personal interests, attitudes, motivational structure, social background, and cultural influences. Existing personal cognitive structures will also affect ... the individual. (Chisnall, 1985)

By extension, perception is also important in the judgement consumers make of the quality of a product or service. Wilkie (1986) argued that two key factors determine how something is perceived: its stimulus characteristics and the characteristics of the consumer. The question of individually perceived service standards underlines the problem for managers seeking to design and deliver services satisfying the expectations of many clients. Others have discussed the significance of the point, and the difficulties which result.

> Customer perceived quality is rather a blend of objective facts and subjective judgements, of knowledge as well as ignorance ... Nor can manufacturers consider themselves experts ... Quality has become an integrating concept between production orientation and marketing orientation. (Gummesson, 1988)

SERVQUAL and gaps between expectations and service experiences

The study of consumer satisfaction is often based on identifying and understanding the gaps which may be perceived by customers between what they had anticipated, and their experiences of the service, as shown in Table 2.4 and

Table 2.4 General service gaps

1 Differences between consumer expectations and management perceptions of consumer expectations
2 Differences between management perceptions of consumer expectations and service quality specifications
3 Differences between service quality specifications and the service actually delivered
4 Differences between service delivery and what is communicated about the service to consumers
5 Differences between consumer expectations and perceptions of the quality of the service received; depending on the size and direction of the other four gaps

(Based on Parasuraman, Zeithmal and Berry, 1985)

Figure 2.4. Various approaches exist to conceptualize expectations. Clow et al. (1997) suggest that the predicted level of service is based on what the firm promises in its advertising, word of mouth and past experiences. The consumerist-gap model argues that the expectations which a customer has prior to a service influence their evaluation of the firm's performance, and affect their satisfaction. Another approach regards expectations as the level of performance the customer wants from the firm, and is the basis for the SERVQUAL instrument.

The general SERVQUAL model combines perceptions of service quality on five dimensions: *tangibles*, *reliability*, *responsiveness*, *assurance* and *empathy* (Parasuraman, Zeithmal and Berry, 1988). These were reduced from ten items in the earliest version, 'Assurance' encompasses the dimensions of *Competence*, *Courtesy*, *Credibility* and *Security*; while 'Empathy' includes *Access*, *Communications* and *Understanding the customer*. The team of three researchers developed a method to identify positive and negative gaps in the firm's performance on the five service quality dimensions. This was achieved using two sets of twenty statements which compare customers' expectations with their perceptions of the firm's service performance, each rated on a seven point Likert scale. Zeithmal, Parasuraman and Berry (1990) explain their method in the following terms we followed well established procedures for devising scales to measure constructs that are not directly observable. We developed 97 items capturing the ten dimensions of service quality identified in our exploratory phase. We then recast each item into a pair of statements – one to measure expectations about firms in general within the service category being investigated, and the other to measure perceptions about the particular firm whose service quality was being assessed ... A seven point scale accompanied each statement.

Discussing their findings from a comparative study of four service industries, Banking, Long distance telephone, Repair and maintenance and Credit cards, Zeithmal and her co-authors show that reliability was regarded as the most critical dimension of service quality to their research samples in each service sector studied. Reliability means the 'ability to perform the promised service dependably and accurately'.

SERVQUAL and tourism

Zeithmal et al. pointed out that the other factors may be more significant as cues influencing potential customers. The factor which mattered least to current customers was tangibles (the appearance of physical facilities, equipment, personnel and communications materials). There is evidence which directly refutes this, as tangibles have been shown in many studies to be significant in tourism, both in consumer choice and in their service experiences. A senior airline manager once remarked to me that when confronted with a broken reading light one passenger had loudly demanded to see the aircraft's maintenance log, fearing that the engines might be in the same condition!

In Figure 2.4, it can be seen that each of the five SERVQUAL gaps can potentially cause dissatisfaction with a holiday. Gap 1 is the result of any mismatch between what customers expect and managers' perceptions of what customers want from their holiday. Even if gap 1 does not cause problems, further difficulties might cause dissatisfaction. Gap 2 relates to problems in the technical specifications for a holiday, for example the tour operator might schedule a 6 a.m. departure to optimize use of an aircraft. However, this departure time could necessitate an extra night's hotel accommodation and additional expense for those passengers unable to reach the airport from home at that hour. Gap 3 describes the varied set of circumstances such as travel delays which sometimes occur. Gap 4 can arise from exaggerated advertising claims. Any or all of these four gaps contribute to Gap 5 which is comparable to the consumerist-gap acid test discussed earlier in which the customer compares his or her own experiences with what was expected from the service.

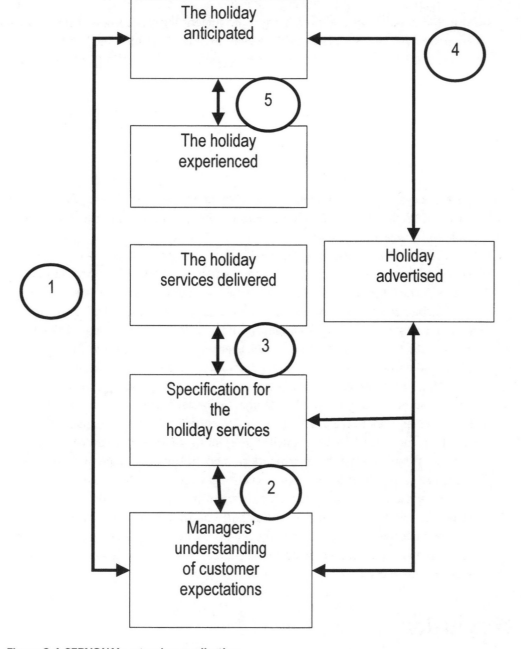

Figure 2.4 SERVQUAL: a tourism application

The SERVQUAL debate

SERVQUAL has been criticized both for its underlying conceptualization and its methodology (Johns, 1999; Teas, 1994; Brown, Churchill and Peter, 1993; Carmen, 1990). Some researchers even question the continuing use of SERV-QUAL.

> At best, it can be argued that SERVQUAL is applicable to contexts close to its original setting, that is, appliance repair, retail banking, long distance telephone ... it is questionable ... whether it is measuring service quality at all. (Robinson, 1999: 29)

Nevertheless, it has been applied to tourism in a number of studies, for example Fick and Ritchie (1991), Saleh and Ryan (1992), Tribe and Snaith (1998), and Mok and Armstrong (1998).

Debate still continues on the appropriateness of the gap approach, including its core constructs of consumer satisfaction, expectations and quality (Chadee and Mattson, 1996). Bitner, Booms and Tetreault (1990) have suggested that perceived service quality, in contrast to the quality of individual service transactions, may be similar to an individual's general attitude towards the service firm, a point of view which echoes Gronroos's three factor model discussed earlier.

Many contemporary researchers investigating the related issues of service quality and the ways in which customers experience service episodes continue to refer their work to the SERVQUAL model, either by directly employing some or all of its constructs, or by explicitly attempting to differentiate their analysis from what has become the benchmark of modern service management research. Although it has been subjected to severe criticism, SERVQUAL (developed and refined by Zeithmal, Berry and Parasuraman in a series of articles and books spanning more than a decade and a half) continues to serve us well in two important respects: it highlights unequivocally the centrality of quality in service research and management, and it emphasizes the complexity of managing service experiences.

Conclusion

This chapter has introduced service management theory and discussed its relevance to tourism marketing. It is clear that managers need to take a broad perspective on their roles when dealing with services such as tourism where customer experience is paramount. It is the customer's judgement of service quality which is the most important performance objective, not criteria specified by an organization's management. Yet each customer has individual needs and expectations, so the challenge is to find ways to understand the individual customers quality expectations, and combine the company's resources with the skills of its staff in a flexible design which allows for individuality. This is the subject of Chapter 3.

Bibliography

Band, W. A. (1991) *Creating Value for Customers: Designing and Implementing a Total Corporate Strategy*. New York: John Wiley and Sons.

Brown, T., Churchill, G. and Peter, J. (1993) 'Improving the measurement of service quality', *Journal of Retailing* 69 (1), 127–39.

Bitner, M. J., Booms, B. H. and Tetreault, M. S. (1990) 'The service encounter: diagnosing favorable and unfavorable incidents', *Journal of Marketing* 54 (January), 71–84.

Carmen, J. M. (1990) 'Consumers' perceptions of service quality', *Journal of Retailing* 66 (1), 33–55.

Chadee, D. and Mattson, J. (1996) 'An empirical assessment of customer satisfaction in tourism', *Service Industries Journal* 16 (3), 305–20.

Chisnall, P. M. (1985) *Marketing, a Behavioural Analysis*. London: McGraw Hill.

Clow, K., Kurz, D., Ozment, J. and Beng Soo Ong (1997) 'The antecedents of consumer expectations of services: an empirical study across four industries', *Journal of Services Marketing* 11, 230–48.

Cowell, D. W. (1986) *The Marketing of Services*. London: Heinemann.

Deshpande, R. (1983) '"Paradigm lost": on theory and method in research in marketing', *Journal of Marketing* 47 (Fall), 101–10.

Feigenbaum, A. (1956) 'Total quality control', *Harvard Business Review* (November–December), 94–8.

Fick, G. and Ritchie, J. (1991) 'Measuring service quality', *Journal of Travel Research* 30 (2), 2–9.

Garvin, D. A. (1988) *Managing Quality, the Strategic and Competitive Edge*. New York: Free Press.

Gronroos, C. (1990) *Service Management and Marketing, Managing the Moments of Truth in Service Competition*. Lexington, Mass.: Lexington Books.

Gummesson, E. (1988) 'Service quality and product quality combined', *Review of Business* 9(3), 1–11.

Harington, D and Akehurst, G. (1996) 'An exploratory investigation into managerial perceptions of service quality in UK hotels', *Progress in Tourism and Hospitality Research* 2 (2), 135–50.

Horovitz, J. and Panak, M. J. (1992) *Total Customer Satisfaction: Lessons from 50 European Companies with Top Service*. London: Financial Times/Pitman.

Johns, N. (1999) 'Quality management', in Brotherton, B. (ed.) *The Handbook of Contemporary Hospitality Management Research*. Chichester: Wiley, 333–49.

Laws, E. (1986) 'Identifying and managing the consumerist gap', *Service Industries Journal* 6 (2), 131–43.

— (2001) *The Design, Analysis and Improvement of Tourism Service Systems*. Sagamore, Ill.: electronic book.

Locke, E. A. and Schweiger, D. M. (1979) 'Participation in decision making, one more look', in Staw, B. M. (ed.) *Research in Organisational Behaviour*. Greenwich, Conn.: JAI Press.

Mok, C. and Armstrong, R. (1996) 'Sources of information used by Hong Kong and Taiwanese leisure travellers', *Australian Journal of Hospitality Management* 3 (1), 31–5.

Nyquist, J. D., Bitner, M. J. and Booms, B. H. (1985) 'Identifying communication difficulties in the service encounter: a critical incident approach', in Czepiel, J. A., Soloman, M. R. and Surprenant, C. F. (eds) *The Service Encounter*. Lexington, Mass.: Lexington Books.

Normann, R. (1991) *Service Management: Strategy and Leadership in Service Businesses*. Chichester: Wiley.

Parasuraman, A., Zeithmal, V. A. and Berry, L. L. (1985) 'A conceptual model of service quality and its implications for future research', *Journal of Marketing* 49, 41–50.

— (1988) 'SERVQUAL: multiple item scale for measuring consumer perceptions of service quality', *Journal of Retailing* 64 (1) (Spring), 12–40.

Saleh, F. and Ryan, C. (1992) 'Conviviality: a source of satisfaction for hotel guests? An application of the SERVQUAL model', in Johnson, P. and Thomas, B. (eds) *Choice and Demand in Tourism*. London: Mansell.

Shostack, L. (1985) 'Planning the service encounter', in Czepiel, J. A., Soloman, M. R. and Surprenant, C. F. (eds) *The Service Encounter*. Lexington, Mass.: Lexington Books, pp. 243–53.

Teas, K. (1994) 'Expectations as a comparison of standards in measuring service quality, an assessment and reassessment', *Journal of Marketing* 58 (1), 132–9.

Wilkie, W. L. (1986) *Consumer Behaviour*. New York: Wiley.

Zeithmal, V. A., Parasuraman, A. and Berry, L. L. (1990) *Delivering Quality Service*. New York: Free Press/Macmillan.

36

3 Managing Tourism Services

Eric Laws

Introduction

This chapter considers the complexity facing tourism managers which results from the fragmented but interdependent business activities which contribute to its products. The chapter introduces service blueprinting and related techniques by which the design of a service can be evaluated from the perspective of its customers' perceptions. The point is also made that managers are unable to control all factors which might influence their customers' satisfaction.

Consumer purchasing decision theory is summarized and the nature and consequences of consumer dissatisfaction are discussed.

Management issues

Almost all the services bought by tourists have to be delivered at the time and place at which they are produced, for example in a restaurant, aircraft or hotel. As a consequence, the quality of the social interaction between the provider of the service, such as the waiter, flight attendant or hotel receptionist, and the consumers is part of the product being purchased by tourists. 'If aspects of the social interaction are unsatisfactory ... then what is purchased is in effect a different service. The problem results from the fact that the production of such consumer services cannot be entirely carried out backstage, away from the gaze of the tourist' (Urry, 1990).

Much of what determines customers' satisfaction is the contacts they have with service staff who deliver the technical features of the service. Normann (1991) referred to the points of interaction in a service episode as 'moments of truth', a phrase which Carlzon had adopted as the title of his perceptive book (1987) reflecting on his experiences at the Scandinavian tour operator Vingressor and it parent airline, SAS. Both Carlzon and Normann have demonstrated that each of the moments of truth is an occurrence used by customers to judge the overall quality of the service and the organization. In complex services such as undertaking a journey or going on a holiday, it is not just the main organization's staff who provide services to clients; subcontracting organizations also have direct contact with the client, raising further issues for managers dealing with partners in the service chain. In the case of a tour operator, clients are actually served by transport companies, hotels, restaurants and a variety of tourist attractions in the destination.

The emphasis on customers' expectations and perceptions of the service experience is a fundamental distinguishing point when contrasting services and manufactured products. In the traditional organization, the heirarchy of communication and control is strictly downwards, flowing from the chief executive to senior managers and through middle managers to the production workers. Customers seldom even feature in the organizational structure. In contrast, Zemke and Schaaf (1989) place customers in the centre of a triangle whose base is the service system and the people involved in it, while the organization's service strategy forms the apex. Figure 3.1 implies that the function of management is to ensure effective service to its clients through resourcing the delivery system and supporting contact staff. Many managers are evidently uncomfortable with this approach to organizational structure, but it has been shown to be very effective for service companies (see for example Case Chapter C), and inspired managers have succeeded in turning around companies on the brink of failure by adopting this approach, as shown in Case Chapter B.

Laszlo (1999) has analysed how Southwest Airlines built operational and administrative excellence on a foundation of management commitment, customer focus, and employee involvement, and were awarded a Canada Award for Excellence. At Southwest Airlines the focus is on human interactions, and technology is regarded as there to provide the tools for those interactions. Laszlo states that legendary customer service comes from the heart not from cumbersome systems. As part of the efforts to keep simplifying administration and operation, meetings and reports are regularly reviewed to ensure that they serve an ongoing need. The operating philosophy at Southwest Airlines is to 'make an everyday reality their credo that customers come second to employees and still get great service'. Legendary customer service requires passion that transcends techniques and procedures: since commitment to service is a personal value, it must come from the heart.

From this point of view, two primary functions can be identified for service-

Figure 3.1 The triangle of service
(Based on Zemke and Schaaf, 1989)

sector managers. One is fundamentally concerned with designing and resourcing an appropriate delivery system which also defines the parameters for
service encounters between staff and customers. The second function is concerned with staff selection and training, and beyond that, the development of an
organizational culture which empowers staff to solve problems on behalf of
customers, within the company's cost or profit policies, and rewards them for
contributing to customer satisfaction. The first management function, service
design, underpins successful service delivery; if successful, it minimizes dys-
function and maximizes effective service transactions, providing satisfying
experiences for customers.

Service delivery systems: the customer interfaces

The objectives of designing and managing service systems are to enable the organization to deliver appropriate, satisfying services to the clients it serves, and to do this in ways which satisfy organizational objectives, whether these be profit, growth, efficiency or excellence. So the organization's resources, including the skills and professionalism of its managers and staff, should be focused on customer needs and presented in ways which customers can enjoy. Many services take place over extended periods, a couple of hours for a restaurant meal, a day and a night for a hotel stay, a week or a month for a holiday. This presents the customer with multiple points and types of interaction, the moments of truth in which he or she tests and evaluates service quality. The importance of contact with the organization's equipment and staff, and with those of service partners has been noted. Customers also notice and respond to the service setting; the ambience of the restaurant interior, even its accessibility in good weather or inclement, are factored into their evaluation of the total service quality. So is the behaviour of other clients, as this too can impact on service experiences, adding to one client's pleasure, or detracting from his or her own enjoyment.

Analysis of customer correspondence (Laws, 1991) indicates that people do not experience a service, which had essentially similar characteristics for each of them, in the same way. An explanation for this phenomenon is that each person interprets selected aspects of the tourism service in his or her own terms and thus may find the experience more or less satisfying than other passengers. The significance of this lies in the limitations it implies for universal quality standards and control systems in tourism. Indeed, this line of study suggests that the criteria of tourism quality are determined by three sets of people, the client and contact staff during the delivery processes, as well as management who are mainly responsible for strategic decisions such as the design of the service system. The quality of any tourism service is therefore a complex concept defined in the interaction between producer and client. Effective management of tourism quality therefore depends on a close match between the intentions and actions of the service provider and the expectations of clients.

Service blueprinting

The foregoing discussion has indicated that satisfactory service experiences call for a systematic approach to the management of quality. This suggests both that the organization should be designed around good service delivery, and that its management should be constantly focused on quality issues, designing the system from that perspective. Berkeley (1996) recommends blueprinting as 'one of the most sophisticated and promising approaches to service design ... it ... provides service designers with a way to visualise service processes and to identify opportunities for improvement'. Traditionally, a blueprint is an ordered technical drawing in which the symbols represent instructions to technicians which they use as a template in manufacturing processes, or in wiring electrical circuitry.

Lynn Shostack, in her pioneering paper of 1984, first identified the need to systematically analyse service delivery systems and described the blueprinting method, demonstrating its application to the analysis of quality and performance in service systems. Shostack, then Director of an American bank, was critical of poor service design, of managers who failed to recognize responsibility for defining what it actually is that their organization provides. She advocated service blueprinting as a way of analysing an existing service, gaining a customer perspective on it and identifying potential problem areas, the fail points which it was critical for managers to address. The technique has been extended and further refined, and now embraces service mapping and perceptual service mapping. The purpose of these techniques is essentially the same: to try to understand what customers expect from a service, the sequence of events they experience during a service and how the underlying technology contributes to their satisfaction. The customer's perspective can be presented as a flow chart, and then matched to the processes involved in delivering the service, even though many of these are invisible to the customer. Mismatches become the focus of investigation, to identify causes, evaluate the cost of potential consequences and of remedial action. It is the designed service which encapsulates the organization's vision of its distinctive offering, and this is the basis for communication between the organization's managers and its customers, staff and suppliers.

The value of service blueprinting is that the many interactions between clients and the providers of complex services can be identified from the underlying technical design. Blueprinting a service in this way shows that in many instances little of the service is actually visible to the consumer. Shostack called this phenomenon the service iceberg, the implication for service managers is that all aspects of the service design have to be managed from the perspective of how they impinge on customers' experiences. She noted that particular attention should be paid to the invisible processes which consumers are unaware of, because these are the basis for the service and can cause success or failure.

The basic service blueprint should have three main features (Shostack, 1984). It must incorporate within the design a time dimension, enabling the researcher to follow the customer's progress through the service delivery process. Secondly, it should show the main functions which together comprise the service, and show their interconnectedness. Shostack presented her original blueprint with a single horizontal dividing line to distinguish the front of house events visible to clients from those which are invisible to them, occurring off-stage, but which underpin service delivery.

Shostack argued that the third feature of a blueprint is that it should incorporate performance standards for each stage of the process. This introduces a further feature of service blueprints, they can be used to identify fail points, the parts of a service which are most likely to cause errors (George and Gibson, 1988).

The detailed events in service tasks can be built into a service blueprint, but the resulting complexity detracts from their main advantage of showing the entire process at a glance. Each of the events in a service is actually composed of many steps; the amount of detail in service designs can be overwhelming. Figure 3.2 shows some of the various procedures involved in restaurant meal service (many more steps are involved than shown in this simplified diagram).

Development of service blueprinting

The basic blueprint model can be developed in two significant ways, by including consideration of the pre- and post-service as well as the core events, or by replacing the simple line of visibility with a zone within which the service technology is visible to clients to a greater or lesser extent. The discussion of service procedures suggests that a customer experiences the service as a series of events occuring in several phases. Lalonde and Zinzer (1976) distinguished three phases, pre-transaction, transaction and post-transaction. From the point of view of the outcomes of the service system, the significance of the pre-transaction phase is that these events can influence the way a customer approaches the core service. For example, a difficult journey to the airport is quite a common experience for travellers, and there is little that the airline can do to alleviate the passenger's stress and concern that he might miss the flight. (Amongst the strategies to overcome this aspect is the inclusion in the price of premium tickets of a limo service within a limited distance of the airport on departure and return, particularly in heavily competed markets such as London.) In less difficult conditions, the customer might hardly be aware of the journey to the airport, but when problems arise the customer's awareness is

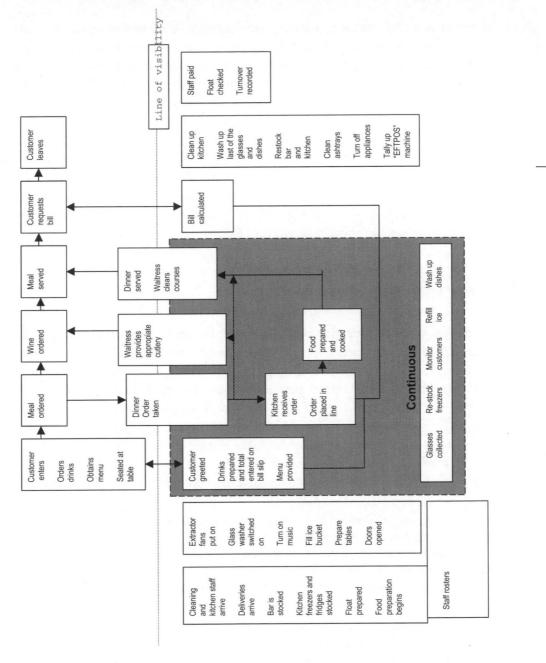

Figure 3.2 Blueprint of a pizza restaurant service

heightened. The customer actively evaluates each phase of the service, and his or her overall satisfaction with it, against what had been anticipated. If the customer is in a bad mood when he or she first has contact with the service provider, staff are confronted with the need to calm the customer down to make him or her receptive to the service process. This may partly explain the offer by some airlines of a complimentary limo service between home or office and airport for premium-class passengers.

The second major refinement to service blueprinting recognizes that the range of tasks which constitute a service vary in the degree to which they are visible to clients, suggesting a zone of visibility rather than a line clearly delineating aspects of the service which customers see from others which are not at all visible to them.

Perceptual blueprinting

Another type of blueprint was developed by Senior and Akehurst (1992), organized around trying to understand customer's perceptions of a service system, or their experiences of using it. This approach emphasizes the service events from the customers' perspectives and is based on interviews, focus groups and participant observation techniques. It is used by researchers interested in service interactions and customer attitudes, and places less detailed emphasis on the complex variety of tasks needed to deliver a service.

Whereas operations research is concerned with physically structured problems, soft-systems methodology and perceptual blueprinting look at

> unstructured problem situations in which unpredictable human behaviour is a determining influence on the success or failure of a system ... Systems are coexisting technical and social systems which cannot be treated in isolation, yet design efforts often concentrate so much on the hard technical aspects that they neglect the soft social and less mechanical aspects. (Senior and Akehurst, 1992)

This is particularly helpful, because it is widely accepted that customers' perceptions of service events differ, and that individual quality judgements are based on the divergence of the service experiences from service anticipated. It takes on some of the characteristics of iterative or action research, in which managers are interrogated about the operational meaning (and validity) of their clients' commentary on the existing service delivery system. A subsequent phase explores the setting of managerial priorities and the remedial action to be taken in redressing the fail points identified earlier.

Mapping tourism services

Service mapping is distinguished from service blueprinting notably by the increased levels of delivery system analysis it offers. Service maps add complexity back into the basic blueprinting concept, with additional information layers (or levels) which record additional factors such as the interactions between customer and contact staff, between contact staff and support staff, and between staff and managers, who may be remote from the service delivery location.

Service mapping has been described as a process which

> visually defines a service system, displaying each sub-process within the sequence ... The map should revolve around the explicit actions the customer takes to receive the service ... The specific contacts the customer has with contact personnel are mapped, as are the internal services (invisible to the customer) that support contact services. (Berry, 1995)

Shostack and Kingman-Brundage (1991) have together generalized the management procedures needed for service development, emphasizing the iterative nature of defining services, analysing the data, synthesis and drawing conclusions. Their joint view is that blueprinting and its developments contribute to the master design of the service and facilitate improvement and redesign as a result of continually increasing knowledge. Commenting on this, Gummesson (1991) noted: 'The strength of the procedural models ... is ... that they directly emanate from empirical material on service development where blueprinting was applied. It is in part inductive research and an application of grounded theory.'

Figure 3.3 is a perceptual map of an inclusive holiday. The tourist experiences a series of events such as the flight, the hotel and so on shown by the boxes 1–11 in the upper section. These extend across the line of visibility into the zone of visibility in the form of a series of service encounters. Invisible to the client, the company carries out a sequence of technical tasks such as contracting for the flights. A number of fail points which might occur are noted below the main service map, giving short examples. Research for a tour operator to determine for what aspects of their holiday clients considered the company responsible elicited the typical responses shown in the bottom row of Figure 3.3.

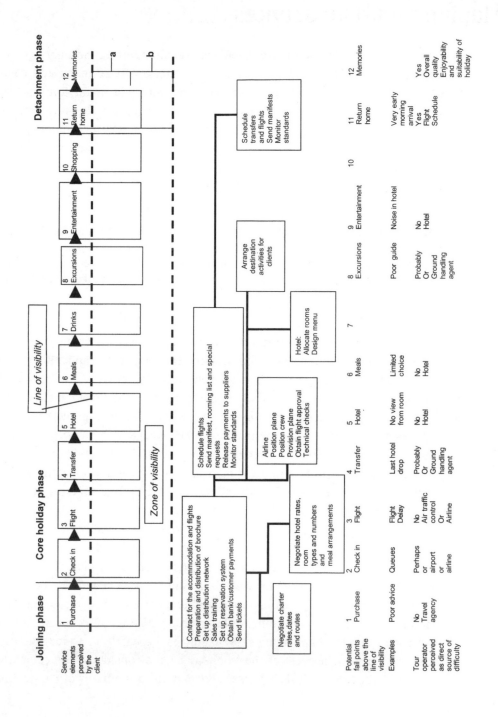

Figure 3.3 Perceptual map of an inclusive holiday

The limits of management control

The complexity of service-industry transactions is a major theme in this book with many factors impinging on customer satisfaction. Hollins and Hollins (1991) have advocated a process of continuous improvements, relying on a view, which also underlies service blueprinting, that the service is a chain of events which the customer experiences. They regard the stage of designing the service as its managers' main opportunity to determine the characteristics of the service offered to customers. Zeithmal, Berry and Parasuraman (1996) report that many organizations 'have instituted measurement and management approaches to improve their service ... the issue of highest priority today involves understanding the impact of service quality on profit and other financial outcomes of the organisation.' However, 'the link between service quality and profits is neither straightforward nor clear'.

Noe (1999) notes that problems such as those the weather can cause to travellers are not under the direct control of managers, but they may trigger strong emotional responses amongst guests adversely affected by them. Table 3.1 lists a number of factors under the control of managers, and others which they cannot normally control.

Table 3.1

Service factors managers can control
1. Access
2. Communications
3. Competence
4. Courtesy
5. Credibility
6. Reliability
7. Responsiveness
8. Security
9. Tangibles
10. Understanding the customer

Service factors managers have little control over
1. The customer's attitude, influenced by word of mouth recommendation
2. The customer's personal needs
3. Any past experience he may have had with that company.

(Based on Zeithmal, Berry and Parasuraman, 1988)

Managing partnerships and channels in tourism services

It is almost certain that tourists will be served by staff from other companies at certain stages in a holiday, as was shown in Figure 3.4. The dependency of one company on the performance of others has been discussed in the following terms.

> A company can be viewed as a node in an ever-widening pattern of interactions, in some of which it is a direct participant, some of which affect it indirectly and some of which occur independently of it. This web of interactions is so complex and multifarious as to deny full description or analysis. (Ford, Hakansson and Johansson, 1986)

Poon (1993) has argued that this is one of the most critical areas of study in the tourism industry.

Relationship marketing is the term applied by the Nordic school of service researchers to the networks within which organizations create and distribute their services. For example, an airline's distribution network consists of travel retailers selling to clients, tour operators who purchase blocks of seats, and its supplier network consists of complex sets of specialists at each airport it serves. These include check-in agents, caterers, baggage handlers and the technical engineering and flight preparation services. Different organizations provide each of these at airports remote from the airline's home base. In fact, its competitors are often the suppliers, the airline reciprocating the arrangement at its base airport. If any of these aspects fail, the service is likely to be less enjoyable for the customer and less profitable for the organizations involved in the value chain. Viewed in this way, the traditional perceptions of firms as competitors in a defined marketplace is only a partial analysis. In many instances, the management priority is to establish and maintain cooperative relationships with other organizations. Case Chapters C, E, F and J examine some of these issues.

Loyalty

The assumptions underlying traditional marketing as epitomized by mix models outlined in the first chapter are that marketing activity has the primary purpose of attracting new customers and that the market consists of a large number of potential customers. In this simplified approach to marketing the needs of all customers were regarded as very similar, and it was thought to be easy to replace any who desert with new customers so there was little concern with methods of retaining existing customers. In contrast, service marketing and contemporary approaches to marketing in other sectors emphasize the importance of developing long-term relationships with customers.

> A firm can through long term relationships with customers get access to detailed and useful knowledge about the customer . . . develop a core of satisfied committed customers . . . Service firms have started to identify their customers, which enables them to be more focused in their marketing. (McCarthy, 1960)

Increasingly the concern expressed by tourism managers is how to understand the factors which are central in motivating clients to remain loyal to their original supplier when there are so many alternative offers of similar services, and so many different services and products to enjoy, with limited funds and time.

Purchasing decisions and consumer involvement

Holidays represent a period of time when the individual is relatively free from everyday constraints, and is able to indulge his or her wishes. Holidays also represent a deliberate purchase, in which limited financial resources are invested in buying time in a chosen resort, implying both that the tourist cannot visit alternative resorts during that vacation, and that he or she has chosen not to spend money and time on alternative products. Consumers' degrees of interest and 'involvement' in purchasing particular products or services range from low to high. Involvement is likely to be high when the purchase has functional and symbolic significance, and entails some financial risk (Asseal, 1987).

The purchasing decisions of customers, whether past, present or potential, are crucial to any company; existing customers generate flows of both revenue and information. The perceptions, attitudes and preferences of current clients are important data to companies seeking to understand their behaviour. A valuable distinction has been drawn between the attitudes of customers to whom a particular purchase has personal importance (high involvement), and those to whom it has merely utilitarian or routine significance (Chase, 1978). Customers whose involvement with tourism services is high are likely to undertake extensive search behaviour, and as the model developed in this section suggests, they are likely to be concerned with the enhanced aspects of the core product.

Four aspects of holidays suggest that many tourists experience a high degree of involvement in choosing their holiday destination.

- Holidays are expensive
- Holidays are complex both to purchase and experience
- There is a risk that the resort may not prove satisfying
- The resort reflects the holidaymaker's personality

It is arguable that high-involvement customers become loyal to their normal supplier, and are less likely to switch to alternative suppliers. In addition, they may be more tolerant of minor service failures, in part because of a deeper understanding of the service delivery system. This theory suggests that in high-involvement pre-purchase decision situations a consumer will compare brands in a detailed and systematic manner. Similarly, after purchase the consumer will evaluate the chosen brand's performance. Satisfaction will reinforce the consumer's judgement and that brand is more likely to be repurchased in the future. If dissatisfaction occurs the consumer will re-assess his choice, and repurchase of that brand is much less likely to occur.

Low-involvement decision-making occurs where the consumer does not consider the product particularly important to his belief system and does not strongly identify with the product. Low-involvement buying behaviour is typified by brand switching which can easily be stimulated by reduced price offers treating all options as broadly similar commodities. However, much of the argument in marketing literature, and many of the actions of marketing managers, assume that customers are very interested in their product, when in reality they are often not. In contrast to the rational, information-processing model of high-involvement behaviour, the consumer who has low involvement with a particular product is likely to be a passive recipient of information about it. When a purchasing need or desire arises, one brand is likely to be purchased rather than others on the basis of some token advantage, such as ease of access, schedule convenience or familiarity; and it is widely believed that this can be gained through repetitive advertising linked to low relative prices.

The low-involvement consumer will, however, be relatively neutral towards any brand as it (and the product) has no strong association with any of his important beliefs. Low-involvement products offer solutions to consumers' problems rather than optimizing the benefits. Services are purchased on the basis of price or convenience since the consumer has no basis for distinguishing between the benefits of various brands.

The concept of involvement is consumer related rather than product related. Asseal (1987) has suggested that the degree of consumer involvement is the critical factor in both consumer behaviour and in setting marketing strategy. This leads to four levels of consumer involvement, with four distinct managerial strategies. It follows that the features of a service which its managers believe distinguish it from competitors' should be defined in terms of the consumers' evaluation of the importance of each service attribute. The varying extent of consumer involvement can be measured on an individual level, and this understanding can be used as a basis for segmented approaches to a general market. Table 3.2 applies this conceptually to model satisfaction outcomes contingent upon passenger involvement of contrasting service strategies.

Table 3.2 Consumer involvement and choice between brands

Involvement	Low	High
Service features		
Core	Sufficient	Insufficient
Enhanced	Grateful	Expected

(Based on Asseal, 1987)

Low-involvement passengers are satisfied if an airline provides an on-time flight with reasonable standards of comfort and catering. Any service enhancements such as a sophisticated entertainment system or fine meals are received with pleasure. In contrast, a high-involvement passenger expects that enhanced service as a minimum requirement and looks for additional evidence of superior service such as the latest style of seating or enhanced facilities at the airport. The basic core service is insufficient to please a high-involvement passenger.

Exaggerated service claims

Given the intangible nature of services, and the close association of their consumption with customers' self images (Asseal, 1987), many service providers use imagery and text emphasizing high quality in their advertising, and thereby raise customers' expectations of service standards to a sometimes unsustainable level. There is a temptation to overstate the enhanced benefits on offer. Airlines often feature stylish, individual attention in their advertising, but it seldom feels like that, even to travellers in premium-class cabins. Bennett (1991) has warned against this practice.

We used to believe it was good policy to exaggerate in our advertising, to promise more than we would deliver. We were sure that the consumer would understand what was happening and the lawyers even invented a phrase 'permissible puffery'. Today it has become clear that overblown claims can lead to disaster in the tourism business.

Two sets of issues arise, the level of service to provide, and the way it is experienced by clients. If an arbitrary decision is taken, the service provided may not match what clients anticipate. The revised standards could exceed expectations, thus increasing the company's costs unnecessarily, or alternatively too low a standard of service would offend clients, and the company would risk the loss of some of its business. The problem with service promises that are not kept is that they lead to dissatisfaction which is quite easy for consumers to articulate by pointing to the discrepancy between offer and experience. In the consumerist-gap terms described in Chapter 2, the anticipated service A_0 is raised to A_1 so even if the company performs well it may not reach the level which customers believe was promised to them, inevitably opening a consumerist gap which normal service delivery cannot bridge.

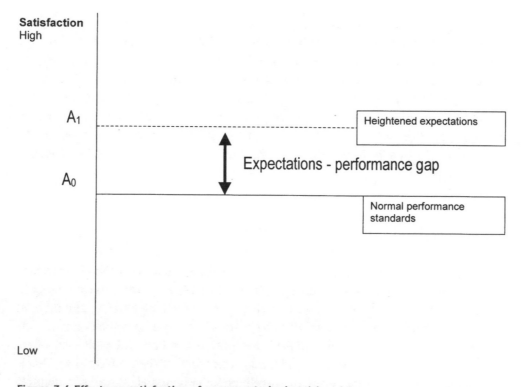

Figure 3.4 Effects on satisfaction of exaggerated advertising claims

The difficulty is compounded when the expectation of a particular type and standard of holiday service is created by promises about a destination. Laws and Cooper (1998) noted that 'resorts are comprised of a constantly shifting mosaic of stakeholders and value systems. Each of these groups has a different view of the role and future of tourism at the resort and therefore the adoption of strategies becomes a political process of conflict resolution and consensus.' A key difficulty is that the standards promised or implied in advertisements may not be matched by the reality of visitors' experiences during their stay. This is significant because clients cannot sample the destination before committing themselves to a visit, and because the fragmented nature of the tourism industry means that many organizations are involved in delivering services to tourists during their stay, with the potential for lack of coherent service standards. Dissatisfied customers are unlikely to repeat their visit, and, furthermore, they tend to share their unpleasant memories with friends on returning home.

Dissatisfaction with services

The opposite of service quality is service failure, the consequence of which is customer dissatisfaction. Dissatisfaction has been defined as a state of cognitive or affective discomfort. The consumer has allocated some of his or her resources, spending money and time and building up an anticipation of satisfaction, but if the customer's judgement of the service experienced is that it did not meet expectations, the customer will experience cognitive dissonance (Festinger, 1957). The response to any dissonant experience is an effort to correct the situation, or a determination to avoid it in the future. Nevertheless, passengers often have to travel with airlines which had previously provided a dissatisfying flight either because they were already ticketed for a further journey, or because of factors such as the convenience of that airline's schedules, its pricing, or because their itineraries are booked by their employers or a tour operator.

Dissatisfaction with the products of any organization has consequences for the organization and the customer. From the company's point of view, dissatisfaction represents a potential loss of that customer's future business as he or she can easily migrate to an alternative provider in the hope of experiencing better outcomes. An extension of this argument is that the disappointed customer will tell his friends, relatives and colleagues about the poor experience, and this may also cause that company a loss of potential business. Furthermore, dissatisfied customers often complain, and this causes extra work for staff and trying to placate an irate customer can be emotionally draining and time consuming, often in situations where other customers require speedy attention to their routine needs. If the complainant is still dissatisfied, formal complaints require the attention of managers and may escalate to legal procedures tying up yet more of the company's resources

Research suggests that competent technical responses to any problem, such as moving the passenger who expresses discomfort to a preferred seat, are judged by the passenger in terms of the perceived attitude of staff. His or her satisfaction will be boosted more by what he perceives to be a caring response to a fault in the service than by someone who is merely competent in rectifying the presenting problem. Grudging service when remedying a defect, even when efficient in hard performance measures, may prejudice a future repurchase of that company's services.

The significance of the contact staff's attitudes is greater when the technical response to a problem proves inadequate; and in the bounded conditions of an aircraft in flight this has often been observed to be the case. However, when staff are concerned to help the passenger, and are seen trying to overcome the particular difficulty he or she encountered, they can minimize overall dissatisfaction, thus keeping open the possibility of a future sale. In summary, responses to an initial problem can accentuate or attenuate the dissatisfaction caused by a service interruption (of whatever nature).

The costs of managing service quality

Several studies have established positive links between quality and a firm's bottom-line performance (Rapert and Wren, 1998). Organizations incur costs from any service failure, but implementing a quality control system to minimize problems also imposes costs (Bejou and Palmer, 1998; Leppard and Molyneux, 1994). These costs result from actions taken to get a service right from the start, auditing that it is correctly delivered and the expenses of responding to any failure. Further costs are incurred in implementing preventive measures to reduce future dissatisfaction, including the redesign of service delivery systems or training and motivational programmes for staff.

These costs have to be considered against the probability that dissatisfied customers will take their future business elsewhere. It has also been demonstrated that they are likely to discuss their negative experiences with many friends and colleagues, thereby further undermining the company's market place credibility (Anderson, 1998).

There are many organizations in tourism, particularly certain hotels and restaurants, whose service strengths provide an excellent basis from which to gain the advantages of branding (see Case Chapter C). Other businesses, including some major airlines, have been able to achieve success across a range of measures starting from the catalyst of a crisis, usually related to a significant change in their operating environments brought about by deregulation or by privatization. Carlzon (1987) has described how this was done in SAS, the Scandinavian airline. Laws (1991) has reported on the management turnaround at British Airways in the mid 1980s. In this book Case Chapter B examines the revival of Continental Airlines.

Service problem or service crisis

Dissatisfaction with some elements of a complex service is probably a common occurrence in the tourism industry. In most cases, a service problem is not immediately a service crisis, although it may escalate into one: Basil Fawlty knew intuitively how to deal with his clients' and staff's concerns! On the other hand, a group of ornithologists experienced several serious difficulties during a visit to Venezuela. One flight was missed when their bus broke down, their leader and guide were left behind for another flight, and twice their hotel was changed. 'About 20 people made the trip, how many were satisfied? Surprise! At the end, all spoke of what a great trip it had been and were enthusiastic at the prospect of a future expedition' (Swann and Bowers, 1998).

There are three phases to dealing with service problems, as indicated in Figure 3.5. The immediate challenge is to recognize that a problem has occurred. The response should be to remedy the defect promptly and without drama. A clean fork can easily be substituted for a dirty one. But the defect is a service problem too. This is addressed by waiters who respond to the client, perhaps

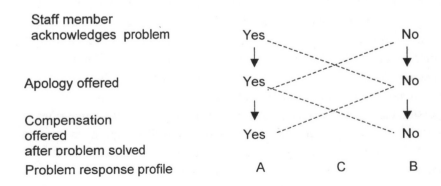

Figure 3.5 Responses to problems

spending extra time with them, or by suggesting an addition to the meal ordered, and if they have the authority, on a complimentary basis. The third phase is normally the responsibility of managers rather than contact staff, although many are empowered to offer compensation such as an upgrade, a glass of cognac or a voucher discounting any future purchase. Beyond that, the organization can learn from the customer's experience.

Fornell and Wernerfelt (1987) reported that in over half the cases which they investigated by following up written complaints, employees' responses to the situation had aggravated the complaint. This is significant because an even greater proportion of complainants reported that they would tell others about the events when their complaint was unresolved. However, in few cases was there a need for financial compensation – it was more likely that the complainant wanted better communications and a more pleasant response to his problem.

Lewis and Morris (1987) have distinguished between individual complaint handling, determined by the long-term value of future purchases of an individual complainant and that person's word-of-mouth impact upon other consumers, and aggregate complaint analysis, identifying and resolving common consumer problems thus avoiding their recurrence, and typically calling for a change in the firm's marketing mix.

However, reliance on customers' unsolicited comments is subject to limitations, such as those identified by Lewis and Morris (1987). They pointed to differences in personal behavioural characteristics tending to make complaints by an individual more or less likely, and addressed the organizational consequences of customer complaints, suggesting that interdepartmental communications might be suppressed because of various behavioural barriers in particular organizations. In particular, the higher the rate of consumer complaints, the more isolated is the complaint handling function likely to become.

Complaints are not always directed formally to the organization supplying a service. Many customers, whether dissatisfied or pleased with a service, discuss their experiences with friends, relatives or colleagues. The significance of word-of-mouth communications in social interactions is that dissatisfied customers are likely to tell many friends and business colleagues about their (perceived) bad experiences (Stafford, 1966). They may thereby influence their contacts away from that supplier. However, if the dissatisfied passenger can be persuaded to direct his or her complaint to the airline, the company then has a second chance to put matters right, and in addition to placating one customer (and his travelling party), may also gain favourable word-of-mouth recommendations amongst the passenger's circle of influence.

The value of complaints lies both in their power as a communications device and as a means of giving the firm a chance to turn a dissatisfied customer into a satisfied and loyal customer (Fornell, 1981). The foregoing analysis suggests that marketing-oriented managers should encourage complaining behaviour; but the key to long-term benefits lies in effective analytical techniques to identify appropriate response strategies.

Conclusion

Once a service has been designed, managers face the challenges of ensuring that it is delivered to clients in a consistent way which yet recognizes their individual needs and concerns, but they also have to respond to service problems.

This chapter has demonstrated how the consumerist-gap method focuses on customer satisfaction as the dependent variable of service encounters, technology and management. By examining the factors influencing passengers' changing satisfaction, another measure of the effectiveness of any quality control systems in place can be activated; and the benefits of additional quality control systems can be assessed. The appropriateness of the technical design of delivery systems can also be explored and, together with an understanding of the meaning to customers of their experiences, is helpful to managers seeking to develop a competitive position, then maintain the advantages gained.

Bibliography

Anderson, E. (1998) 'Customer satisfaction and word of mouth', *Journal of Service Research* 1 (1), 5–17.

Asseal, H. (1987) *Consumer Behaviour and Marketing Action*. Boston: Kent Publication Co.

Bejou, D. and Palmer, A. (1998) 'Service failure and loyalty, an exploratory empirical study of airline customers', *Journal of Service Marketing* 12(1), 7–22.

Bennett, R. (1991) 'The marketing of tourist destinations: why customer service is so important', *Proceedings of the Customer Service in a Global Environment Conference*, Montreal: McGill University, 15–19.

Berkeley, B. (1996) 'Analysing service blueprints using phase distribution', *European Journal of Operational Research* 88 (1), 152–64.

Berry, L. (1995) *On Great Service, a Framework For Action*. New York: Free Press.

Carlzon, J. (1987) *Moments of Truth*. New York: Harper and Row.

Chase, R. B. (1978) 'Where does the customer fit in a service organisation?', *Harvard Business Review* November–December, 137–42.

Festinger, L. A. (1957) *A Theory of Cognitive Dissonance*. Stamford University Press.

Ford, D., Hakansson H. and Johansson J. (1986) 'How do companies interact?', *Industrial Marketing and Purchasing* 1 (1), 34–48.

Fornell, C. (1981) 'Increasing the organisational influence of corporate consumer affairs departments', *Journal of Consumer Affairs* 15, Winter, 191–213.

Fornell, C. and Wernerfelt, B. (1987) 'Defensive marketing strategy by customer complaint management: a theoeretical analysis', *Journal of Marketing Research* 24, November, 337–46.

George, W. R. and Gibson B. E. (1988) *Blueprinting: a Tool for Managing Quality in Organisations*. Sweden: QUIS Symposium at the University of Karlstad, August.

Gummesson, E. (1991) *Qualitative Methods in Management Research*. London: Sage.

Hollins, G. and Hollins, B. (1991) *Total Design, Managing the Design Process in the Service Sector*. London: Pitman.

Lalonde, B. J. and Zinszer, P. H. (1976) *Customer Service: Meaning and Measurement*. Chicago: NCPDM.

Laszlo, G. P. (1999) 'Southwest Airlines – living total quality in a service organisation', *Managing Service Quality* 9 (2), 90–95.

Laws, E. (1991) *Tourism Marketing, Service and Quality Management Perspectives*. Cheltenham: Stanley Thornes.

Laws, E. and Cooper, C. (1998) 'Inclusive tours and commodification: the marketing constraints for mass market resorts', *Journal of Vacation Marketing* 4 (4), 337–52.

Leppard J. and Molyneux L. (1994) *Auditing your Customer Service*. London: Routledge.

Lewis, R. C. and Morris, S. V. (1987) 'The positive side of guest complaints', *Cornell Hotel and Restaurant Administration Quarterly* 27, 13–15.

McCarthy, J. (1960) *Basic Marketing: a Management Approach*. Homewood, Ill.: Irwin.

Noe, F. (1999) *Tourist Service Satisfaction: Hotel, Transport and Recreation*. Champagne, Ill.: Sagamore.

Normann, R. (1991) *Service Management: Strategy and Leadership in Service Businesses*. Chichester: Wiley.

Poon, A. (1993) *Tourism, Technology and Competitive Strategies*. Wallingford: CAB International.

Rapert, M. and Wren, B. (1998) 'Service quality as a competitive opportunity', *Journal of Services Marketing* 12 (3), 223–35.

Senior, M. and Akehurst, C. (1992) 'The perceptual service blueprinting paradigm', *Proceedings of the Second QUIS Conference*, New York: St John's University, 177–92.

Shostack, L. (1984) 'Designing services that deliver', *Harvard Business Review* 62, January–February, 133–9.

Shostack, L. and Kingman-Brundage, J. (1991) 'How to design a service', in Congram, C. and Friedman, L. (eds) *The AMA Handbook of Marketing for Service Industries*. New York: AMA.

Stafford, J. E. (1966) 'Effects of group influence on consumer brand preference', *Journal of Marketing Research* 3, 68–75.

Swann, J. and Bowers, M. (1998) 'Services quality and satisfaction: the process of people doing things together', *Journal of Service Marketing* 12 (1), 59–72.

Urry, J. (1990) *The Tourist Gaze*. London: Sage Publications.

Zeithaml, V. A., Berry, L. A. and Parasuraman, A. (1988) 'Communication and control processes in the delivery of service quality', *Journal of Marketing* 52, April, 35–48.

— (1996) 'The behavioural consequences of service quality', *Journal of Marketing* 60, 31–46.

Zemke, R. and Schaaf, D. (1989) *The Service Edge*. New York: NAL/Penguin.

4 Marketing Destinations, Service Quality and Systems Considerations

Eric Laws

Introduction

Attention now turns to the implications for destination marketing of service quality approaches. Destinations are the core of tourism, an industry which is generally defined as temporary travel away from home and the activities undertaken there. This emphasis on destination places and activities should be seen in the broader context of those same places being home to destination-area residents. Consequently the effects of tourists' activities, although not stressed in this book, are extremely important; see Laws (1995) for a discussion.

Tourist destinations

From a customer perspective, a destination can seem to be like any other 'product' to be chosen amongst a range of competing alternatives offering broadly similar benefits. Product branding provides destination managers with a way to highlight the particular features of a destination and retain customer interest by creating customer identification with products based on their attributes and benefits. Brand marketing involves a series of steps (need arousal, information search, purchase and usage). For example, influencing need arousal in favour of a specific destination involves promoting the particular tourism characteristics of that type of destination and strongly linking that type to the specific place in the consumer's mind. Alternatively a travel-agent familiarization tour may be used to demonstrate the tourism brand through direct experience and hence influence a travel agent in selling that destination. The ultimate aim for development of a brand is a high brand awareness and favourable brand attitude throughout the consumer/trade channels.

Dellaert, Ettema and Lindh (1998) note that most studies of travel deci-sions are concerned with destination choices: 'In some studies, this element is combined with decision-making processes.' They comment that the two main factors investigated are the activities that may influence consumer choice, and the attributes of the destination itself, but note also that traveller character-istics can influence travel choices and report their findings that 'more attention might be paid to interrelate tourists' choices of various components of travel decision-making, which jointly affect tourists' ultimate travel choices'.

Peterman (1997) found that the desire to achieve goals guides people's approach to acquiring information. Van Raaij and Francken (1984) introduced a generic 'vacation sequence' model in which five steps (generic decision, infor-mation acquisition, decision-making, vacation activities and satisfaction or complaints) provide the framework for consumer choice and behaviour. Van Raaij (1986) argued that consumers can be classified along a number of dimensions according to their behaviours to 'discover a natural grouping of tourists into segments'. The purposes are essentially operational, that is, to identify how to influence that segment's behaviour.

Awareness of travel destinations is created and enhanced by travel reporting in the media, guide books and other documentaries such as nature films (Laws, 1995). Electronic online systems are regarded as increasingly important information sources (and booking avenues) for the future (Buhalis, 2000). Table 4.1 lists the following order of importance of most major infor-mation sources predicted for the year 2005.

Table 4.1 Information sources

1 Online information via Internet, teletext, etc.
2 Radio, TV features, videos
3 Reports from recommendations of acquaintances and family
4 Other books, magazines
5 Travel guides
6 Information, travel agency advice
7 Travel destination decision reached without using these information sources
8 Travel operators' catalogues, brochures

(Based on Muller, 1998)

Many researchers agree that personal sources of information, including previous experience and word-of-mouth recommendations from friends and acquaintances is the most important factor in risk-reduction strategies when trip planning (Fodness and Murray, 1997). The risks under consideration here are mainly psychic, notably the possibility of choosing a destination, hotel or activity which the tourist does not actually enjoy, thereby spending both money and time unwisely, and also the chance that a more interesting holiday alternative might have been overlooked.

Dellaert, Ettema and Lindh (1998) argue that tourists' decisions are complex with multifaceted elements, which are interrelated and evolve over time. The key factors in holiday choice are varied, and can include cost, availability or various psychic benefits such as the exclusivity or relative newness of a particular type of holiday component including specific hotels, modes of transport or available activities. Thus, tourist information search is a lengthy process involving a sequence of steps. Table 4.2 synthesizes the points outlined above, highlighting the information implications of the various aspects of choice including complexity and risk in making a choice, and the role of experience in subsequent evaluation of satisfaction with it.

Table 4.2 Information, choice and risk

Aspect of choice	Destination issue	Role of information	Most salient sources
Complexity	**Where?**	Answers specific queries; raises other issues; compounds the difficulty of choice	Travel agent; visitor information centres (etc.); media; advertising; Internet
Risk	**Will it be: fun? safe? too costly?**	Reassurance	Experience; friends; travel writers; travel agent
Choice	**Would an alternative have been better?**	Information streams coming from competing destinations	Friends' holiday anecdotes; travel writers
Experience	**Quality and style**	n/a	Destination services
Evaluation	**Future bookings by this client and friends**	n/a	Experience; friends' anecdotes

In contrast to tour operators and travel principals who rely largely on price as their main marketing tool, destinations generally seek to promote distinctive images. Crompton (1979) defined vacation destination images as being 'the sum of beliefs, ideas and impressions that a person has of a destination'. The crucial role of image in marketing strategies for destinations has been noted in many studies (Bramwell and Rawding, 1996; Goodall, 1998). A comprehensive review of the literature on destination image confirms that it is a critical component in the traveller's destination selection process (Baloglu, 1997).

The effectiveness of image-management techniques depends on an understanding of potential visitors' knowledge, interests and attitudes regarding the destination. Appropriate images can establish a meaningful position for the destination in the minds of selected segments of the public as being a place which is different from other destinations offering similar primary attractions (Ahmed, 1994). The significance of imagery in tourism marketing has been summed up by Buck (1993).

> Tourism is an industry based on imagery; its overriding concern is to construct, through multiple representations of paradise, an imagery (of the destination) that entices the outsider to place himself or herself into the symbol-defined space.

Tourist destinations can be differentiated by mapping the structure of destination images in perceptual space, recognizing that 'places evoke all sorts of emotional experiences' (Walmesley and Young, 1998). Selecting which aspects of a specific destination to feature in the marketplace where tourists choose their holiday destination depends on two steps:

- identifying the destination's special advantages (its attributes)
- understanding how to entice those visitors which the destination hopes to attract (its benefits).

Destination branding

The purpose of branding is to differentiate the goods or services of one seller or group of sellers from those of competitors (Kotler, 1998). Brand management is increasingly recognized as a strategic management tool rather than as an abstract concept (Lawson and Balakrishnan, 1998). They discuss an earlier study which advocated the need for managers to select one of three approaches to branding, and to develop subsequent brand-image and positioning statements consistent with either functional, symbolic or experiential concepts.

Kim and Chung (1997) have argued that the two key variables in the success of global brands are brand popularity and country image: 'Brands originating from a particular country seem to create intangible assets or liabilities that are shared by those brands originating from the same country.' See Case Chapters D, E, I, J and K for examples.

Pritchard and Morgan (1998) note a general agreement that branding can be applied to tourist destinations, but comment that there is 'less certainty about how the concept translates into practical marketing activity ... destination managers face three unique challenges in (branding) initiatives: a lack of control over the total marketing mix, relatively limited budgets and political considerations.'

The essential advantage of branding is that it creates a favourable position for the destination and its integral products, enabling clients to distinguish it from competitors on attributes which are significant to their motivations. This can be expressed as the destination's brand personality: branding provides a way of building an emotional link between product and consumer, appealing to holiday-makers' self-image and life-style concepts. Destination branding is a process that can be likened generically to destination image management, requiring development of a destination image that is well positioned in relationship to the needs and wants of the target market, the image of competitor destinations and, of course, the deliverable attributes of the destination.

Market positioning in turn enables the destination organization to develop a detailed marketing mix for its product, based on research to establish visitors' buying behaviour and alternative destinations in the visitors' consideration set. Brand advantage is obtained by image building which emphasizes specific benefits and contributes to an overall impression of one brand's superiority. The goal is to position a brand in the visitor's mind as occupying a unique and desirable market niche. The imagery used to promote the destination has to be consistent with the self-image of the target customers: to become branded, a place must offer added values which match tourists' needs closely, and are different from those promoted by competitors (De Chernatony and McDonald, 1992).

Place imagery

Discussing the commoditization of cities, Meethan (1996) has shown how selection and interpretation of the city's features reflects the interests of dominant group.

> We can talk of the existence of spatial narratives, that is, ways of interpreting or reading a townscape as the repository of a particular set of values ... The creation and interpretation of these narratives, therefore, depends on the prior interests or positions of dominant groups who have vested interests and control over the urban environment as much as those who are residents or visitors.

Vickers (1989) has discussed the evolution of the (western) image of Bali. He recounts how, in the nineteenth century, Bali was regarded as positively threatening, whereas now the image seen in travel brochures seems positive, evoking fertility, beauty and the charm of its people. The brochure 'is the main marketing tool used to sell tourism packages ... The selling techniques used in brochures are colour photographs depicting the highlights of the holiday, promotional pricing designed to attract the consumer's attention and the quality of the layout' (Vellas and Becherel, 1995).

Gilbert and Houghton (1991) have listed several considerations in order to maximize consumer selection and use of brochures, including how they are displayed, how the consultant uses them in advising clients, and a number of 'consumer filters' such as the clarity with which they convey information, the brand names, and the relevance of the images which they present to the personal needs of intended clients.

A review of the literature on destination image confirms it as 'a critical component in the destination selection process.' Balgolu (1997) also points out that 'according to geographers, perception refers to the apprehension of environmental information by our senses and concerns the filters which distort the world around us ... However, psychologists treat the perception and image similarly because psychologically people cannot make the distinction between the two.' Case Chapters D, I and J illustrate these points.

The chief problems faced by resorts are their distance from origin markets, linked to their need to promote into many countries, and the competition their messages and images face in any source market from all other resorts trying to obtain business there. As a result of these factors, visitors' most likely source of information about destinations is brochures produced by particular places, or tour operators' brochures featuring many potential destination choices. Small or new destinations' brochures may suffer from a number of drawbacks in competing for the attention of potential visitors. They are often produced to a very restricted budget, and may therefore be unattractive in comparison with other place-promotional material. Secondly, their editorial approach and values may seem rather parochial, particularly in the marketplace for international visitors, although this local emphasis may also act as an attractor to those visitors in search of 'new' or 'authentic' destinations. Thirdly, the limited budget also restricts both the number of brochures printed and their placement in origin markets. Tour operators' priorities are to attract customers to their holiday products, and therefore they are less concerned about selling any particular resort: their advertising literature and imagery is often rather generalized, promoting generic holiday benefits such as stylish living, exotic flora and fauna, or the romantic, social or sporting opportunities offered by their holiday concepts.

Although they offer a wide choice of resorts, most tour operators serve clients from only one origin market. They can therefore focus their market spend in spatial terms more closely than resorts, but their appeals also have to be directed accurately to the segments of the market for which their holiday products have been designed. This is particularly apparent in their brochures, where close market segmentation is compounded by constraints of space and by stylistic considerations, resulting in representations for each resort featured which tend to emphasize place similarities.

Travel retail agencies have the most general approach to resort promotion of any tourism industry sector, offering any resort featured by the range of principals and operators whose licenses they hold. The overall result of tour operators' and travel retailers' marketing strength in the origin market is that resorts become substitutable at the point of sale, because the emphasis is on the experiences offered by a holiday, or considerations such as departure convenience or price, rather than the unique attributes of a specific place.

Destination commodification

Many mass-market resorts have reached a critical stage in their life cycle (Butler, 1980) where vigorous growth has given way to stagnation or decline as tourists choose alternative, newer resorts with better amenities. As a consequence, business revenues and the area's tax base fall, and it becomes impossible for individual organizations or the local authorities to maintain or improve standards, resulting in further losses of tourist business.

It has been noted that in many mature destinations, the authorities are taking proactive decisions about their product and market portfolios; this involves choosing facilities to offer, anticipating the demands and changing tastes of their visitors and attempting to influence the nature of their experiences (Laws and Cooper, 1998). This proactive approach contrasts to the often ad hoc, opportunistic entrepreneurial responses which characterized the early development of many resorts (Laws, 1995). A strategic approach has become increasingly common where decisions are taken in terms of the direction of the product offering and the markets to target. Strategic market planning provides an effective framework for the consideration of these issues, whilst also providing clear advantages for resorts (Cooper, 1995).

> The process of goal setting provides a common sense of ownership and direction for the many stakeholders in the resort, whilst at the same time sharpening the guiding objectives. The coherence provided by the approach provides a framework for joint initiatives between the commercial and public sectors and demands the clear identification of roles and responsibilities. (Laws and Cooper, 1998)

As concepts such as destination branding gain wider acceptance, approaches to the management of resort areas have become increasingly sophisticated. These approaches have evolved from the simple view that resorts are places which people visit for their holidays, to a position where they are treated as marketable products (Kotler, Haider and Rein, 1993; Ashworth and Goodall, 1990; Heath and Wall, 1992).

In many established resorts, authorities are beginning to take decisions about their product/market portfolios by choosing facilities to offer, trying to anticipate the demands and changing tastes of their visitors, and attempting to influence the nature of their experiences, in contrast to the often ad hoc, opportunistic entrepreneurial responses which have characterized the early development of many of the original mass-market resorts.

Ashwood and Voogd (1994) discuss a key issue arising from the range of destination attractions and services, arguing that the destination product is not

> the totality of all possible or potential elements ... it is a packaged selection. If it is the package that is the product then the two basic questions of definition and identification concern the nature of this packaging process and who performs it.

The two main candidates suggested are tour operators and government agencies. Poon (1993), advocating new forms of tourism based on an understanding of the contribution which various types of business can make to the tourism value chain, notes that 'distribution is the most important activity along the tourism chain. Without adequate air access and product distribution channels in the market place, the best destinations in the world would find if difficult to survive.'

The view that holidays are a high-involvement purchase (see Chapter 3) leads to a presumption that considerable care will be invested in the choice of resort, with potential tourists undertaking detailed and extended study of brochures, reading and watching holiday advertising, and visiting travel agencies for advice to identify suitable places to visit. However, it could also be argued that holidaymakers' involvement is often with the concept of holiday, rather than the attraction of a given destination. From this perspective, the destination itself may become a subsidiary choice, since the tourist is effectively choosing from the range of holidays (rather than destinations) offered by retail agencies and tour operators on the basis of utilities such as accessibility or price comparisons. Increasingly, the choice of place to visit is determined by tour operators' and retailers' objectives of growth, cost reduction, unit profitability or increased market share, and their relative selling strength compared to the resort.

Collaboration in destination marketing

Destination marketing is usually organized by a coordinating body, but only some of the local tourism operators belong, raising the issue of leadership in promoting destination areas through marketing partnerships. Given the variety of businesses operating from a particular destination, and the geographic dispersion of source markets, cooperative marketing arrangements are quite common. Palmer (1998) has observed that these occur at various levels from local to national, or supra-national. Nevertheless, the preponderance of small businesses in resorts and the diversity of objectives of the larger organizations is an impediment to the implementation of strategic destination marketing.

Interest in the collaborative relationships between organizations operating in a defined marketplace is increasing, exemplified by theories of relationship marketing (McKenna, 1991), and organizational networking (Gummesson, 1995). These approaches have been applied to the functioning of tourist destinations (Laws, 1997; Poon, 1993). Poon advocated new forms of tourism based on an understanding of the contribution which various types of business can make to the tourism value chain. She argued that strategic alliances can lead to improvements in productivity and profits.

See Case Chapters E, F, and K for more examples.

Tourism systems

A systems approach is fundamental to understanding the complex interactions of tourism services. Three stages can be identified in general models of system processes. Inputs are required in the form of equipment, skills, resources and client's demands for the industry's outputs: holiday packages. But a system's outputs also include the profit and work which it creates, and the effects of its operations on other interests, notably those of the destination's residents. The intermediate stage of systems analysis connecting inputs with outputs is concerned with the internal processes whereby organizations transform those inputs into outputs. The various components or elements of the system are interlinked, and the efficiency of the system operating within its boundary will be affected by changes to any of the elements of which it is composed. In general, a system can be described as an ordered set of components; each component is affected by being part of the system: its behaviour is constrained by the needs and conditions of its setting, and the entire system is affected if one component changes. Taking a view of a system is to recognize particular systems boundaries; setting a clear boundary around the system under investigation emphasizes the inputs and outputs for investigation. Outside the boundary of any system are a range of other entities which influence its activities, and which are affected by them: the system is itself part of the environment for other systems. Proponents of systems analysis also recognize the need for an organization to monitor the external environment within which it operates. Chapter 1 and many of the case chapters examine the network of supplier and support organizations with which tourist organizations typically interact.

For effective management of a tourism system two aspects need to be clearly understood: the effects on outputs of any change to its inputs, and secondly the ways in which its processes are organized and controlled. Control over the quality and consistency of a system's outputs requires regular monitoring of its products, and an effective feedback channel between the monitoring and decision-making sub-systems within the organization.

Business organizations can be seen as purposeful social systems, taking resources from their environment and using the skills of their employees to produce outputs to satisfy their clients, and the organization's own objectives. Although the systems approach can be applied to the separate operating units of the industry such as tour operators, travel retailers, airlines, hotels and tourist attractions at destinations, it is at its most powerful when focused on the complex issues of destinations (Laws, 1995) or, as in the case of this book, the entire industry. A systems approach enables the goals, organization, resource and output decisions of management to be examined, in order to understand the effects of their decisions on other groups affected by the organization's activities. Constraints such as competition and regulatory environments may also be studied to understand how levels of efficiency are affected in the industry. Figure 4.1 shows how these systems concepts can be applied to the inclusive holiday industry.

Kaspar (1989) has recommended the systems approach in analysing tourism because it encourages the abandonment of one-dimensional thinking so that multiplex factors can be recognized and analysed from a variety of disciplinary perspectives. Interest is focused on psychological, economic, social, technological, political and ecological contexts to tourism management decisions. He pointed out that a theoretical image of reality can be gained in three ways: by reductionistic, holistic or systemic approaches. Reductionism dissects a whole entity into separate, isolated units (others have called this approach atomization). That method places the focus on the elements of a system, rather than the interrelationships between them. Holism represents the contrary approach; its proponents regard the whole as nonseparable and therefore non-

68

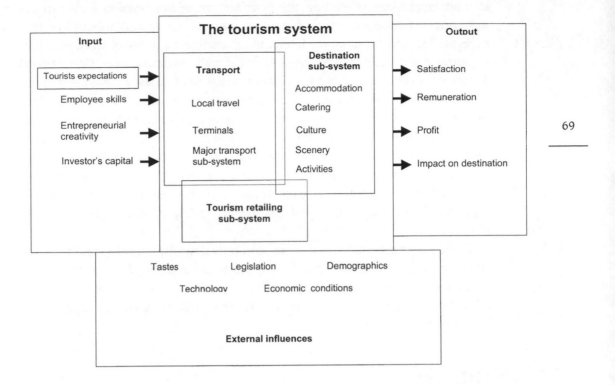

Figure 4.1 The tourism industry system

analysable. Neither of these is a particularly helpful approach. Kaspar (1989) quoted Kuhne's view that these limitations are sufficient to abandon both approaches and to search for 'a perspective which enables one to grasp the peculiarities of the whole and the specific properties of the parts at the same time'.

The various components or elements of the system are interlinked, and the efficiency of the system operating within its boundary will be affected by changes to any of the sub-systems of which it is composed or the processes they employ. The systems view of any organization emphasizes that it exists to carry out the activities and processes related to achieving its aims. Furthermore it controls its activities and interacts with the environment in order to obtain resources and attract support for its products. In a competitive and constantly developing industry, effective service management means a relentless pursuit of new goals of quality improvement.

The analysis of tourism services as a system gives the advantage of identifying the main groups of people acting in it, or influenced by it: particularly the managers, staff and tourists. The systems view provides a framework to understand the effects on all stakeholders of the system's operation, including the residents of a destination area. If the system inputs are the expectations and spending of clients, the skills and attitudes of staff, and the resources and skills of management, then the appropriateness and effectiveness of the system design and its operation can be assessed by comparing the system inputs with the outcomes for each stakeholder group, that is the satisfaction experienced by clients of the system; the remuneration, work satisfaction and career development of staff; while profit and growth of the organization can be regarded as proprietors' and managerial outcomes. While these outcomes are accepted as important for staff and managers, this study is predominantly concerned with outcomes for clients and it is the significance of those for organizational success which provides the feedback loop making the argument iterative.

The systems perspective has not been fully developed in analysing tourism services, but it has the potential to emphasize the importance of ensuring that all components of the service function effectively, not just as separate aspects of a holiday, but in conjunction, and in ways which deliver satisfying experiences to customers.

Conclusion

This chapter concludes the brief theoretical discussion of tourism services marketing. It has shown that destinations, because they are complex and often informal alliances between businesses and are also people's homes, require special attention from tourism marketing managers. They are also competing in a very cluttered marketplace where few tourists have any particular loyalty to the destination they choose to visit. This makes it important to try to develop distinctive brands and to position them competitively, but also emphasizes the need to go beyond destination promotion and to address issues of tourism service quality within the destination.

Branding has not been effectively managed in most destinations because the methods used for manufactured products do not really address the concerns of tourists, particularly in terms of the risk that a particular place may not meet their holiday wishes. Information about destinations comes from many sources, most of which are also intent on conveying messages about other places people might consider, so the unique features of a particular destination are not fully conveyed in typical tour operators' brochures, where the imagery, although quite striking, is seldom specific to one place. This is at once the cause and the result of commodification, the drive to offer as wide a range of holidays as possible, and the resultant need to sell volume on the basis of price rather than intrinsic place benefits.

Another development mitigating against strong destination marketing can be identified. Attention in marketing tourism by tour operators and other intermediaries is shifting away from emphasizing the place attractions of particular destinations to appeals based on the range of activities and special interests featured in the operator's programmes. Examples range from scuba diving, to gastronomy tours or cooking lessons as the main theme of a given holiday product which the tour operator can locate in many different destinations.

The complexity and interrelated nature of each destination can best be understood by considering how it functions as a system. But all destinations function within the broader context of the tourism industry system, and its characteristics of complexity, competition and change introduce a high degree of uncertainty to the interactions of the various elements of each destination. Part 2 now provides readers with a dozen case studies written for this book by a group of international experts which illustrate, and extend, the analysis of tourism services marketing.

Bibliography

Ashwood, G. and Voogd, H. (1994) 'Marketing of tourism places: what are we doing?' in Uysal, M. (ed.) *Global Tourist Behaviour*. New York: Haworth Press.

Ashworth, G. and Goodall B. (eds) (1990) *Marketing Tourism Places*. London: Routledge.

Baloglu, S. (1997) 'The relationship between destination images and sociodemographic and trip characteristics of international travellers', *Journal of Vacation Marketing* 3 (3), 221–33.

Bramwell, B. and Rawding, L. (1996) 'Tourism marketing images of industrial cities', *Annals of Tourism Research* 23 (1), 201–21.

Buck, E. (1993) *Paradise Remade, the Politics of Culture and History in Hawaii*. Philadelphia: Temple Press.

Buhalis, D. (2000) 'Tourism and information technologies: past, present and future', *Tourism Recreation Research* 25 (1), 41–58.

Butler, R. (1980) 'The concept of a tourist area cycle of evolution: implications for management of resources', *Canadian Geography* 24 (1), 5–12.

Cooper, C. (1995) 'Strategic planning for sustainable tourism: the case of the off shore islands of the UK', *Journal of Sustainable Tourism* 3 (4), 1–19.

Crompton, J. (1979) 'Motivations for pleasure vacations', *Annals of Tourism Research* 4 (1), 25–35.

De Chernatony, L. and McDonald, M. (1992) *'Creating Powerful Brands: the Strategic Route to Success in Consumer Industrial and Service Markets*. Oxford: Butterworth Heinemann.

Dellaert, B., Ettema, D. and Lindh, C. (1998) 'Multi-faceted tourist travel decisions: a constraint-based conceptual framework to describe tourists' sequential choices of travel components', *Tourism Management* 19 (4), 313–20.

Fodness, D. and Murray, B. (1997) 'Tourist information search', *Annals of Tourism Research* 24 (3), 503–23.

Gilbert, D. C. and Houghton, P. (1991) 'An exploratory investigation of format, design, and use of UK tour operators' brochures', *Journal of Travel Research* 30 (2), 20–25.

Gummesson, E. (1995) 'Making relationship marketing operational', *International Journal of Service Industry Management* 5 (5), 5–20.

Heath, E. and Wall, G. (1992) *Marketing Tourism Resorts*. New York: Wiley

Kaspar, C. (1989) 'Recent developments in tourism research and education at university level', in Witt, S. F. and Moutinho, L. (eds) *Tourism Marketing and Management Handbook*. London: Prentice Hall.

Kim, C. and Chung, J. (1997) 'Brand popularity, country image and market share: an empirical study', *Journal of International Business Studies*, Second Quarter, 361–85.

Kotler, P. (1998) *Marketing*. 4th edn. New York and Sydney: Prentice.

Kotler, P., Haider, D. H. and Rein, I. (1993) *Marketing Places*. New York: Free Press.

Laws, E. (1995) *Tourist Resort Management, Issues, Analysis and Policies*. London: Routledge.

—— (1997) *Managing Packaged Tourism, Relationships, Responsibility and Service Quality in the Inclusive Holiday Industry*. London: International Thomson Business Press.

Laws, E. and Cooper C. (1998) 'Inclusive tours and commodification: the marketing constraints for mass market resorts', *The Journal of Vacation Marketing* 4 (4), 337–52.

Lawson, R. and Balakrishnan, W. (1998) 'Developing and managing brand image and brand concept strategies', *American Marketing Association* (Winter), 121–6.

McKenna, R. (1994) *Relationship Marketing, Successful Strategies for the Age of the Customer*. Reading, Mass.: Addison Wesley.

Meethan, K. (1996) 'Consuming (in) the civilised city', *Annals of Tourism Research* 23 (2), 322–40.

Muller, H. (1998) 'Long-haul tourism 2005 – Delphi Study', *Journal of Vacation Marketing* 4 (2), 193–201.

Palmer, A. (1998) 'Evaluating the governance style of marketing groups', *Annals of Tourism Research* 25 (1), 185–201.

Peterman, M. (1997) 'The effects of concrete and abstract consumer goals on information processing', *Journal of Psychology and Marketing* 14 (6), 561–82.

Poon, A. (1993) *Tourism, Technology and Competitive Strategies*. Wallingford: C.A.B. International Press.

Pritchard, A. and Morgan, N. (1998) 'Mood marketing – the new destination marketing stratetgy: a case study of "Wales the Brand" ', *Journal of Vacation Marketing* 4 (3), 215–29.

Van Raaij, F. (1986) 'Consumer research on mental and behavioural constructs', *Annals of Tourism Research* 13, 1–9.

Van Raaij, F and Francken, D. (1984) 'Vacation decisions: activities and satisfactions', *Annals of Tourism Research* 7 (1), 101–12.

Vellas, F. and Becherel, L. (1995) *International Tourism*. Basingstoke: Macmillan.

Vickers, A. (1989) *Bali: A Paradise Created*. Berkeley, Calif.: Berkeley Publishing.

Walmesley, D. and Young, M. (1998) 'Evaluative images and tourism: the use of personal constructs to describe the structure of destination images', *Journal of Travel Research* 36 (Winter), 65–9.

72

2 Case chapters in tourism marketing, quality and service management

A Mystery Shopping: Theory and Practice

John Tribe

Introduction

This chapter discusses Mystery Shopping as a method for assessing customer satisfaction and includes discussion of two case studies which reproduce Mystery Shopper assignments undertaken by the author in Spain and the UK. According to Baker (1996), £20 millions is spent by organizations on Mystery Shopper programmes, but what place does Mystery Shopping have in contributing to effective marketing in tourism? The link is tourism satisfaction and in order to probe this question thoroughly it is necessary to first unpack the concept of Mystery Shopping, second to understand the techniques of Mystery Shopping within a wider methodological framework and third to perform an evaluation of different approaches to Mystery Shopping.

Mystery Shopping

There are several definitions of Mystery Shopping. Baker (1996:16) defines it as

> A carefully planned programme whereby unidentified customers test the services of organisations who want to check that standards are being maintained, identify needs or benchmark competitors.

Mayland, cited in Schlossberg (1991:10) offers the following definition:

> a process for measuring service quality, with feedback, that is understandable to the front-line people.

Erstad (1998:34) suggests that Mystery Shopper programmes 'are defined as a tool for evaluating and improving customer service', whilst for hotels Bare (2000:14) describes the Mystery Shopper's job as being 'to discreetly observe the hotel's operations and objectively report his/her observations to management'. None of these definitions are entirely satisfactory. Mayland and Erstad each omit what is perhaps the most important aspect of Mystery Shopping – its mysteriousness. This is a crucial aspect of the concept, which is captured by Bare as 'discreet observation' and by Baker in the deployment of 'unidentified customers'. On the other hand Baker overly restricts the definition by insisting on 'a carefully planned' process, as does Bare by assuming that 'management' is the only possible audience. Mystery Shopping can involve an unstructured visit and its report may be directed at audiences other than managers – consumers for example. There is also some variation on what is to be observed in each definition – 'standards', 'operations', 'service' and 'quality'. All of these are in fact covered in the last of these terms – quality. Bearing this in mind it is proposed to define Mystery Shopping in tourism as 'the reporting of the quality of a tourism experience by an undercover customer'. Having established a sufficiently inclusive definition, attention may be turned to the different techniques and purposes of Mystery Shopping.

Since purpose determines technique, this will be addressed first. In general terms the purpose of Mystery Shopping may be to provide information for two potential audiences – management and customers. Mystery Shopping can provide management information in a number of ways. Baker (1996:16) identifies the following:

to increase the volume of repeat customers
to ensure franchisees meet company standards
to ensure staff are performing as well as they should
to benchmark standards against competitors
to motivate staff to perform better
to evaluate training programmes
to highlight areas for service improvements
to identify strengths and weaknesses of outlets across the country
to evaluate homogeneous standards across the company.

To this could be added the use of Mystery Shopping to report on the prices and standards of competitors. In this respect, Clive Nicolaou of Scher Associates (quoted in Baker, 1996:16) notes the long-established practice of 'pop[ping] down to the corner shop to check out the prices of the competition'. Spooner (1985) provides a similar list which concentrates mainly on human resource issues. In fact the above list somewhat confuses the aims of Mystery Shopping (to increase the volume of repeat customers and to motivate staff) with its objectives (reporting information evaluating the quality of provision).

But not all Mystery Shopping is performed for management reasons. There is a considerable area of Mystery Shopping that is undertaken to inform consumers. In this category should be included reviews of restaurants, holidays and tourism attractions. Whilst these types of Mystery Shopping aim to inform consumers they also have the purpose of selling the media that they are published in, typically newspapers and magazines. It should be noted that 'sponsored' reviews (e.g. holidays that are paid for by the holiday company which is being reported on) should not be counted as Mystery Shopping on two counts. First, the shopper will no longer be undercover and indeed is likely to receive preferential treatment, and second, the objectivity of the shopper may be affected by the sponsorship. For both of these reasons the shopping experience would not be a valid representation of a typical experience.

What then are the different techniques for Mystery Shopping? There are two key factors here which relate to who is to be the Mystery Shopper and how the Mystery Shopping is to be conducted. The choice of who to use is between someone internal to the organization and someone external. Internal Shoppers are usually Head Office experts in quality management (Stefanelli, 1994). Their advantages include knowledge of the company's products but they face problems of being recognized (Erstad, 1998). Another potential problem is that they will be infused with the company culture and this may affect their objectivity and they may be unable to see problems which stem from company policy.

External Shoppers are likely to be cheaper and can be selected to be representative of a company's actual shoppers. Baker (1996:17) explains the importance of matching the Mystery Shopper to the typical customer profile of, for example, the hotel under assessment. Information is supplied by the client which 'takes into account such aspects as age, sex, economic grouping and appearance' and this information is used to select appropriate Shoppers. Mystery Shopping for consumer reports will clearly employ external Shoppers and a potential problem here is that they may not reflect the typical customer profile – would a middle-aged food columnist give a valid report on a TGI Friday restaurant?

Discussion moves now to how to carry out a Mystery Shopping assignment. There are three main approaches to Mystery Shopping. These are structured, semi-structured and open. Erstad (1998) describes a process for constructing a structured questionnaire for Mystery Shopping. She suggests that a number of sources of information are used. First, she advocates the use of input from front-line customer-contact employees 'to prepare a list of characteristics the employees view as important to customers' (p. 35) Second, 'information from customer focus groups' ratings, information from customer satisfaction surveys, and comment cards' (p. 35) should be added to determine the key issues. The issue formulated can be used as a basis for open or closed questions. Spooner (1985) argues for open-ended questions whilst Cramp (1994), Leeds (1995) and Bruno (1998) favour the checklist approach since it is less time consuming to complete and analyse. The structured approach can adopt a more quantitative approach by using a points system to rate service (Schlossberg, 1991). Gofton (1995) explains a system in which a welcoming smile scores four points and a well-dressed server scores two. The UK Seaside Awards are judged by Mystery Shoppers who visit resorts with a checklist of items ranging from dog mess on the beach to toilet paper in the lavatories and lifeguards on duty. Awards are granted to resorts which score beyond a minimum threshold.

Bare (2000) explains the mechanism of a semi-structured Mystery Shop for a hotel. He suggests an agenda of aspects to be observed:

1 Satisfactory or exceptional employee performance
2 Integrity issues
3 Training opportunities
4 Housekeeping
5 Revenue-building opportunities
6 Facility maintenance. (p. 14)

The Mystery Shop would begin 'with making a reservation and continue through to check out' (p. 14). The Shopper would make discrete written or dictated notes and provide 'a complete written report of all observations' (p. 14). An open approach to Mystery Shopping involves nothing more than a blank sheet of paper. Here there is more onus on the Mystery Shopper to be inquisitive, and to be skilled in perceiving significant issues and recording data that is likely to be rich and complex. The skills of insight and intuition are important here.

Methodologies

The discussion now turns to the methodological framework within which Mystery Shopping can be evaluated. Ryan (1995) provides a comprehensive overview of methods for researching tourist satisfaction. Ryan distinguishes between qualitative and quantitative research methods. Under qualitative methods he identifies the two broad categories of field research and open-ended interviewing techniques. Case studies, participant observation and the use of conversations are cited as examples of the former category, with focus groups and structured and unstructured interviews falling into the latter category. The questionnaire is perhaps the prime example of a quantitative method but this heading also includes numerical findings from qualitative research and statistical techniques such as correlation performed on secondary statistics.

Walle (1997) also makes a distinction between qualitative and quantitative methods, which he distils into a comparison of scientific method versus qualitative research. But whereas Ryan is merely descriptive about the range of methods, Walle is evaluative. Walle identifies the importance of scientific method when 'adequate data can be gathered' (p. 531) and emphasizes the fact that data collection can be 'performed by people with a minimum of training' (p. 531). Scientific method certainly ensures rigour, clarity and credibility. But Walle points up the fact that whilst 'science provides a powerful methodology ... it tends to eliminate the investigation of topics that are not easily attacked by its methods' (p. 532). It may be that complex concepts such as satisfaction cannot readily be measured by quantitative methods and that numerical measures or summaries of satisfaction are meaningless. Here Walle's account of qualitative methods which admit intuition and insight offers perhaps a more appropriate approach. Tribe and Snaith (1998), investigating holiday satisfaction in Cuba, argue that 'satisfaction is a very slippery term ... hence a more interpretive methodology might be appropriate. Here meaning is not ascribed by the researcher who freezes the research world into an object of his or her particular view or understanding' (p. 26). This opens up the important issue of voice in research. As Tribe and Snaith observe 'those researched by means of a survey are not very much encouraged to find their own voice' (p. 26). The point being that the issues have often been pre-selected by the researcher.

The three techniques of Mystery Shopping previously discussed may be evaluated in the light of methodological considerations. Mystery Shopping can be located as being a form of participant observation. At one extreme is the structured, point-scoring, quantitative approach. The advantage of this method is that its structure enables uniformity and this allows for comparison of results against set benchmarks, and comparison over time and between different outlets. Point-scoring generates quantitative data that can be readily analysed and summarized. Data collection itself is relatively unskilled and therefore minimizes expense and training. Problems however include the fact that assessment of satisfaction is shoe-horned into pre-selected indicators which may not allow the richness of the concept to emerge. Additionally any numerical summary of satisfaction whilst appearing credible in fact has no logical meaning.

However, Erstad's explanation of the development of a Shopper evaluation form does to some extent tackle the problem of the location of 'voice' in Mystery Shopping. This is because both employee and consumer attitudes are used to construct the question set. This is less obvious in Bare's agenda for Mystery

Shopping reports. The problem here is that this may only represent a managerial view of customer satisfaction issues so that the customer voice is not necessarily found. On the other hand, the semi-structured approach does escape some of the straitjacket restrictions of investigation and recording satisfaction imposed by a structured system. Whilst the Shopper is offered guidance, the data collected is qualitative and the written system of reporting enables explanation and more of the richness of an encounter to be recorded.

The open technique of Mystery Shopping comes closest to what Walle refers to as artistic or emic methods within a qualitative paradigm. Its success rests heavily on the ability of the Shopper to generate an agenda specific to a situation. Its disadvantage is that it always offers a unique case study so that comparisons are not easily made over time or between outlets. Also it is necessary for the Shopper to have highly developed skills of observation, analysis and recording. The power ascribed to the Shopper means that it is his or her 'voice' rather than that of a typical consumer that is heard, i.e. it is highly subjective. However, there are two strong advantages to the open approach. First, the problem of company ideology or organizational culture, or closeness and over-defensiveness is avoided. The problem here is that it is often difficult for research where the agenda is largely set within an organization to escape 'the company view of things' and offer itself for open criticism. A combination of the open approach and an external Shopper enables things to be seen with a fresh set of eyes. The second advantage is that the report of an open Mystery Shop is likely to make its points in a colourful and memorable way. The report is part of the art of this type of Mystery Shopping.

This chapter continues by reproducing two examples of the open method of Mystery Shopping followed by a commentary on these.

Case study 1 Port Aventura, Spain: hot, wet and wicked

As we approached Port Aventura, Europe's second biggest theme park, Dragon Khan loomed out of the heat haze. It emitted an ominous low roaring. 'Wicked,' said Jamie aged 12. 'I'm not going on that,' said Tom aged 9.

I was still thinking through my position when I was frog-marched by children across continents, from Polynesia to China. 7.02: entered queue for Dragon Khan. 7.07: stuffed into cart. 7.08: heart attempts to drill its way out through ribs as our cart is cranked up. 7.09: plunged earthward at 70 mph, looped loops, took in a corkscrew. 7.10: the pneumatics release us from a yellow plastic grip of iron.

Awesome.

Getting to Port Aventura is a breeze – access from the autopista, a rail station, bus and coach services. Admission is Pts 4000 for adults (Pts 3100 for children under 13). We had worries about heat and queues, so we plumped for night tickets (Pts 2500/1900), which were just over £40 for a family of five.

Jelly-legged after Dragon Khan, I fancied a live show (choice of 11) but instead I was bundled into El Diablo, a runaway mine train with no queue. Next was our only real wait – 40 minutes for Silver River Flume. It is a good-humoured queue, clapping to country music as we near the logs. Some strip to their underwear while others don macs – these portents of a drenching are borne out. 8.20: slither off log.

Wild Buffaloes turn out to be dodgem cars – my three children bear down on me. Grand Canyon Rapids next – the three minute queue is rapid, the effects are grand and another mild drenching is had by all. Tutuki Splash is a volcano-themed water coaster. We are dumped from great heights into splash pools. Our boatload can't get enough. 'Otra, otra,' (More, more) they chant. With no queue, their wish is granted.

We opt next for a takeaway snack. Instant service, about £2.50 per head. It is dark now and I sip my ice-cold beer. Heaven. We could have eaten in any of 14 restaurants serving food from different themed areas.

Forget coffee, it's on to Kontiki Wave, a giant swingboat, after which we encounter a problem. Tifon needs 36 people to run and the queue fails to reach its critical mass. We wait for 20 minutes. Note to management – Tifon needs better signage and its operators must drum up custom. It eventually lurches into action like a giant cocktail shaker. An hour to go and we fit in Serpiente Emplumada, Trono de Pacal, and an extra spin on El Diablo and Dragon Khan.

Two moans. Our high-tech photo souvenirs needed a low-tech plastic bag, and Stampida was closed.

But Port Aventura is the business, it's good value made better by the strong pound. The park is well designed, handling people flows well and avoiding long waits. It has wide appeal – white knucklers, family rides and shows. The heat is kept at bay by water and shaded queuing stalls. Themed areas are tasteful. It is managed well – litter free, spotless toilets, cheerful operatives – and the rides ran right up to the advertised time of midnight. We left after five hours feeling thoroughly entertained and exhilarated. In short, we had a lot of fun.

This article first appeared in *Leisure Management*.

Case study 2 Segaworld, London: Queue! What a torture

'Welcome to the next generation of futuractive theme parks.' And what better place for an indoor park than in the middle of a city which is wet and cold for at least half of the year? We 'take the rocket escalator to another dimension', and it feels good – the steep, long escalator ride to the apex of the Trocadero centre excites the senses. We are on the threshold of 'a galaxy of futuristic experiences in one world'.

The kids – there are 12 of them in our party – just cannot wait to encounter The Beast in Darkness. They push and crane their necks round every corner. Eventually, after a 45-minute wait in a queue, we reach its lair – dark but not terribly beastly. There is the occasional roar through some speakers and a few video screens showing a beast going about its daily routines. Then the floor becomes uneven. But the next bit had us all leaping out of our skins – a Segaperson jumped out on us from around a corner. An old trick, but a good one.

He put us on a ride. Now the kids were scared again. Where were they going? They fought to be with an adult. As our cart set off I recalled my first theme-park experience: the Black Hole at Disneyland, California, some 20 years ago. When that cart shot off into the dark, I could only scream out involuntary oaths as it hurtled round its impossible track. It was pure sensation, exhilaration, entertainment.

But the cart in the Beast's lair just trundled. The commentary said something like 'The beast has escaped, it's going to get you.' But my sweat glands were not activated, my pulse didn't miss a beat, my adrenalin pump failed to kick in. Matthew, aged 8, yawned. And that was The Beast in Darkness.

Points. Futuricity: 1970s. Beastliness 1/10. Pulse Rate: 72 beats per minute. Screamometer: 0 decibels.

We skirted the Combat Zone, an arcade full of computer games, and arrived at our next queue for Aqua Planet. Aqua Planet was worth the 45-minute wait. We were strapped into seats, and plunged headlong into a breathless journey. It was virtually real. Things jumped out from the screen, we ducked instinctively to avoid collisions. The illusion worked. It was old technology – 3-D plastic specs, and tilting seats – but as the brochure brags, 'Try telling your brain it's not real.'

Points. Excitement: 7/10. Fun: 8/10.

We pass another hangar of computer games – Race Track – down a floor to Space Mission. Unfortunately it's mission impossible due to maintenance problems.

Points. Length of Kids' Faces: Very long. Robustness of Ride: 0/10 (it was only a few weeks old).

Down another level and we try to join the queue for Ghost Hunt. It's just malfunctioned so we have to wait five minutes before we can start to queue. The queue, once reached, is long, hot, boring and slow moving. You 'try telling your brain it's not real' but this is no virtual queue. Over and above the malfunction, Ghost Hunt has technical problems. It's only working at half capacity. Ghost Hunt is bizarre. You get in another cart on another train. You trundle round. Targets appear in front of you. You try to shoot them down. It's just like a regular amusement arcade machine, only you're in a cart. Weird.

Points. What *was* the point?

We spill out of Ghost Hunt to witness a now familiar vista: another sea of computer games, called The Carnival. We spot the next ride – The House of Grandish. The queue is posted as 30 minutes. It hardly moves. As we near the front, the reason becomes clear. This ride is shoebox-sized. It takes four people at a time. Each session takes four and a half minutes. As we crawl to the front of the queue, Segaworld is suddenly revealed to me as a glitzy con-trick.

'We anticipate that a true Segaworld experience will take four hours,' so we arrived at 2 pm for a 6 pm departure. It is now 4.30, a Segaperson tells me that queues are over an hour downstairs, so we are going to miss out on three out of eight rides. That's two and a half hours of queues and malfunctions, punctuated by the (very) occasional thrill. In view of the queues 'the wildest car chase of our life' gets the Denver boot.

The floor manager is summoned. Virtual tough luck, mate. Shouldn't come at a busy time. As prickly as Sonic the Hedgehog. I ask to see the Segaboss. Paul Smith, Operations Manager arrives. Yes it's very busy, but we are nowhere near our fire certificate capacity. We are the victims of our own success. If you've got a complaint write in on Monday.

Some victim, some success. We, the customers, are the victims, it seems. While Segaworld counts the money, we stand in queues. Well I have got a complaint – four, as it happens. Complaint number one is that you are sold something that Sega does not have the capacity to fulfil. But you've paid your money up-front. It's rather like paying in advance to get into a supermarket and then finding most of the shelves half-empty. Complaint number two is the temperamental technology. Complaint number three is that the rides are a sideshow. The main space is devoted to playing computer games – acres of them. And complaint number four is that the future has sadly not arrived. The rides are unimaginative, largely old-tech. This is not how I understand interactive virtual reality. There is little total immersion. You are not in control of much. Interactivity is confined to mindlessly bashing a fire button. You do not make choices, you do not interact with other people, you follow a set path. It all lacks sophistication.

I asked for a Sega comment on all this and I am told that when queues have developed pay machines have been put on freeplay. A team of engineers from Japan have been working to achieve a '100 per cent efficiency' which should reduce waiting. I am also told that Sega has the largest research and development department in its industry putting it 'at the leading edge of virtual reality'.

Let's hope next year is the year of the hedgehog.

This article first appeared in *The Times*.

Discussion of cases

Both of these cases were written by someone external to the target organizations paying for their own entrance tickets. Their format is open rather than structured or semi-structured. Their intended audience is the consumer. This has a number of results. On the negative side, the lack of structure presents problems for the use of this approach. It means that there is no systematic account of the full encounter. Some of the detail that might be of interest to the management of these attractions is not reported on (for example the cleanliness of the toilets at Segaworld). Then there is the question of 'voice'. The Mystery Shopper of Segaworld is a father of three children. It may therefore be suggested that he is not a typical Segaworld customer and therefore some of the criticisms are invalid. Also open Mystery Shopping expeditions are by nature time-consuming and labour intensive. They are inevitably a 'one off'. This can invite a question over their reliability. For example if the visit to Segaworld happened to take place on a bad day its conclusions may be less significant. This problem is less likely to occur with the less labour intensive structured Mystery Shop which can take place more often and therefore an average view can be formed. For example Domino's Pizza used 'mystery shoppers for 26 shopping visits a year at each of the 4200 outlets' (Bruno, 1988: 24). This latter type of Mystery Shopping is therefore more useful for comparisons over time and to provide a regular quality audit.

On the other hand, a very powerful picture of customer discontent emerges from the Segaworld case, which is a direct function of the open technique used. The story is not cluttered, as it would be as a structured Mystery Shop, by references to whether the toilets were clean or whether the attendants were welcoming or a whole series of standard questions. Instead a story of a customer journey is elaborated, starting with the expectation and anticipation of the visit but then demonstrating increasing frustration as the visit proceeds. The agenda emerges from the experience as encountered. The problems at Segaworld jump out of the page. Similarly a strong sense of satisfaction with the whole experience emerges for the Port Aventura case. This kind of overall feeling is rarely communicated by a structured Mystery Shop which takes a logical (but unemotional) journey through an attraction. Another advantage of the truly independent Mystery Shopper is that he or she sees problems that may be so entrenched that internal Shoppers may fail to notice. This is particularly noticeable in the Segaworld case where the Mystery Shopper sees queues as a real problem but the operations manager sees them as inevitable on busy days and even an indication of the success of the attraction. Queues had become part of the culture of Segaworld. Erstad (1998:34) reports that 'the hotels and casino group Stakis expands the scope of the mystery shopping objective to include not only front-line employees but also senior management'. The Segaworld case shows how most of the problems encountered were indeed those that could only be tackled at a very senior level.

Conclusion

Mystery Shopping has become an important part of the quality management aspect of the marketing of tourism organizations. For example, of the 110 clients of the UK specialist firm Scher Associates, the major bulk come from 'the restaurant industry, closely followed by hotels, then cinemas and leisure' (Baker, 1996). It is the favoured method of the UK Consumer Association (*Holiday Which?* 1998). This chapter has reviewed the definition of Mystery Shopping and discussed the various types that take place under this heading. It is clear that different techniques have competing strengths and weaknesses and that considerable thought needs to be given to the construction of a Mystery Shopping programme so that it is appropriate to its aims. These aims may be to provide information to consumers or to managers. In the latter case the quality loop must be closed by using the results to improve service delivery. Amongst other things this will involve the provision of appropriate feedback, the redesign of systems, the use of findings in staff induction and training, and the provision of performance related rewards. However, Mystery Shopping should be an important part of any tourism organization's self-evaluation. Whilst Segaworld London struggled to survive, Port Aventura continues to be a huge success.

Bibliography

Baker, J. (1996) 'Mystery shopping', *Hospitality* 154, 16–17.

Bare, M. L. (2000) 'Blueprints for the proper use of a mystery shopper report', *Bottomline* 15 (6), 14–15.

Bruno, K. (1988) 'Today's mystery guest is ... a food spy, hired by management, to check service', *Nation's Restaurant News* 22 (11), 24.

Cramp, B. (1994) 'Industrious espionage', *Marketing* 18 August, 17.

Erstad, M. (1998) 'Mystery shopping programmes and human resource management', *International Journal of Contemporary Hospitality Management* 10 (1), 34–8.

Gofton, K. (1995) 'Service without a smile; customer service, marketing guides, customer loyalty', *Marketing* (2 February), 3.

Holiday Which (1999) 'Which travel agent?', *Holiday Which?* (Autumn), 162–5.

Leeds, B. (1995) 'Mystery Shopping: from novelty to necessity', *Bank Marketing* 27 (6), 7.

Ryan, C. (1995) *'Researching Tourist Satisfaction: Issues, Concepts, Problems*. London: Routledge.

Schlossberg, H. (1991) 'There's no mystery in how to retain customers', *Marketing News* 25 (3), 10.

Spooner, L. (1985) 'Mystery Shoppers uncover keys to sales and service', *Savings Institutions*, 92.

Steffaneli, J. (1994) 'Using mystery shoppers to maintain hospitality company service standards', *Hospitality and Tourism Educator* 6 (1), 17–18.

Tribe, J. and T. Snaith. (1998) 'From SERVQUAL to HOLSAT: holiday satisfaction in Varadero, Cuba', *Tourism Management* 19, 25–34.

Walle, A. (1997) 'Quantitative versus qualitative tourism research', *Annals of Tourism Research* 24, 524–36.

B Continental Airlines: Turnaround through Customer-Focused Strategies

Agnes Lee DeFranco, Ed.D., CHE and Connie Mok, PhD, CHE

The Humble Beginnings

Approaching nearly 70 years of age, Continental Airlines, just as many other successful businesses, started small. In 1934, Walter T. Varney and his partner Louis Mueller founded Varney Speed Lines. Its maiden voyage was on a single-engine Lockheed aircraft and took place between the cities of El Paso, Texas and Pueblo, Colorado with stops in Las Vegas, Santa Fe and Albuquerque. In the later part of the year, Varney gave complete control of the airline to Mueller, and three years later, Mueller sold 40 per cent of the business to Robert F. Six. Six took the business and ran it for forty plus years with many ups and downs. It was Six who changed the name of Varney into Continental Airlines in 1937, and moved the headquarters from El Paso, Texas to Denver, Colorado.

War and Peace years: the 1940s to the 1960s

Continental also played a role in World War II and the Vietnam War. During the Years before World War II, Continental built the Denver Modification Center and assisted the war efforts by modifying B-17 Flying Fortresses and B-29 Super Fortresses. After World War II, Continental assumed its growth path in the civilian sector. In 1951, Continental made over $7 million in profits and spent a similar amount to update its fleet. In 1953, it merged with Pioneer Airlines, which added another sixteen cities and routes in Texas and New Mexico for

Continental, and made Continental the largest airline in Texas. Other growth indicators in the post-war years also included adding jets in the late 1950s and purchasing and maintaining its first jet fleet, a small Boeing 707 fleet.

To ensure proper care of its products, Continental instituted a 'progressive maintenance' programme. This programme was very detailed and took care of the safety and care issues. In addition, due to the great maintenance, Continental was able to fly its fleet on sixteen-hour days every day. This provided a great source of revenue for the company and Continental was on its way to being a better and more successful enterprise.

The 1960s also brought many changes to Continental. Six decided that a new image needed to go with the continued success. Thus, in 1963, Six moved the headquarters once again to a more prestigious address – Los Angeles, California. Then, Six also decided to once again assist in the war efforts. This time, Continental helped by contracting with the United States military to transport its troops to Vietnam. This move propelled the beginning of Continental's entering of the Pacific market. In 1968, Air Micronesia was formed and in 1969, Continental began its service to the Island of Hawaii.

From management to product failure to bankruptcies

The forming years of Continental proved to be successful and until the early 1970s, Continental really enjoyed good growth in the business. However, certain events led to a downturn. When President Carter approved new travel routes from Los Angeles to New Zealand and Australia in 1977, with its headquarters in Los Angeles, Continental did not think twice about expanding its fleet to take on this new venture. So, DC 10s were added to its already large inventory of planes, which were getting old and difficult to maintain. The deregulation in the airline industry in 1978 also hit Continental hard in the late 1970s. In addition, the rising oil prices that followed put Continental in a very peculiar dilemma. To save the business, Continental merged with Frank Lorenzo's Texas International in 1982. This move, which was supposed to save Continental, proved to be a poison pill for the airline.

First, the labour unions that represented Continental employees voiced objections to this merger. Second, Lorenzo moved the headquarters once again, this time to Houston. The employees never supported Lorenzo. The union employees never saw him as one of their own. Although the name of the company was still Continental and although the logo was still the same, this marriage never worked. By then, Continental had 112 aircraft flying routes to four different continents. With a labour force that was not cooperating, the relationship ended in a strike a year later, dealing the deathblow to Continental and Lorenzo. In 1983 Lorenzo was forced to file for Chapter 11 bankruptcy.

Lorenzo was not an individual who would give up easily. He immediately began the reorganization of the company and was able to post profits in 1984. By 1985, Continental began non-stop flights to London and eventually added other major cities, such as Paris, Munich, Frankfurt, and Madrid. These proved to be very profitable routes and helped Continental to be strong once again. To continue the uphill climb, Lorenzo sought other mergers with companies such as Frontier Airlines and People Express, making Continental the third largest airline in the United States.

Continental also began to take care of its customers by establishing the 'One Pass' frequent-flyer programme in 1987. A year later, they also formed the first global alliance with Scandinavian Airlines System. In 1990, Lorenzo sold most of his Continental investments and resigned as the head of the airline. Good news was still on its way as the airline announced its new logo in February of 1991 and also began its Business First service on overseas flights in October of 1992. This service was extended to its domestic flights a year later. In 1993, Continental also ordered ninety-two 737s, 757s, 767s and 777s from Boeing. This time Continental was not plagued by internal factors. Rather, the Gulf War began brewing in 1990 and the effects it had on oil prices forced Continental into its second bankruptcy in a ten-year period.

The critical years: a broken Continental

A second bankruptcy in a decade was very devastating to a company that had tried its best through various means to become once again a giant player in the sky. However, many other problems in addition to the rising oil price were plaguing Continental silently but surely.

Continental was ranked in last place in the United States Transportation Department's ranking of the nation's airlines. Both flight departures and arrivals were often not on time. Baggage handling was another challenge. Baggage was often lost or mis-routed. All this led to customer dissatisfaction and complaints, and none of it was good news for the ailing company. Continental did not have a concept or even a product that it could be proud of. It was trying to compete with the low-fare airlines by offering Continental Lite (CALite – the low-cost, short-haul, point-to-point subsidiary) as a competing brand, but this was a losing proposition from the very beginning. Brands such as Southwest were dominating this niche of the market and the CALite product was not able to pierce through the competitive barriers.

As for products, when an airline could not depart and arrive on schedule, lost luggage and gave poor service, there was not much of a product to be proud of. In addition, the 'physical' product itself was not in good condition. The carpeting in the waiting areas for the flights was in need of replacement. Paint was also peeling off. The aircraft were in such sad shape due to all the mergers that there were four different paint schemes, also peeling off, and seven different interior layouts. In other words, there was not 'one' identity to the product.

Continental had an unstable management team that managed the company with incompatible management strategies. Its management team could be said to assume the characteristics of a revolving door.

Continental went through ten Chief Executive Officers in ten years. They were mostly financial people who managed the company with financial goals and not market-driven customer goals. For instance, management would give out incentives for cost cutting. In doing so, and without realizing the negative effects, the situation became worse. In order to obtain the added bonuses and incentives, pilots would cut costs by flying at economy cruise to save fuel. The on-time arrival goal, which is more important to the customers, was neglected. This obviously led to customer dissatisfaction.

Continental also did not have employees who liked their jobs. With management giving out conflicting signals in the last decades due to all the various mergers, employees of Continental felt that they were being used in all these 'financial deals'. Some were made redundant by the company while others received wage cuts. They began to distrust management. For those who stayed on, some would even remove the Continental patch from their uniform as they did not like to be seen associated with an airline that was such a 'mess'.

Continental was in a dire financial situation with very little cash in hand: a total of $700 million. Orders for aircraft had been placed and contracts had been signed, and the CALite concept also committed Continental to leasing an additional fleet. Interest payments were due. With the CALite concept not going well, Continental still had to somehow fulfil the commitment in the aircraft leases.

The fixing team: Bethune and Brenneman

On the verge of a third bankruptcy, Gordon Bethune took control as Continental's Chief Executive Officer (CEO) in November of 1994. Bethune had been a Boeing man who held the position of Vice President and General Manager of the Boeing Commercial Airplane Group's Renton Division, which produced the Boeing 737 and 757. He also held the position of Vice President of Boeing's Customer Service Division. Thus, Bethune knew the importance of the customer in any industry. He had airline experience and had also served with the US Navy. He had worked his way up in the ranks of the Navy and became an aircraft maintenance officer.

Bethune knew that taking over Continental was not an easy task. Thus, he wasted no time in appointing Greg Brenneman as President and Chief Operating Officer (COO). Brenneman was then a 33-year-old Vice President at Bain & Co. Inc. and was the 'turnaround man' of the firm. Together Bethune and Brenneman gave Continental its blue print for a huge turnaround known as the Go Forward Plan.

The Go Forward Plan: build the customer base and profits will come

As the 'Fixing Team' described this plan, it was plain and simple – back to basics. What Continental needed was either a plan to better its product or to better its people. Of course, it would be best to have both. And the two men did just that by launching the Go Forward Plan. The plan is simple and only has four points: Fly to win, fund the future, make reliability a reality, and work together.

The four points

Fly to Win. Bethune and Brenneman took the concept of economic value-added to heart. They managed the company as if they were putting together a team to win. They began with the first point of 'Fly to Win', a strategy to provide a vision for both external and internal parties. Bethune and Brenneman analysed Continental, took the strengths of the airline and expanded on such factors, discontinuing operations that were taking away the value of Continental. First, CALite was a drain on Continental's resources and was thus cancelled. Its low-fare concept did not blend well with Continental's existing concept and it confused the customers more than helping the airline. Second, Continental wanted the 'coats and ties' group who liked service and would be willing to pay for better service. Once they knew what the customer wanted, they provided such service and adjusted the ticket prices to maximize the yield. Third, all routes were examined and those that were unlikely to make a profit were dropped. Fourth, they negotiated with international carriers to form alliances for their customers. All in all, if a strategy added value to Continental, Bethune and Brenneman would pursue it.

Fund the Future. There will only be a future if there are enough monetary resources to fund it. As mentioned, coming out of a second bankruptcy in one decade with only $700 million in cash did not provide much in the way of resources. By 1994 when Bethune became CEO, this amount was down to $300 million. Therefore, Bethune and Brenneman also worked on the financial side of the house.

To fund the future, they first looked at all the debt Continental had taken on and began negotiations to extend the amortization schedule thus lowering the amount of interest due. One of the major players that helped Continental in this regard was General Electric (GE), which gave Continental more cash in the short run to perform many of the needed repairs and concentrate on its fleets and hub sites.

Turning the focus onto its fleet: there were outstanding orders to Boeing for deliveries of new aircraft. Like GE, Boeing was under no obligation to help. However, with Bethune's ties with his former company, and wanting to keep Continental as a long term customer, Boeing let Continental defer the delivery of the aircraft and returned some of the deposits to Continental, giving Continental more cash for the rough times ahead.

The CALite programme also committed Continental to a lease for a number of Airbus A300s. With this programme now eliminated, Continental still owed the agreed amount to the lessors. Thus, Bethune and Brenneman needed to work out a plan to lease such aircraft to other airlines.

In addition to all the above measures, Continental also had to raise cash to cover all its other obligations. To do so, Continental issued convertible notes that could be converted into shares at $13 a share. Other strategies included using convertible preferred stock, enhancing equipment trusts and debt that was convertible into common stock, refinancing old higher-interest debts into new lower-interest ones. From the convertible preferred stock, $500 million was raised. This was used to retire the high-interest debt and pay off some previously issued convertible debt. As there is an obligation to pay interest on debt but dividends can be accrued, this strategy helped increase the cash flow of Continental.

Make Reliability a Reality. Continental had been rated worst on all counts by the Department of Transportation. Thus, the goal at this point of the Go Forward Plan was product specific. Continental was to produce a reliable product that the customer demanded and employees were proud to sell and be associated with. This translated into better on-time departures and arrivals, prompt baggage handling and few customer complaints. The cost-saving incentives were gone, and, with that, the pilot would pay more attention to on-time measures, which would increase customer satisfaction. Management rewarded people because of who they were – employees and associates of the company. Bethune and Brenneman also approved the distribution of bonuses, but this time such bonuses were tied to factors that would satisfy the customers and not costs.

Continental did not just ask its employees to meet all company goals without helping them to attain the goals. Little things such as painting more detailed aeroplane pathways so that crowded planes do not block each other and better positioning the baggage carts on the tarmac, so that baggage from connecting flights would not be misplaced, were just part of a more comprehensive list. Continental also launched a complex rescheduling effort in every hub by employing an aerospace model used by NASA to test routings and schedules.

Another example of an improved product under the Go Forward Plan was the meal schedule. Customers who paid hundreds of dollars for a one-way ticket would like to be served more than a small pack of nuts and a soft drink. To cut costs, Continental had a policy of not serving food on flights that were less than two-and-a-half hours. To make this work, Continental had been flying point-to-point on short-hauls rather than non-stop. This 'policy' saved money on food costs but also caused Continental to have an undesirable product. Thus, this policy was also changed.

To add to the product column, Continental also brought back all services of its frequent flyer programme that had been lost through the cost cutting of the last few years. It also expanded its first class so as to provide more opportunities for its frequent flyers in the coach class to enjoy upgrades. Again, the goal here was to provide a safe, clean, on-time airline competitive in the market.

To ensure that the customers were getting what they wanted, Continental also set up a 24-hour hot line to handle complaints. Instead of staffing this hot line with receptionists, there would always be a pilot, a flight attendant, a mechanic and a reservations agent. By doing so, two purposes were served. First, these staff members would be able to hear any complaints first hand and would also be best to deal with the issues brought forth. Second, from the customers' point of view, it was always better to talk to somebody who could relate to them rather than a person who was purely relaying the message. This hot line was also instructed to let the customers know that they would receive a response to their suggestion and concern within 48 hours.

Those customers who would rather voice their opinions in writing were encouraged by Continental to do so. Response cards were inserted in all the Continental in-flight magazines so that customers could access them easily. By opening these lines of communications, Continental produced a product that lowered customer complaints significantly.

Working Together. Employees and management of Continental were like ene-mies, which was not a healthy situation. Strikes, bankruptcies, redundancies and wage cuts were fresh in many people's mind. Distrust was the way of life. Thus, the fourth point was to work with the internal customers – the employees, and to start with a clean slate, making Continental a place where people enjoyed coming to work rather than tearing off the Continental patches on their uniform. To achieve this, many management practices were changed or instituted. Management now rewarded cooperation and adopted an open-door policy. Before this 'Working Together' concept, senior level management, including vice presidents, were not able to see the president or CEO without an appointment. This practice fostered paranoia and ill will. In addition, there were security cameras on the executive floors of the Houston headquarters. To show the trust they had for their own employees, Bethune and Brenneman took away all such cameras. To make himself 'one of the regulars', Bethune also instituted dress-down Fridays.

Continental also practised empowerment by letting employees make their own judgements. This was a very powerful message, as trust was passed from the top down. They did away with the old employee manual by burning it at the headquarters in Houston. To replace that, Continental now had a set of 'guidelines', only about a third as thick as the old policy manual.

The Go Forward Plan was summarized and the results were printed in the Go Forward Bulletins that were widely distributed to all the employees. A monthly newsletter was also published. Bethune himself would record a mes-sage every week that could be accessed by all his employees. The message would invariably summarize the events of the past week, things that would happen in the coming week, and the thank-yous that he wanted his people to have. Moreover, monthly open houses were held in Houston, and Bethune would visit new employees at their training classes. He would talk to the new blood about the culture of Continental. Thus, other channels of communication were also established between management and employees to make Continental a real team, and a real family.

The rewards and awards

The impact of this plan on Continental was absolutely astounding. In 1994, Continental ranked last in all three categories of services (on-time performance, customer complaints and lost baggage) as measured by the Department of Transportation. By 20 January 1995, Continental was ranked seventh. Bethune also announced on that day that every employee would get a $65 monthly bonus if Continental were rated in the top five for that particular month. This move tied the four points in the Go Forward Plan together. In order to have a good product, employees would have to work together. With people working together and with a good product, business would increase and the financial position would stabilize. This is exactly what 'Fly to Win' was set out to do!

This encouragement, a $65 monthly bonus announced in January, only took a month to materialize. By February, Continental was rated fourth. All employees were given this extra cheque with a note from management that said 'Thank you for helping us be on time.' By March, just one more month, Continental was ranked first and held that position for many months to come. By late 1995, Bethune wanted to change the $65 top-five bonus to $100 if Continental were ranked in the top three. This was supposed to come into effect in January 1996. However, when Continental was ranked first again in December 1995, everybody received the $100 rather than the $65. Thus, Bethune not only exceeded the expectations of Continental's customers but also Continental's employees.

One might argue that these bonuses might cripple a cash-short Continental. However, in total these bonuses were far less than the money Continental had had to spend on accommodating passengers who were stranded due to delayed flights.

This move boosted employee morale tremendously. Continental employees were proud to be identified with the 'winning team' that 'flies to win' and the staff turnover rate dropped by 33 per cent.

The awards that Continental and its officers received included but were not limited to:

- 1995, J. D. Power and Associates and *Frequent Flyer* magazine named Continental as the top US, long-haul airline in achieving customer satisfaction.
- 1995, the Power survey also rated Continental in a tie for second place among short-haul carriers.
- 1995, *Entrepreneur* magazine cited Continental as the airline with the best transatlantic business class.
- 1995, *InsideFlyer* magazine rated Continental's as the best elite-level frequent-flier programme.
- 1995, New York Stock Exchange (NYSE) named *Business Week* and Continental the NYSE Shares of the Year.
- 1995, *Fortune* called Continental the best investment of 1995.
- 1996, *Business Week* named Bethune as one of the Top 25 Business Managers of 1996.
- 1996, October, Continental was ranked by the Department of Transportation as one of the top three airlines in on-time arrivals, baggage handling and fewest customer complaints.

Financial order restored

Since Funding the Future was one of the four points, the Go Forward Plan had an enormous financial impact. In October 1996, Continental had $865 million in cash reserves and its stock price had more than tripled, from $4 to $13 a share. Kellner, the chief financial officer, credited this to the 'margin' concept rather than the cost alone. He also admitted that Continental needed to learn how to spend its money properly.

In 1995, Continental earned net revenue of $224 million and was named by the NYSE as one of its Stocks of the Year. In the first half of 1996, Continental was also able to raise $650 million to finance new aircraft. Bethune and his team had really turned the company around. By 1998, revenues reached $7.9 billion and pre-tax profit was a record $770 million. Cash balances at the end of 1998 were in excess of $1 billion, and earnings per share increased from $4.17 in 1996 to $5.02 in 1998.

From the employees' viewpoint, Continental has paid a total of $270 million in profit sharing since 1996. In 1998 alone, Continental employees received $23 million in on-time bonuses.

Other new strides

Besides the strategies of the Go Forward plan, there were many other positive moves that made Continental what it is today.

Working with global and diverse suppliers

To aid in its turnaround, Continental knew that it could not rely on a few sources of supplies. Thus, it began to work with many suppliers in a diverse and global fashion. From aerospace companies to uniform suppliers, from firms who produce hand-sewn leather seat covers to Subway sandwiches, to Rolls-Royce engines to electronic data management systems, Continental works with all its partners in the same way as it works with its customers and employees.

Flexible maintenance plan

In 1993, Continental did more than 90 per cent of its maintenance inhouse, at a cost of over $770 million. By 1996, this amount was reduced by about 30 per cent through careful out-sourcing. At that time, the maintenance market outside the airline industry had extra capacity, and thus was willing to negotiate with customers like Continental. So, Continental was able to negotiate some reasonable contract services rates. By out-sourcing some of the maintenance work which could be done more efficiently and effectively, Continental was also able to concentrate its efforts on other areas such as overnight servicing to improve dispatch reliability and reduce delays and maintenance cancellations.

Web site and e-ticket

Joining the information highway, Continental also instituted a user-friendly web site so that its customers could check for departures, arrivals, frequent-flyer accounts, and even special promotions and discounts. The e-ticket concept, which began in mid 1995, was a bold step forward that has also received much positive feedback. It provides a venue for the more 'high-tech' preferred travellers to 'zip' through the check-in process. This also lessens the amount of waiting time for the rest of the travellers who prefer to be taken care of by an agent.

Global alliances and new routes

In early 1998, Continental allied with Northwest Airlines to code share. This also enabled Continental to work with Northwest partners such as KLM. All these alliances gave Continental's customers more choices and more services. The non-stop flight from Houston to Tokyo in late 1988 represented another milestone for Continental.

Conclusion

All in all, Continental, through its Go Forward Plan, switched the company's philosophy around from financial only to people friendly, not only to its customers but also to its employees. It recognized the importance of empowering its employees to perform and good performance is rewarded. Customer's needs are carefully studied and satisfied to stay competitive in the marketplace. Customers are happy with the product and become more loyal. Employees feel the sense of belonging and pride; and the financial community sees the black rather than red in Continental's future. Continental turned around by executing a strong service concept; they do things better than their competitors; they listen carefully to employees and customers; they invest in the performers of the service; they strive to exceed customers' expectations; and they always try to improve their service performance. In 1997, Continental won its second J. D.

Power Award and was also named Airline of the Year by Air Transport World. Its One Pass frequent flyer programme also received many accolades. What a 'turnaround' story in the airline industry!

Bibliography

Continental Annual Report, 1998.
www.hoovers.com/premium
www.quicken.excite.com
www.continental.com
www.onepass.com
'The top managers of 1996', *Business Week* (13 January, 1997).
'Continental Airlines: a Texas turnaround', *Aviation Week & Space Technology* (16 December, 1996). Advertiser Sponsor Market Supplement S1–S19.
'Airline of the Year: Continental Airlines', *Air Transport World* (February 1997). Awards Issue.
'Going Forward: Gordon Bethune has taken Continental from the bottom to the top', *Travel Agent* (6 January, 1997).
McCartney, S. (1995) 'How to make an airline run on schedule', *Wall Street Journal*. 22 December.
O'Brian, B. (1995) 'Continental Airlines is not climbing toward a profit', *Wall Street Journal* 22 June.

C Air 2000

John Gountas

History

On 11 April 1987 the Owners Abroad Group launched a new charter airline, Air 2000. The mission was to create a new kind of leisure airline combining exceptional value for money with unprecedented levels of service, reliability and performance. The name of Air 2000 was deliberately chosen to convey the message of an airline of 'tomorrow for the leisure travellers of today' (air2000.co.uk website, 2001).

For the company's first season two new Boeing 757s were operated, enabling the airline to undertake some 35 flights per week from its Manchester base to 12 popular Mediterranean destinations. By 1990, the fleet had grown to eight 757s plus a single 148-seat Boeing 737–300. By this time the carrier was flying an intensive series of inclusive tours (IT) services from Manchester and Glasgow to the Mediterranean and Orlando, Florida. Air 2000 also added Gatwick as one of its UK departure points, providing seats for operators other than its parent company, Owners Abroad. Other long-haul routes were soon added including Kenya, Mexico and the Caribbean.

Over the years, the number of routes and services increased and the airline entered the scheduled short-haul market by providing new services for the hybrid market of the business and leisure travellers.

In its fifteen-year history, at the time of publication, Air 2000 has established itself as a leading leisure airline by listening to its customers and introducing innovative practices ahead of its competitors. The changing attitudes of the UK travelling public necessitate the constant adaptation of the service provisions (Gountas and Carey, 2000). Since 1990 when the coveted Golden Globe Award was established, Air 2000 has won it for the 'Best UK

Charter Airline' seven times. This achievement reinforces the airline's claims of being one of the leading leisure airlines. The award formally recognizes all the efforts by the Air 2000 employees and it is a tangible appreciation by the air passengers.

> Commenting on the award, Ken Smith, Air 2000 MD, said this is a magnificent achievement and a tribute to the consistently high standard set by all who work for Air 2000. Winning the award in 1999 sets the seal on our ambition to be 'The Holiday Airline' for the new millennium. Immediately after regaining the award in 1998, we set ourselves the target of holding on to it into the year 2000 and beyond. I am delighted that we have been successful. Receiving the Golden Globe Award from the travel industry for a second consecutive year running is a recognition of our success to date. (air2000.co.uk website, 2001)

Following a change of senior management in 1995, the Owners Abroad group, which owned Air 2000, was re-branded as First Choice Holidays PLC. Some two-thirds of Air 2000's passengers are First Choice clients, with more than 120 other tour operators and groups making up the balance.

In 1997, Air 2000 together with Landor, a recognized leader in airline corporate-identity design, undertook the first re-branding of its image. The idea was to create a design which would, by incorporating various cultural icons, reflect the destinations to which the airline flies. 'Displaying the tapestry of colours theme on our aircraft tells the world at a glance that we fly our customers to different exotic and many fun places where they can sample the delights of foreign cultures for themselves.'

In October 1998, the First Choice Group and Air 2000 became a fully vertically integrated tour operator with the announcement of its distribution strategy and creation of a retail division. By the end of 1999, the Group had a retail presence in over 607 shop equivalents. First Choice Holidays PLC's principal areas of activity are:

• Air Inclusive Holidays
• Charter Airline Operations
• Travel Retailing
• Yachting and Watersports Holidays.

Air 2000 flies from fifteen regional airports in the UK and Ireland carrying nearly seven million passengers to more than fifty destinations around the world. Air 2000 operates scheduled flights from the UK to Cyprus, the Canary Islands, mainland Spain and Portugal.

Based on the experience gained by operating scheduled flights to Cyprus since 1993, Air 2000 expanded the scheduled services network by a further 46 routes for Summer 2001. The new routes provide a new cost-effective option to both holiday-makers and business travellers alike and supplement the existing scheduled services to Cyprus. The number of scheduled return flights now offered by Air 2000 is over 100 per week. The company's mission has been adapted somewhat from the one in 1987, by recognizing the vital importance of the distribution network and vertical integration of the company. According to Prahalad and Hamel (1990), corporations need to rethink the core competencies and identify new strategic approaches in order to grow. For the Tour Operations corporations the international competition is growing and major competitors have already achieved a high degree of vertical integration.

Key dates in the history of Air 2000 and First Choice

- 1973 Owners Abroad (Wholesale Ltd) formed from merger of Continental Air Brokers and Economy World Travel.
- 1982 Owners Abroad becomes Owners Abroad Group PLC and is floated on USM.
- 1983 Acquisition of Falcon. 1984 Acquisition of 2wentys.
- 1987 Formulation of Air 2000 and full stock-market listing. In 1988, 25 per cent stake in ITH, Canada.
- 1990 Acquisition of Sovereign.
- 1991 Air 2000 voted Best UK Charter Airline.
- 1992 Relocation of Head Office to Crawley, West Sussex, England. Air 2000 voted Best UK Charter Airline.
- 1993 Hostile Airtours bid defeated, new Chairman and Chief Executive appointed. Air 2000 voted Best UK Charter Airline.
- 1994 ITH, Canada becomes 100 per cent owned.
- 1995 Owners Abroad re-launched as First Choice (new brands, new corporate identity, new management structure, new head office).
- 1995 ITH re-launched as Signature Vacations. Acquisition of JWT Holidays and SkiBound. Air 2000 voted Best UK Charter Airline.
- 1998 Acquisition of Unijet PLC. Acquisition of Hayes and Jarvis. Holiday Hypermarkets joint venture with West Midlands Cooperative Society, United Norwest Co-operative Society and First Choice Holidays PLC launched. Acquisition of Intatravel.
- 1999 Air 2000 voted Best UK Charter Airline. First Choice voted Best Short Haul UK Tour Operator. Acquisition of Meon Travel. Acquisition of Sunsail International Limited. Acquisition of FlexiGroup. Travel Choice Direct opens, complementing the retail network of Travel Choice shops and Travel Choice Express outlets. Announced intention to increase to 100 per cent shareholding in Holiday Hypermarkets. In 2001, acquired French long haul specialist and Italian specialist I Viaggi Del Turchese S.R.L.

Overall Group Divisional Structure

The Company has five Operating Divisions, with Chief Executive, Peter Long.

UK and Ireland

Its principal businesses are structured into three main areas: Tour Operations, Distribution and Airline and Aviation.

Tour Operations division includes four major areas of business:

- The First Choice Holidays Divisions (leading mainstream brands) include: First Choice, Unijet, Falcon, JWT, Eclipse, Sunquest, 2wentys, Ski, Lakes and Mountains, Flexiski, Sunmed and Sunstart.
- The First Choice Independent Travel Division (Specialist Businesses) includes: Flights (First Choice, Unijet, Air 2000), Suncars (Worldwide Car Hire), Hays and Jarvis, Meon Villas, Longshot Golf Holidays and Flexi Conferences.
- Citalia Holidays (leading premium specialist tour operator).
- Sunshine Cruises (joint venture Cruise Business together with RCCL 'island').

Distribution includes Retail shops (Travel Choice, Bakers Dolphin, and strategic retail partner Hays Travel).

Airline and Aviation includes Air 2000 and Viking Aviation.

Barceló Travel

A number of separate companies operate within this division covering the Spanish, Portuguese and Latin American markets.

European specialist business

This division covers all operations in France, Germany, Austria, Switzerland, Belgium and Italy.

Canada

This division covers operations in Canada (Signature Vacations, Sun Holidays, Franchise offices of the American Express Travel services), and the American Express Leisure Travel.

First Choice Marine

This includes all the 'Watersports' types of operations (Sunsail International, Crown Blue Line and Stardust).

The Group's human resources

The airline Air 2000 is an integral part of the First Choice Group of companies, and currently employs approximately 2,500 staff as follows: 350 pilots, 1500 cabin crew, 200 engineering staff, 125 ground operations and 325 ground administration. However, the First Choice group of companies as a whole employs over 11,000 people, operating from ten countries worldwide and carrying five million holidaymakers in the year 2000.

Air 2000's performance from 1997–2000 has shown a healthy growth in turnover and number of employees.

Year Ended October	1997	1998	1999
Turnover (£'000s)	275,341	319,451	477,499
Total Number of staff	1,297	1,383	2,345

Training Policy

Air 2000 believes that the quality of the staff is the most important asset for the success of the company. All staff in all departments, from the cabin service to engineering, are highly trained individuals. The training programmes are systematic and consistent over a long period of time to ensure up-skilling of all staff. This is reflected in a number of ways, from the extensive Safety Training for all the cabin crew and flight deck, to the high level of training for aircraft maintenance and operations staff. Training is also carried out to cover subjects such as human factors and general familiarization for the Boeing 757 and 767 aircraft. This training is carried out at Commonwealth House, which houses a total of eight fully enclosed classrooms.

More technical training opportunities are available because Air 2000 Engineering headquarters are located in purpose-built offices at Manchester

International airport. Air 2000 currently conducts aircraft type training to ATA 104 level 3.

Extensive and continuous training opportunities exist throughout the Group of First Choice companies for customer service, Information Technology, overseas operations, sales and marketing and other types of operations-related training. The location of the training can be the UK or various overseas destinations, depending on the type and level of training.

The successful operations of Air 2000 are the result of a tremendous team effort in all areas of operations such as route licensing, engineering, cabin crew training and catering. Bateson and Hoffman (1999) suggest that every employee in a direct or indirect way has an influence on the quality of service delivered. Investing in the development of the employees' skills means the airline's service is likely to improve.

Types of aircraft and safety issues

The airline's growth has been consistent and steady over the past 14 years.

- The fleet now has a total of 29 aircraft (four 767s, 16 757s, five A321s and four A320s). Air 2000 is now the second largest UK leisure airline, operating 30,000 flights a year, flying from fifteen regional airports in the UK and Ireland, carrying nearly eight million passengers to more than fifty destinations around the world.
- In 1992 the introduction of the four Airbus A320 aircraft brought about a significant change in the company's engineering philosophy. Air 2000 retained airworthiness and engineering control of the A320 fleet. In July 1992, a line maintenance facility was set up at Bristol.
- In 1993, it was decided to extend Air 2000's airworthiness control and for engineering to encompass the Boeing 757 fleet in addition to the A320 fleet. This exercise was phased in between November 1993 and April 1994. Air 2000 now exercises complete airworthiness and engineering control of all the aircraft in the fleet, contracting, where appropriate, base and line maintenance.
- In 1998, Air 2000's parent company First Choice Holidays PLC acquired Unijet and Hayes and Jarvis. This in turn increased the fleet size due to the acquisition of Leisure International, which was part of Unijet.
- Air 2000 currently offers line-maintenance services to Airtours, Britannia, Monarch, JMC, Transaer and Air Mauritius and is actively involved with a number of leasing companies dealing with aircraft acceptance and lease returns. Air 2000 also has the capability to support other operators with management services. These services include, but are not limited to, Technical Services, Technical Records, Production Planning, Powerplant Management, Maintenance Control, Reliability and Development, Materials Control and Aircraft Projects.
- At Air 2000, operational safety is the main priority and takes precedence over all other areas of the company's business. The airline's management ensures that they meet the

highest levels of safety and comply with all the regulatory standards in order to maintain the confidence and trust of the passengers.

Current Air 2000 destinations/product range

The *charter flights* cover an extensive range of destinations throughout Europe, the Caribbean islands, USA, Mexico and Brazil. Passengers can fly out of all the UK regional airports (see the air2000 web site on flights for a detailed breakdown of all available charter and scheduled flights).

The *scheduled services* go to all the major holiday and travel destinations in which the group of companies operate. Based on the past experience gained by operating scheduled flights, Air 2000 expanded the scheduled services network by a further 46 routes for summer 2001.

Air 2000 now operates the following scheduled services

- From Birmingham, London Gatwick, Manchester and Newcastle to Alicante, Malaga, Larnaca, Paphos, Palma, Tenerife, Lanzarote and Faro.
- From Bristol to Alicante, Malaga, Palma, Lanzarote and (new for summer 2001) Faro.
- From Cardiff to Alicante, Malaga, Palma, Tenerife, Faro, Lanzarote and (new for Summer 2001) Larnaca and Paphos.
- From Glasgow to Alicante, Malaga, Lanzarote, Tenerife, Larnaca, Paphos, Faro and (new for Summer 2001) Palma.
- From London Stansted to Lanzarote, Tenerife and (new for Summer 2001) Paphos.

Air 2000 has a range of flights to suit different needs. The existing scheduled services allow passengers maximum flexibility to satisfy their needs by offering one-way tickets for a short break or for a longer stay abroad.

Air 2000's varied fleet of aircraft enables the airline to fly regularly *ad-hoc air services* for various sizes of groups to any route around the world. The fleet operates on short-, medium- and long-haul routes with the ability to fly to some of the world's most difficult and demanding airfields.

Air 2000 operates *VIP flights* with two dedicated Boeing 757 aircraft with all the 'VIP' configurations of just 92 seats during the winter months of November to April (northern hemisphere). Since 1996, the airline has flown numerous private jet tours to destinations not readily accessible to the everyday traveller including several 'around the world' tours. These trips have been successfully organized and promoted by a US-based company to various groups including university alumni associations and museum study groups as well as to the public in general.

Distribution of Air 2000 seat capacity

Viking Aviation is the worldwide sales and marketing department for aircraft seats for all the companies of the vertically integrated group of First Choice companies. The sister company Air 2000 benefits directly for all the flight requirements for the short-haul and long-haul destinations. The aircraft seat capacities are sold to a wide cross-section of tour operators including of course all the tour operating companies of First Choice (Unijet, Hayes and Jarvis and Falcon Ireland).

Viking Aviation is responsible for the sale and purchase of nearly 5 million seats annually, of which over 3 million are with Air 2000. The remaining business is with other leading British and European charter airlines. Given the volumes that Viking purchase, Air 2000 is well placed to be competitive in a highly volatile market with strong emphasis on price, quality and range of products and flexibility of services. The vertical integration allows Air 2000 to be both innovative and flexible with the services that it offers to the different market segments.

Selling benefits to differentiate from the competition

Air 2000 has a reputation for high standards for pre-flight and in-flight services provided on all types of charter, ad-hoc, VIP and scheduled flights. For long-haul flights Air 2000 offers a choice of Classic Premium or 'Classic' flights. With the Air 2000 *Classic Premium long-haul flights*, passengers can enjoy the comforts that make a real difference to a long-haul flight, without breaking the bank. The benefits that differentiate this service are

- A dedicated cabin with 38 seats; more comfortable seats with extra leg room, greater width and complimentary drinks (excluding champagne).
- A personal video player with a choice of 10 films.
- Choice of three hot meal entrees outbound and two hot meal entrees inbound (with stainless steel cutlery) including cheese and fruit service.
- Fast check in (within 90 minutes). A dedicated check in is provided at the UK and overseas airports (where available). There are also VIP airport lounge facilities where available (for a small additional surcharge); a luggage allowance of 30 kilograms and all this at competitive prices.

The *'Classic' service* offers great value for short-haul flights. This is a scheduled service which has been upgraded by the addition of various benefits to make it as pleasant as possible. Some of the benefits included in the 'Classic' service are:

- Complimentary glass of wine with dinner.
- Free headset to enjoy a full range of in-flight entertainment and complimentary children's fun-pack
- For ease and comfort and at no extra charge, passengers travelling on the scheduled services are automatically pre-seated together onboard.

The passengers on the luxury private jets either on the *VIP or ad-hoc services* experience top class service with a dedicated on-board chef, silver service and dedicated aircrew, who remain with the aircraft for the entire programme.

The usual benefits that *all Air 2000 passengers* enjoy are

- Passengers can visit the flight deck onboard of the aircraft or they can experience flying one of the Boeing jets by using the Virtual Cockpit facility provided by Air 2000. (Visits to the flight deck were suspended by all airlines following the terrorist attacks in the USA on 11th September 2001.)
- Through the Air 2000 website up-to-date information and advice is provided for transportation needs, for international dialling codes, details for health issues such as immunization and online consultation worldwide.
- The airline provides general information websites and contact details regarding political situations overseas (e.g. Foreign and Commonwealth Office).
- Organization of parking facilities such as NCP operated airport car parks in ten UK airports offering convenient facilities close to the terminal buildings and with special price deals.
- Free online weather information pages and pre-booking facility for seats and advanced luggage checking.
- Flying with Air 2000, customers can take advantage of BAA's airport upgrade packages and enjoy access to some special services before they fly.
- The GatwickPLUS package includes Fast Track security clearance, entries to the VIP Lounge, commission free foreign currency exchange and a range of special shopping and eating offers.
- Passengers who plan to travel to the airport by car can add Valet Parking to their package by simply pulling up in front of the airport departures building and Air 2000 will park the car and deliver it back again when they return.

In-flight entertainment (benefits) for children and adults

Air 2000 offers its passengers a choice of in-flight entertainment for kids and adults using a dedicated onboard system with controls at every seat. On all flights greater than three hours, one of the latest Hollywood blockbuster movies is normally shown. A different film is played on the outbound and inbound flights. For shorter flights, a selection of classic TV comedy, travel programmes and weekly updates is usually shown. Passengers can order a box of Thornton's Luxury Truffle Assortment at £5.00, Daim Bars at £4.00 or Thornton's special toffee at £4.00 to enjoy during the film.

Even a short journey can seem long to children, so the airline has designed a Kid's Pack. It's specially designed to keep active hands and minds occupied and entertained. Kids can also tune in to a special audio channel designed just for them. There is provision of special children's meals at reasonable prices. However, these must be booked before departure with Customer Relations. If the holiday is booked at least 56 days prior to flight departure the airline can pre-book children's meals free of charge. There are up to 10 channels (Boeing 757) of audio entertainment accessible from every seat. The selection has been carefully designed to appeal to most tastes e.g. The Comfort Zone, Best of the 90s, Comedy, Rock, Pop, Country, Classics, Jazz, Kids and Kiss FM.

Service provision

The management team at Air 2000 is progressive and proactive in its thinking of how to improve and innovate in order to stay ahead of the competition. Ongoing market surveys are essential (Malhotra, 1999) because they can reveal accurately the overall standard of performance. The surveys conducted by Air 2000 show that the overall satisfaction rates are high on all areas of the service interaction: checking in, ground-staff service, on-board facilities and services, entertainment, food and beverages and overall standards of cleanliness and appearance of staff and aircraft. Air 2000 competes effectively with all other leisure airlines and reaches the standards of some of the top performing scheduled airlines in terms of in-flight comforts. It provides as wide a range of services as offered by all other competing scheduled and charter airlines.

However Air 2000, like all other airlines, is not always able to match the high standards of home entertainment that the modern travelling public is used to. The airline through continuous marketing research identifies the needs of the travelling public and provides the services that are feasible and most preferable. Air 2000 continuously raises the bar of service quality in all the aspects of flying operations. Lovelock, Patterson and Walker (1998) suggest that customer satisfaction is a moving target and therefore the organization needs to improve its service levels constantly.

Environmental policy

While the economics of leisure operation dictate the need to make high utilization of aircraft, including night-time operations where permitted, Air 2000 fully recognizes the wider environmental need to minimize disturbance to those who live near airports and thus keeps night flying to a minimum.

Through the use of new technologies, the average global fuel consumption of a new passenger jet is half its level of 20 years ago. Between 1991 and 1994 alone, the carbon dioxide, nitrogen oxide and carbon monoxide content in emissions was reduced on average by 17 per cent and there was a 40 per cent drop in the content of incombustible hydrocarbons.

Nonetheless, intensive development work is still required to better protect the environment while satisfying the human demand for mobility. To that end Air 2000 exceeds the requirements of most relevant environmental legislation by operating a modern, fuel-efficient, low-level emission fleet of aircraft, all of which fall into the quietest noise categories for their type set by the Department of Transport. In addition, and wherever practical, Air 2000 recycles its in-flight catering equipment and packaging both to ensure efficient usage of the world's limited resources and to minimize pollution.

Corporate Strategy summary

The First Choice group of companies sees itself as a leading European leisure travel company comprising mainstream and specialist tour operations, travel retail and aviation businesses

In 1994 the company was restructured and was re-branded as First Choice Holidays PLC. Following Board level changes a new Group Managing Director, Peter Long, was installed together with Executive Deputy Chairman, Ian Clubb, and a strengthened management team. A three-year recovery plan was implemented, the UK Expansion and Distribution Strategy 1998-2000. Throughout the recovery period the company grew by acquisition and the implementation of a distribution strategy, which transformed First Choice into a fully vertically integrated and successful travel group. The UK travel industry rapidly began to consolidate in the late 1980s and 1990s. First Choice played an active role by acquiring, in June 1998, two key UK tour operators, the Unijet Travel Group and Hayes and Jarvis.

In the same year, other acquisitions included the retail agencies Bakers Dolphin and Intatravel, to complement the opening of new travel shops under the name of Travel Choice and Travel Choice Express, and the initial stake (25 per cent) in Holiday Hypermarkets, the out-of-town travel superstores. UK acquisitions in 1999 were of premium-niche-market operators: Meon (Meon Villas and Longshot Golf Holidays), Flexigroup (ski holidays and conferences) and Sunsail (leading yacht charter and watersports club operator). Within retail, Ferrychoice, a small regional agency chain and a number of small Irish agents were also acquired.

In May 2000 First Choice announced the acquisition of the remaining outstanding interest in Holiday Hypermarkets, previously a joint venture between West Midlands Co-operative Society, United Norwest Co-operative Society and First Choice. Holiday Hypermarkets now holds the number one position in the growing out-of-town travel-retailing sector with 27 sites across the UK, as at October 2000.

As part of its strategy to play a major part in the consolidation of the European travel industry, First Choice announced the following in the first six months of 2000: a strategic alliance and £200 million investment in First Choice Holidays by Royal Caribbean Cruises Ltd, the acquisition of Ten Tour Group's European Tour Operating Businesses and Barceló Travel Division plus the option of a hotel joint venture. First Choice now has a presence in France, Spain, Belgium, Germany, Austria, Switzerland and Southern Ireland.

Transforming the First Choice Group

Following the completion of the three-year recovery target to return the Group to profitability and achieve industry-average margins, First Choice now believes it has the highest UK tour-operating margins of the major UK tour operators. As outlined in the 2000 preliminary results the next stage in the Company's strategy is to build upon the transformation of the Company into a leading leisure-travel company. There is a clear vision to differentiate from competitors through specialization, providing lifestyle holidays for its customers. Mintzberg, Quinn and Ghoshal (1998) and Kotler and Armstrong (1999) suggest that the most effective way to achieve a sustainable competitive advantage is through differentiation of the services offered.

Strategy 2000 saw the commencement of the anticipated consolidation within the European tour-operating industry. In particular there was a con-vergence of a small number of European participants principally in the UK and Germany, the two most dominant markets in Europe. First Choice has not participated in this mass-market consolidation, clearly setting out a strategy to differentiate from the traditional main competitors. The year 2000 was a year of achievement and change for the First Choice Group. The group commenced its transformation from a UK tour operator into a leading European leisure travel group. Thus far the overall strategic objectives have been

- To continue to improve the profit margins within the core UK tour-operating business through capacity control and effective yield-management techniques.
- To further develop distribution capabilities and increase the percentage of sales via direct routes to market.
- To continue investment in those specialist businesses, both in the UK and Europe, which can provide above-industry-average margins and are more robust.
- To continue to differentiate the Group from its competitors in the UK and Europe by investing in specialist niche businesses. It is Air 2000's intention to deliver up to 50 per cent of their profits from these businesses within a three-year period.

Financial highlights of year ended 31 October 2000

- Record profits before tax of £68.9m compared to £46.9m, an increase of 47 per cent (1999: profit before tax of £38.0m as restated)
- 33 per cent of profits before goodwill and tax generated from the Specialist Businesses
- Profits on underlying trading up by 19 per cent before restatement
- Record margins of 5.4 per cent in UK Tour Operating
- Shareholders funds up by 250 per cent to £417.3m
- Earnings per share before goodwill amortization up by 36 per cent to 11.3p (9.7 per cent increase before restatement prior to year results)
- Distribution capability enhanced with further plans for Hypermarket and e-commerce development
- Final dividend of 2.6p (1999: 2.4p)
- Total dividend of 3.9p (1999: 3.6p) up by 8 per cent.

Year:	2000	1999**	% Change
Turnover (£'s)	1880.7m	1465.8m	+28%
Profit before taxation* (£'s)	88.8m	63.5m	+40%
Earnings per share	11.3p	8.3p	+36%
Dividend per ordinary share	3.9p	3.6p	+8%

** Where applicable 1999 comparatives are as restated
* Before exceptional items, goodwill amortization and retail losses

For more details of the profit and loss account for the past five years refer to the latest annual report which is available on the First Choice web site (firstchoice.co.uk). For the overall trends and passenger figures carried by all the ATOL licence holders in the UK see the web site of the Civil Aviation Authority (CAA).

¹¹² Bibliography

Bateson, J. E. C. and Hoffman, K. D. (1999) 'Managing Services Marketing, Text and Readings', London: The Dryden Press Harcourt Brace College Publications.

Gountas, J. and Carey, S. (2000) 'The Changing Attitudes to "mass tourism" products', *Journal of Vacation Marketing* 6 (1), 69–75.

Kotler, P. and Armstrong, G. (1999) *Principles of Marketing*. London: Prentice Hall, International Edition.

Lovelock, C. H., Patterson, P. G. and Walker, R. H. (1998) *Services Marketing, Australia and New Zealand*. Sydney: Prentice Hall.

Malhotra, N. K. (1999) *Marketing Research, An Applied Orientation*. 3rd edn. London: Prentice Hall, International Edition.

Mintzberg, H., Quinn, J. B. and Ghoshal S. (1998) *The Strategy Process* London: Prentice Hall, Rev. European edn.

Prahalad, C. K. and Hamel, G. (1990) 'The core competence of the corporation', *Harvard Business Review* (May–June).

D Chinese Tourism: Emerging Markets

Grace Wen Pan

Introduction

As part of the strategy to modernize China, the country entered an era of economic reform under the leadership of Deng Xiaoping, beginning in 1978. Gradually and cautiously, it began to open the gates in the bamboo curtain to world commerce and tourism. The 'Socialist market economy', as it was called by Chinese leaders, was adopted in 1992. It is meant to imply that much of China's economy is to be guided by market forces (Thomm, 1996). Because of China's confidence in its economic reforms through experimentation with this market economy, the nation has enjoyed political stability and economic prosperity. Between 1979 and 1997, China's economy grew by 9.8 per cent on an annual basis, 6.5 per cent higher than the world average, 7.3 per cent higher than developed countries and 4.8 per cent higher than developing countries (*Beijing Review*, 1999).

This case study examines how tourism in China has developed in three steps, namely inbound tourism by overseas tourists, domestic tourism by Chinese tourists, and outbound tourism by Chinese tourists (Dou and Dou, 1999). It has been suggested that the development of tourism activity is a barometer of the country's economic prosperity and its political enlightenment (Wang, Zhang and Cai, 1997).

Inbound Tourism in China

Under Mao Zedong's regime China was liberated by the Communist Party from Kuo Mingdang (Chang Kai Chek) in 1949, however, a near total ban on inbound travel for any purpose was enforced between 1949 and 1976. This isolationism fostered widespread interest in China amongst foreigners. The introduction of Deng Xiaoping's economic reform, a radical change in policy, brought the rapid development of inbound tourism in China. However, during the first four years from 1978–82, the government mainly focused on educational and political visits to China. In 1982 the Government recognized tourism as an economic activity, and the three facets of tourism in China have developed.

Before 1978, less than a dozen Chinese cities were open to foreign tourists, and tourist activity in these cities was carefully controlled and monitored by the state government. This number increased to 60 in 1979, more than 200 in 1984 and 496 in 1987 (Ritchter, 1989). There were 1068 cities and counties opened to foreigners by 1994 (Bailey, 1995). By the beginning of the twenty-first century, tourists were at liberty to visit virtually every part of China without restrictions.

Table D.1 International visitor arrivals in China, 1978–1999

Source: *China Statistical Year Book,* (1999)

The tourism industry in China has achieved remarkable growth since 1978 (Table D.1, Table D.2). It should be noted that although there was a severe fall in international arrivals because of the negative effects of the 1989 Tiananmen Square Incident, there was a recovery in the following year.

International visitor arrivals in China increased from 1,809,200 in 1978 to 63,478,400 in 1998, and the international tourism receipts increased from US$263 million in 1978 to US$12,602 million in 1998 (CNTA, 1999). Moreover, China became ranked sixth for international tourist arrivals, and eight for international tourism receipts in 1997 (WTO, 1998). These data highlight the role that China is now playing as an important integral part of the world tourism

Table D.2 Chinese international tourism receipts, 1978–1999

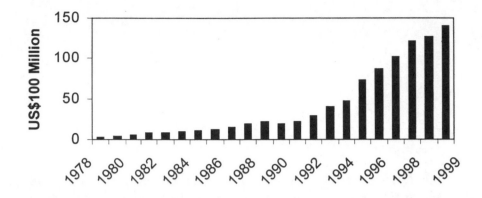

(Source: *China Statistical Year Book*, 1999)

industry. In 1997 Zhou, King and Turner forecast that the Chinese tourism market would be the world's fastest growing tourism market in the following 5–20 years.

The Chinese government categorizes inbound tourists into four categories (*China Statistical Year Book* 1999), that is,

• Foreigners – foreign travellers with other countries' passports
• Overseas Chinese – those who reside in other countries except Hong Kong, Macao and Taiwan
• Compatriots from Hong Kong and Macao – ethnic Chinese residents of Hong Kong and Macao
• Compatriots from Taiwan – ethnic Chinese residents of Taiwan.

Table D.3 summarizes the number of inbound tourist arrivals in China from 1978–98. Among the categories, overseas Chinese are less than 0.2% of total arrivals, but the data are compiled by nationality, which makes difficult the identification of Chinese persons who are citizens of other countries. The Chinese government considers that Hong Kong, Macau and Taiwan are part of China. Hong Kong and Macau have each become a China Special Administration Region, conducting 'one country, two policies', however, Taiwan remains independent. Compatriots are the majority percentage of the total number of inbound tourists to China (Table D.3). Compatriots accounted for 88.6 per cent of total arrivals in 1998.

The Chinese inbound tourism market has grown fast reaching 7,107,700 foreign tourists in 1998, which is more than seven times the number in 1990 (*China Statistical Year Book* 1999). Inbound tourists are almost all stayovers

Table D.3 Summary of inbound tourist arrivals in China, 1978–1998 (10,000s)

Year	Total	Foreigners	Overseas Chinese	Compatriots
1978	180.92	22.9	1.81	156.1
1985	1783.31	137	8.5	1637.8
1991	3334.98	271	13.3	3050.6
1994	4368.45	518.2	11.5	3838.7
1995	4638.65	588.7	11.6	4038.4
1996	5112.75	674.4	15.5	4422.8
1997	5758.79	742.8	9.9	5006.1
1998	6347.84	710.77	12.1	5625

(Source: *China Statistical Year Book* 1999).

due to the geographic distance. Most major origin markets are Asian markets which take advantage of their geographic proximity to China (see Table D.4). However, it should be noted that tourists from North America and the United Kingdom accounted for 16 per cent of foreign tourists in 1998. One of the reasons is that there are large ethnic Chinese populations in these countries. Easier access, the availability of facilities and world-standard accommodation in China have appealed to tourists from all over the world.

Another crucial reason in the attraction of foreign tourists to China is the abandonment of Foreign Exchange Certificates (FECs), an important reform indicating the more mature development of the Chinese tourism market. Chinese currency, RMB yuan, circulated in two forms in China, that is, RMB yuan and FECs from 1980 to 1994. Although both forms officially had the same value, FECs were overpriced and China forced foreign tourists and foreign residents to use them (Kaye, 1994). In 1994, the government officially stopped issuing FECs which were not used at all after 1997. The use of the same currency by both foreign tourists and Chinese citizens eliminated the foreign tourists' confusion through the use of different currencies in China. It also demonstrates that to

Table D.4 Top ten inbound tourist sources by country for China, 1998 (10,000s)

Country	Number	% of total foreign tourists
Japan	157.21	22
Russia	69.20	10
United States	67.73	10
South Korea	63.28	9
Singapore	31.64	4
Malaysia	30.01	4
Mongolia	26.48	4
Philippines	25.65	4
United Kingdom	24.29	3
Canada	19.60	3

(Source: *China Statistical Year Book* 1999).

some extent China has taken the initiative to facilitate foreign tourists' travel in China.

The Development of China's Travel Services

The structure of the travel agency classification, organization and regulation indicates a country's own distribution system. Table D.5 illustrates the development of travel services and policies in China.

China Bureau of Travel and Tourism was established in 1964 under the Foreign Affairs Office within the State Council. It was later upgraded to ministerial level directly under the State Council and was renamed State General Administration for Travel and Tourism (SGATT). It was given its current name, China National Travel Administration (CNTA), in 1983. CNTA is the national administrative body with responsibility for both short-term and long-term

Table D.5 Development of travel services and policies in China

Year	Event
1953	Establishment of Beijing Overseas Chinese Travel Service
1954	Establishment of China International Travel Service (CITS)
1963	Establishment of Overseas Chinese Travel Service
1964	Establishment of China Bureau of Travel and Tourism under Foreign Affairs Office within the State Council
1966	Beginning of Cultural Revolution
1974	Establishment of China Travel Service (CTS) to replace Beijing Overseas Chinese Travel Service
1975	End of Cultural Revolution
1978	Opening of China to tourists
	Upgrading of China Bureau of Travel and Tourism to ministerial level directly under the State Council and renaming to State General Administration for Travel and Tourism (SGATT)
	Provinces and municipalities begin to establish their own Travel and Tourism Bureaus
1979	Establishment of China Youth Travel Service (CYTS)
1983	SGATT renamed China National Tourism Administration (CNTA)
1984	A long-term policy for the government to allocate RMB$5 billion annually to the top 14 tourist cities for project development
1985	Travel agencies allowed to be established by collectives or private citizens
	Travel agencies are categorized into one, two and three
1988	'Provisional Regulations on Administration of Tourist Guides' issued to require tourist guides to be licensed
1990	'Provisional Regulations on Management of Organising Chinese Citizens to Travel to Three Countries in Southeast Asia' issued by CNTA
1992	Decentralization of tourism pricing, all tourism enterprises operating in a market economy environment
1995	'Provisional Regulations on Quality Service Guarantee Funds of Travel Agencies' issued by CNTA
1997	'Provisional Regulations on the Management of Outbound Travel by Chinese Citizens at Their Own Expense' issued by CNTA

(Source: Choy and Can, 1988; Zhang, Chong and Ap, 1999; CNTA 1997)

policies for the development of tourism in China. It is also authorized to plan and coordinate tourism development at a national level (Choy and Can, 1988; Yu, 1992). As a national tourism entity, CNTA has played an important role in the development of the Chinese tourism industry.

The first travel agent, called Beijing Overseas Chinese Travel Service, was established in 1953. From then until 1980, all incoming travellers had to have their arrangements within China organized by either China International Travel Service (CITS), China Travel Service (CTS) and China Youth Travel Service (CYTS). Until 1984, CITS, CTS and CYTS monopolized travel service operations (Zhang, Chong and Ap, 1999). In 1985, travel agencies were first allowed to be established by collectives or private citizens and CNTA now classifies all agencies into three categories. Category one travel agencies are authorized to operate international travel business. In addition to seeking their own clients directly, some of the authorized outbound Category one travel agencies receive passengers from Category two and three travel agencies. Thus, these authorized agencies can be regarded as wholesalers as well. Category two agencies are restricted to arranging tour-related activities for the foreign tourists coordinated by Category one travel agencies and domestic tourists, while Category three agencies are restricted to handling domestic travel. The strength of interest in the tourism industry is demonstrated by the growth of agencies from 1245 in 1987 to 6222 in 1998 following a policy of decentralization and liberalization (*China Statistical Year Book* 1999).

In 1984, a long-term policy was formulated to allocate RMB$5 billion annually to the top 14 tourist cities, such as Beijing, Guangzhou, Xian, Suzhou and Shanghai, for environmental and historical preservation and tourism development. Since then, many unique and historical attractions in China, such as the Great Wall and Palace Museum (the Forbidden City) in Beijing, Terracotta Warriors in Xian and the Grand Canal in Suzhou have been restored or further developed with new and/or improved facilities (Zhang, Chong and Ap, 1999).

During the period 1988–95, the Chinese government further regulated the operation and service quality of travel agencies and tour guides, as there had been many complaints by Westerners about standards of accommodation, meals and transportation. In 1988, CNTA issued rules to regulate all travel agencies. The measures introduced covered operating conditions, approval procedures and penalties in the event of a breach of the rules. Meanwhile 'Provisional Regulations on Administration of Tourist Guides' were issued by CNTA aiming at regulating the qualifications, duties and responsibilities of all tourist guides. All tourist guides were also required to be licensed. In 1992, tourism pricing was decentralized. Tourism corporations were given the right to provide their own prices based on domestic and international tourism demand (Zhang, Chong and

Ap, 1999). In 1995, in order to guarantee the service quality provided by travel agencies, CNTA issued 'Provisional Regulations on Quality Service Guarantee Funds of Travel Agencies' which require all travel agencies to deposit a sum of money with CNTA to ensure the provision of service quality. The development of travel services and policies in China was intended to reassure the world that China had taken inbound tourism seriously, and had made efforts to guarantee the quality of services.

Economic development in China

China remains a low-income country. The affordability of goods and services depends ultimately on incomes and prices (Chai, 1996; Table D.6). The national disposable income per capita in 1998 increased to 5425.0 RMB yuan which was a growth of 55.2 per cent of income levels in 1994. China is moving to a moderate level of prosperity, especially in the three main regions of Beijing, Shanghai and Guangzhou (*Beijing Review*, 1999).

During the period 1979–97, the consumer spending of residents rose 7.3 per cent annually (*Beijing Review*, 1999). However, economic development in China is spatially and structurally uneven. After 1985, the economic gap between the industrial and commercial coastal cities and special development zones, and non-coastal regions became increasingly obvious. The geographic region for outbound markets is concentrated along the coastal zone in major cities, such as Beijing, Shanghai and Guangzhou (Qu and Lam, 1997; Wang and Sheldon, 1995; Wen and Tisdell, 1996; Zhou; King and Turner, 1997). In 1998, the average national total disposable income per person was US$ 655.26 (US$1 = 8.2791 RMB yuan), while the three most developed regions, Guangdong Province, Shanghai and Beijing ranked in the top three of China's 31 regions with disposable incomes of US$1067.71, US$1059.67, and US$1023.30 respectively (*China Statistical Year Book* 1999).

Table D.6 The Chinese national economy, 1994–1998

Year	1994	1995	1996	1997	1998
Population (million)	1198.5	1211.2	1223.9	1236.3	1248.1
GNP (trillion RMB yuan)	4.67	5.75	6.69	7.35	7.80
National disposable income per capita (RMB yuan)	3496.2	4285.9	4868.9	5160.3	5425.0

Domestic tourism development

Until 1979, leisure travel for the Chinese population was almost non-existent. Tourism was looked upon as a major foreign exchange earner rather than an industry that would also provide recreation and leisure activities for its own citizens (Wang, Zhang and Cai, 1997). However, the rapid economic growth and more leisure time increased the Chinese people's desire to travel. This desire continues to grow stronger because of the country's fast-paced economy and relatively enlightened government policies (Wu, Zhu and Xu, 2000). In 1998, 694 million Chinese engaged in domestic travel, and spent 239.1 billion RMB yuan, nearly 30 times that of the expenditure in 1985 (CNTA, 1999).

There are a few major reasons which have caused the increase in domestic travel, resulting in the recent amalgamation by the Chinese Government of Category 1 and 2 agencies to stimulate the development of overseas tourism. Category 1 and 2 agencies to the development of overseas tourism. First, with the reduction of weekly working hours from 48 to 40 hours since 1995, Chinese people have extra time to spend on travel and leisure. In addition, the Chinese government has recently standardized three one-week holidays annually in China: International Labour Day 1–7 May, National Day (1–7 October) and Chinese New Year (also called Spring Festival). Therefore, people are able to travel much longer distances to metropolitan cities and coastal areas, such as Shanghai, Beijing and Guangzhou or even travel overseas. Second, different travel motivations and patterns have emerged with greater similarities to Western tourism markets, such as adventure tours, leisure tours, conventions and business trips, and visiting friends and relatives (VFR) (Wang, Zhang and Cai, 1997). Third, due to the bureaucracy in China, trips had been primarily sponsored by state employers with minimum personal spending. After 1991 an increasing proportion of travellers began to pay their own expenses, and more people joined groups (ibid.).

Due to the economic gap between the different regions of China and the persistent income differential, Chinese tourists have various patterns of domestic travel, from traditional sightseeing with lower expenditure to special-interest tourism with high expenditure in the 1990s (Wu, Zhu and Xu, 2000). Methods of travel are varied, and Chinese tourists can either join a group or a package tour, or travel by themselves. However, Wu, Zhu and Xu maintain that mass tourism still plays the dominant role in the domestic market. Moderately priced short-haul sightseeing and short-haul weekend vacations have become popular tourist products. In addition, it should be noted that alternative tourism has started to develop in China. Eco-tourism, such as going to national parks, and culture tourism, such as visiting places in Yunnan Province of China, have started to develop in China with high demand amongst Chinese tourists (2000).

Chinese outbound tourism development

The experience gained in domestic tourism has helped develop an appetite for international tourism (Wen, 1997). Moreover, since Chinese people are no longer restricted to holidays within their homeland, as it becomes easier to obtain an exit permit, they are increasingly going overseas (Wang, Zhang and Cai, 1997).

Although the national disposable income has continued to increase significantly, the amount required for overseas travel is still prohibitive for many Chinese. Nevertheless, economic growth, relaxation of restrictions and an expanding middle class have led to more Chinese travelling abroad (Office of National Tourism, 1998). Chai (1996) pointed out that it is difficult to define the middle class precisely, but those able to afford international travel are in the top 2 per cent of income earners, a potential market of at least 12 million people.

The Chinese government placed tight restrictions on the outbound tourism market until 1983. The slightly liberalized policy first eased Chinese leisure travel to Hong Kong and Macau, then cross-border travel. At that time, 'outbound travel' was defined as visiting overseas friends and relatives (VFRs). Thus the trip was sponsored financially by overseas relatives and friends so there was no drain on China's foreign-exchange reserves. With the expansion in the number of Chinese people travelling to Hong Kong and Macau, more and more people expressed their desire to visit their relatives in other regions. Consequently, in 1990, with the approval of the State Council, CNTA, the Foreign Ministry, the Public Security Ministry and the Overseas Chinese Affairs Office declared 'the Provisional Regulations on Management of Organising Chinese Citizens to Travel to Three Countries in Southeast Asia' (see table D.5). This regulation enabled Chinese citizens to visit friends and relatives in Thailand, Singapore and Malaysia if sponsored by their overseas relatives and friends (Dou and Dou, 1999). The Philippines joined the group in 1992.

However, with the development of travel services, trips changed from VFR to holiday leisure travel, moreover Chinese tourists prepaid for services such as accommodation and transfers in RMB yuan in China, making travelling overseas much easier, particularly for those who do not have relatives overseas. In 1991, Singapore, Malaysia and Thailand witnessed the rush of the first tour groups from mainland China when the country began to permit its residents to travel to selected Southeast Asian countries for personal and leisure purposes. Subsequently, other Southeast Asian countries were also recognized and awarded Approved Destination Status (ADS) by the Chinese government. Australia and New Zealand were granted ADS in 1999. The total number of Chinese outbound tourists had a rapid growth in 1994–8 (Table D.7). Of the total outbound tourists from China, 54.3 per cent were for business purposes, and 45.7 per cent for private purposes including leisure and VFR (CNTA, 1997). WTO (1998) stated that the number of Chinese outbound tourists in organized tour groups increased by nearly 130 per cent to 1,640,000 between 1993 and 1996 (see Cai, Boger and O'Leary, 1999).

Table D.7 Total Chinese outbound tourists, 1994–1998

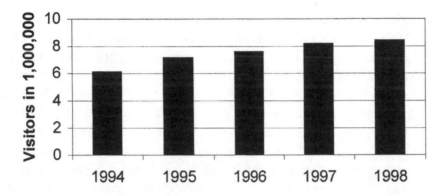

(Source: *China Statistical Year Book*, 1999.)

Three main categories were identified by the National Tourism Administration of the People's Republic of China (PRC) (Table D.8). These are Chinese outbound tours, cross-border tours, Hong Kong and Macau tours. It should be noted that only cross-border tours do not need a visa. Hong Kong has become a Special Administration Region (SAR) of China, and Macau followed suit on 20 December 1999, that is why different regulations for visiting these two areas apply for Chinese outbound tourists. However, Chinese tourists still have to apply for a visa to visiting Hong Kong and Macau. The cross-border tours mean that Chinese tourists do not have to apply for visas to travel to these countries which include Northeast China, Russia, North Korea and Mongolia; in Southwest China, travelling to Vietnam, Cambodia, Laos and Myanmar; in Northwest China, travelling to Russia and other former Soviet Union countries (Dou and Dou, 1999). In 1997, the major destinations of Chinese outbound tourists organized by travel agencies were Hong Kong, Macau, Myanmar, Thailand, Vietnam, Russia, Singapore, Malaysia, North Korea and the Philippines (CNTA, 1997). Hong Kong and Macau are treated as traditional destinations because of ethnic, cultural and political connections (Cai, Boger and O'Leary 1999). Thailand, Singapore, Malaysia and the Philippines currently account for 75 per cent of China's outbound tourism (Wang and Sheldon, 1995; Dorries, 1999).

Table D.8 Major destinations of Chinese outbound tourists

Destinations	Outbound (thousands) 1997	Change (%) over 1996
Thailand	220.7	-2.6
Singapore	86.3	3.0
Malaysia	81.7	0.5
Philippines	13.8	50.0
Myanmar	234.7	-50.3
Vietnam	212.9	44.9
Russia	75.1	14.5
North Korea	52.6	124.8
Hong Kong	465.7	10.9
Macau	333.4	-14.4

(Source: CNTA, 1997)

On the 1 July 1997 the 'Provisional Regulations on the Management of Outbound Travel by Chinese Citizens at Their Own Expense' were issued jointly by the CNTA and the Ministry of Public Security after approval by the State Council (see Table D.5). With this, China established a new management system for outbound travel to meet the growing demand of Chinese citizens for travel outside of China (CNTA, 1997). Under the regulations, outbound tours by Chinese citizens should be conducted in a planned, organized and controlled manner. Only approved travel agencies can handle outbound travel, and they also have to take the responsibilities of managing the outbound travel itself. Sixty-seven Chinese Category A travel agencies have been approved by CNTA to handle Chinese outbound travel services due to the demand for international services. However, only 22 of the 67 Chinese travel agencies were authorized to handle the Chinese tourism market to Australia and New Zealand. These 22 travel agencies are located in Beijing, Shanghai and Guangzhou. The Ministry of Public Security is responsible for the management of passports for outbound travel and the exit and entry procedures are based on the Chinese exit and entry laws and regulations. These regulations determine that the major pattern of the Chinese outbound leisure travel is package tours, not fully independent tours. If Chinese citizens intend to travel overseas, they have to contact authorized Chinese travel agencies to arrange the tour, then join the groups to travel overseas.

A typical all-inclusive package includes international travel, private chartered coach within Australia, sightseeing excursions, local guides, accommodation and meals (mainly Chinese food with some local style meals). This form of tour arrangement can be compared with typical Western inclusive holiday packages (Laws, 1997) providing Chinese clients with similar advantages, particularly the benefit of knowing beforehand what to budget for their holiday, and relieving them of any concerns about difficulties of making their own arrangements in a foreign country.

Conclusion

China is a developing country and has only recently acknowledged tourism as an economic activity. However, it has made progressive improvements in the last two decades, in terms of the development of inbound tourism, domestic tourism and outbound tourism. In this period the tourism industry has been recognized for the first time as a new growth area in the national economy. Most regions in China have supported and encouraged tourism as a pillar or key industry (He, 1999). Although China is still at the early stage of developing its tourism, particularly outbound tourism, CNTA has taken the initiative, on the one hand, to regulate the market, and on the other hand to facilitate both foreign tourists visiting China, and its own citizens visiting other countries.

Bibliography

Bailey, M. (1995) *China, International Tourism Reports*, No. 1, London: Economist Intelligence Unit, pp. 19–37.

Beijing Review (1999) 'China Remains First in GDP Growth' 28, December 1998–3 January 1999, p. 20.

Cai, L., Boger, C. and O'Leary, J. (1999) 'The Chinese travellers to Singapore, Malaysia, and Thailand: a unique Chinese outbound market', *Asia Pacific Journal of Tourism Research* 3 (2), 2–13.

Chai, P. (1996) 'China's Economy, and Tourism to Australia', Bureau of Tourism Research conference paper, Australia.

China National Tourism Administration (CNTA) (1997) *China Tourism Annual Report*, Beijing: National Tourism Administration of the People's Republic of China.

China Statistical Year Book (1999) compiled by the State Statistical Bureau of the People's Republic of China, China Statistical Publishing House, Beijing.

Choy, D. J. L. and Can, Y. Y. (1988) 'The development and organization of travel services in China', *Journal of Travel Research* Summer, 28–34.

Dorries, B. (1999) 'China to deliver tourism bonanza', *Courier Mail* 22 April, p. 9.

Dou, Q. and Dou, J. (1999) 'A study of the Chinese Mainland outbound tourist markets', in *Tourism 2000 Asia Pacific's Role in the New Millennium, Conference Proceedings*, Asia Pacific Tourism Association Fifth Annual Conference, Hong Kong, Vol. II, pp. 751–8.

He, G. (1999) 'To make persistent efforts and positively develop tourism industry as new economic growth point', *Tourism Survey and Research* 1, 3–12.

Kaye, L. (1994) 'Deafened by decree: China's currency and tax reforms spread confusion', *Far Eastern Economic Review*, 13 January, pp. 80–2.

Laws, E., (1997) *Managing Packaged Tourism: Relationships, Responsibilities and Service Quality in the Inclusive Holiday Industry*. London: International Thomson Publishing Company.

Office of National Tourism (1998) 'Tourism industry trends', *Industry Science Resources* 5, October.

Pan, G.W. and Laws, E. (2001) 'Tourism Marketing Opportunities for Australia in China', *Journal of Vacation Marketing* 8 (1), 39–48.

Qu, H. and Lam, S. (1997) 'A travel demand model for Mainland Chinese tourists to Hong Kong', *Tourism Management* 18 (8), 593–7.

Ritchter, L. K. (1989) *The Politics of Tourism in Asia*. Honolulu: University of Hawaii Press.

Thomm, R. (1996) *Business China. A practical insight into doing business in China*, Sydney: Business & Professional Publishing.

Wang, Y. and Sheldon P. (1995) 'The sleeping dragon awakes: the outbound Chinese travel market', *Journal of Travel & Tourism marketing* 4 (4), 41–54.

Wang, H., Zhang, L. and Cai, L. (1997) 'The emerging market of China's domestic tourism', *Travel and Tourism Research Association Conference Proceedings*, pp. 432–7.

Wen, Z. (1997) 'China's domestic tourism: impetus, development and trends', *Tourism Management* 18 (8), 565–71.

Wen, J. and Tisdell, C. (1996) *Regional Inequality and Decentralisation of China's Tourism Industry*, UQ Department of Economics discussion papers, No. 194.

World Tourism Organisation (WTO) (1998) 'Tourism Market Trends East Asia and the Pacific 1988–1997', WTO commission for East Asia and the Pacific, thirty-second meeting, WTO, Madrid.

Wu, B., Zhu, H. and Xu, X. (2000) 'Trends in China's domestic tourism development at the turn of the century', *International Journal of Contemporary Hospitality Management* 12 (5), 296–9.

Yu, L. (1992) 'Emerging markets for China's tourism industry', *Journal of Travel Research* Summer, 10–13.

Zhang, H. Q., Chong, K. and Ap, J. (1999) 'An analysis of tourism policy development in modern China', *Tourism Management* 20, 471–85.

Zhou L., King, B. and Turner L. (1997) 'The China outbound market: An evaluation of key constraints and opportunities', *Journal of Vacation Marketing* 4 (2), 109–19.

125

E Canadian Tourism Commission's Product Clubs

David J. Telfer

Introduction

Within the tourism industry, companies and destinations are increasingly joining forces to market their product. The purpose of this case study is to investigate the Product Club programme facilitated by the Canadian Tourism Commission (CTC). A Product Club is a partnership comprised of participants, often small and medium-sized businesses, with a common vision for the development of a specific tourism product or niche market (www.canadatourism.com/productclubs). The purpose of the Product Clubs is to develop new products or enhance the quality of existing products through partnerships of tourism industry stakeholders. The Product Clubs are encouraged to take an underdeveloped industry sector and facilitate it becoming 'market ready' (www.canadatourism.com/productclubs). The programme was launched in 1996 with six Product Clubs through the CTC's Industry and Product Development Committee and has grown to 31 funded Clubs in 2001. The initiative involves over 250 partner organizations and more than 5000 associated members and businesses. This case study will begin by examining the importance of building strategic alliances for marketing tourism destinations followed by explaining the function of the CTC. The Product Club programme will then be explained in detail and a Table is presented outlining the existing 31 Product Clubs. Conclusions will be presented on the challenges and opportunities facing the CTC's Product Clubs.

Strategic alliances and tourism marketing

The marketing of places has become increasingly competitive and public-sector marketing strategies are becoming ever more sophisticated (Morgan and Pritchard, 1998). 'Competition for place advantage in tourism extends to restaurants, facilities, cultural amenities, and entertainment – there is a competition over which place has the most four-star hotels, best cuisine, most museums and theatres and top-ranked athletic facilities' (ibid., p. 145). In this increasingly competitive environment, tourist destinations are adopting branding strategies in an effort to differentiate their identities. To achieve individuality, destinations are using images and icons to create and reinforce their destination images. In many cases, the images and icons are a culmination of historical, social and economic processes (ibid.). It is recognized, however, that there are more difficulties in branding a destination than a product because for branding to be successful it involves the mobilization of the whole marketing mix (Seaton and Bennett, 1996). As Morgan and Pritchard (1998) suggest, it is more difficult to brand a destination as a single product because it is a composite of different components such as accommodation and catering establishments, tourist attractions, arts, entertainment and cultural venues and the natural environment. In addition, the adoption of a single image for a destination with defined geographic boundaries, can be overly restrictive (Batchelor, 1999). As a solution to this problem, Seaton and Bennett (1996), however, suggest that a destination may present itself in different ways to different groups so that the destination becomes not one brand but many. Similar such efforts have been adopted by the Canadian Tourism Commission in establishing the tourism Product Clubs, which presents different images of Canada to the international and domestic market. The development of the Product Clubs is based on building strategic alliances between related organizations in order to build a common vision and bring products to market.

The value of moving towards strategic alliances in the tourism industry is increasingly being recognized as a strategy to remain innovative and competitive (Telfer, 2000, 2001; Crotts, Buhalis and March, 2000; Bramwell and Lane, 2000). Gulati (1998:293) defines strategic alliances as 'voluntary arrangements between firms involving exchange, sharing, or co-development of products, technologies, or services. They can occur as a result of a wide range of motives and goals and can take a variety of forms, and can occur across vertical and horizontal boundaries.' Strategic alliances in the airline industry such as the Star Alliance and, in the sectors of travel agents, lodging and information technology (Computer Reservation Systems) illustrate the trend of cooperation emerging in the industry (Go and Williams, 1993). In terms of destination marketing, Telfer (2000, 2001) explored the development of strategic alliances in the Niagara Region, which have led to the creation of a regional brand based on food and wine, different from the dominant image of Niagara Falls.

According to the *Four Cs of Strategic Alliances*, strategic alliances should be entered into when (Brouthers and Brouthers, 1993 cited in Brouthers, Brouthers and Wilkinson, 1995):

- complementary skills are offered by the partners,
- cooperative cultures exist between the firms,
- the firms have compatible goals,
- commensurate levels of risk are involved.

Caffyn (2000) developed the Tourism Partnership Lifecycle Model, which clearly presents the importance of building initial trust and innovation in forming partnerships. A cautionary note, however, is also expressed in the model as tourism partnerships over time can stagnate and Caffyn (2000) explores what the possible long-term options are for tourism partnerships. Similar challenges facing the CTC's Products Clubs will be revisited in the conclusion of this case study. In the strategic alliance literature, management recommendations have been proposed on how to improve the chances of a successful international strategic alliance under the categories of the 4 Cs outlined above (Brouthers, Brouthers and Wilkinson, 1995:23). Under *complementary skills* the authors argue that alliances should only be entered into with firms that can contribute to the strength of the venture. The experience, skills and knowledge must be specific and applicable to the product or services offered. Under *co-operative cultures* it is important that managers realize that cooperation is a two-way street and the firms need to learn from each other. It is also important to recognize any cultural differences which exist between firms, especially if they are located in different countries. Managers must also ensure that potential partners must have *compatible goals*, as conflicting goals of partner firms may result in the poor performance of the alliance or restrict the results so that the benefits are not shared equally. Two major areas of risk with alliances are the giving away of corporate competencies and the finding of increased financial pressures because of problem partners. As will be noted later, the funding from the CTC terminates after three years and it is then up to the partnership to carry on with the financial support of its members. It is important to consider all of the risks and ensure that there are *commensurate levels of risk*. One suggested method to safeguard non-alliance information is to set up an information gatekeeper in order for companies to protect themselves (ibid., p. 23). On a similar cautionary note they conclude their article with the following statement: 'strategic alliances themselves are as fraught with peril as the emerging competitive environment, and an inappropriate choice of an alliance partner could prove to be even more dangerous than operating as single firm' (p. 24).

Canadian Tourism Commission

The Canadian Tourism Commission (CTC) is a working partnership between the tourism industry businesses and associations, provincial and territorial governments and the Government of Canada (Goeldner, Ritchie and McIntosh, 2000). The vision and mission statements of the CTC are presented in Figure 1. The mandate of the CTC is to plan, direct, manage and implement programmes to generate and promote tourism to Canada. The purpose of the CTC is to position Canada as a favourable destination for both domestic and international visitors as well as to provide accurate, up-to-date information to the tourism industry to assist in decision-making (ibid.).

Figure E.1 The vision and mission statements of the Canadian Tourism Commission

VISION OF THE CTC
Canada will be the premier four-season destination to connect with nature and to experience diverse cultures and communities.
MISSION OF THE CTC
Canada's tourism industry will deliver world-class cultural and leisure experiences year round, while preserving and sharing Canada's clean, safe and natural environments. The industry will be guided by the values of respect, integrity and empathy.
(CTC, 2001)

The Commission is made up of industry representatives from across the country and it has a yearly budget of up to CDN$ 75 million from the federal government. As evidence of the increasing federal commitment to tourism, this figure is up from CDN$ 15 million five years earlier (Katz, 2001). Some of the main CTC Committees include Europe Marketing Committee, Asia/Pacific Marketing Committee, US Meetings, Conventions and Incentive Travel Marketing Committee, Latin America Marketing Committee, Canada Marketing Committee, Industry and Product Development, US Leisure Marketing Committee, Research Committee, and Technology Committee. As of 2 January 2001, the CTC officially became a Crown Corporation (ibid.). By moving to a Crown Corporation, the CTC is able to act more like a private-sector operation and is no longer constrained by some of the government policies in areas such as hiring and procurement. The CTC is also able to directly benefit from partnerships such as the one signed until 2002 with Roots Canada and Wareaxe Ventures to produce a range of products, clothing and leather goods carrying the CTC logo for more than CDN $ 100 000 per year (ibid.).

The broad goals of the Commission are to coordinate the efforts of the main players in the industry, including hoteliers, airlines, tour operators, attractions, local and provincial associations and government agencies. The CTC brings the private and public sectors together to design and implement marketing strategies and programmes to increase tourism to Canada. These programmes involve gathering data on potential markets, analysis of marketplace opportunities both nationally and internationally, market research and analysis, public relations, promotional projects, advertising, and travel-trade activities (Goeldner, Ritchie and McIntosh, 2000). With its partners, the CTC provides a number of services to the industry to provide them with information. These services include the assessments of the performance of the various sub-sectors of the industry, market studies, gathering data on the economic impact of tourism, and studies on revenues, capacity and tourist consumption of specific products (ibid.). A recent advance in the communication of information has been the development of the Canadian Tourism Exchange (CTX) which is a business-to-business Internet based network, which allows businesses to share information (www.canadatourism.com).

One of the key strategies, which the CTC uses and which is the focus of this case study, is the development of partnership opportunities for marketing, research and industry and product development. The purpose of the industry Product and Development Programme is to assist the industry to develop new products that match global demand. Through a partnership approach the CTC supports new initiatives such as Product Clubs.

Product Clubs

The Product Club programme brings together traditional and non-traditional partners, with a focus on small and medium-sized enterprises. The partnership is also viewed as an opportunity to create business and learning opportunities through the sharing of knowledge, best practices and success stories. The general objectives of the programme are to

- bring new tourism products to market-ready status and encourage their introduction in a national basis
- enhance the quality of existing tourism products and packages in Canada
- increase the diversity of innovative, high quality tourism products and packages
- encourage the delivery of products year round to enhance Canada's position as a four season destination
- extend the seasonality of Canada's tourism product
- increase Canada's tourism competitiveness globally. (www.canadatourism.com/productclubs)

The CTC defines a Product Club as a

partnership or consortium of tourism industry stakeholders, usually in more than one region or province, which pools its efforts in order to increase the range of quality of existing tourism products (packages, events, activities, experiences, etc.) or to develop new products to ultimately make Canada a more attractive and competitive tourism destination. Its strength lies in

1   its capacity to bring Canadian stakeholders together to accomplish activities and strategies that would likely not be achieved alone
2   conducting co-operative market research
3   sharing knowledge and information
4   its ability to bring to market, innovative and/or off-season products which are able to attract a wider segment of travellers. (www.canadatourism.com/productclubs)

The activities of a Product Club can include forging partnerships, building new packages, conducting research on customers' needs, identifying products and markets with high potential, creating product development and marketing strategies, conducting seminars, developing newsletters and other communication tools (business-to-business website) all working towards building a sustainable structure (www.canadatourism.com/productclubs). While the Product Club Programme does allow for the creation of a marketing strategy the CTC does not provide funding for marketing activities such as promotion, advertising, printing of brochures or consumer website development. The CTC does acknowledge that Product Club members may do marketing, however these activities are classified as outside the scope of the programme. As will be illustrated with an example later, the funding of the Product Clubs allows firms to network and develop new products, which later are marketed. Product Club members cover a diverse spectrum including accommodation, operators, attractions, tour operators, outfitters, tourism associations, provincial/territorial governments, other travel industry stakeholders or businesses from outside the tourism industry (www.canadatourism.com/productclubs).

The process of the development of the Product Clubs begins with the CTC surveying the industry and overseas market representatives as part of a needs analysis. The results of this needs analysis are published as areas of tourism demand to the industry (Ohman, 2000). Once this is completed, a call-for-proposals is issued and those in the industry are invited to make their own partnership proposals, which address a specific area of tourism demand. In the guidelines for submissions of proposals, the CTC notes that it builds its marketing around product clusters, which include touring, history and culture, cities and resort, and adventure (www.canadatourism.com/productclubs). Table E.1 contains a list of themes, which the CTC uses to invite new applications and which are believed to have future potential growth. These themes can be grouped under the CTC's marketing clusters listed above. For existing Product Clubs, the CTC organizes the Clubs into five broader themes, which are used in their brochure advertising the Product Clubs. 'Treading Softly on the Land' includes Clubs with an ecotourism and adventure focus. 'Discovering Our Arts and Culture' includes Clubs that focus on heritage and culture. 'Stepping Out and Getting Away' highlights urban and resort Clubs and 'Cruising the Country' presents Clubs that have developed unique touring packages. Finally, 'Making the Most of Winter' presents Clubs which focus on the winter experience (CTC, 2000).

Table E.1 Potential Product Club themes

Learning through leisure	Snowmobiling	City breaks
Language learning	Holiday Season such as Christmas	Bird watching
Cultural network development	Walking	Northern lights
Performing arts	Shopping	Sports travel
Museums	Spa tourism	Cycling
Major cultural events	Attractions	Nature
Gardens/botany	Farm vacations	Horseback riding
Cuisine	Sport fishing	Youth tourism

(Source: www.canadatourism.com/productclubs)

The proposal must include a five-year business plan and a strategy for self-sufficiency after the initial three years. The CTC provides financial support for the first three years and after the initial period it provides support in the form of access to research, cross-sectoral training and enhanced networking opportunities (Ohman, 2000). Approximately CDN$1.5 million over three years is committed to the programme on a matching funds basis to each new round of successful applicants. The average value of previous three-year contracts has ranged from CDN$50,000 to CDN$300,000 and payments are made on the completion of deliverables or proposed projects. As a prerequisite to applying to the programme, applicants need to show they have industry financial support. After the three-year period, Clubs are expected to become self-sustaining (www.canadatourism.com/productclubs). Table E.2 contains a listing of the 31 Product Clubs across Canada. Many of these Product Clubs maintain their own web pages.

One of the key concepts of a successful application is to base it on an 'icon', which defines a region yet can be expanded to include a wider geographic base. The Lighthouse Product Club started out based on using a local lighthouse as a tourist attraction. The concept soon spread to the Maritime Provinces (Eastern Canada) and developed into a Product Club. It even led to a conference on Lighthouse tourism and is now moving to a national level (Ohman, 2001). The key element is to move the idea from a local level and move to inter-provincial and even national level. The key activities include communication, education and research, which includes developing inventories and developing marketing strategies. The Product Club programme will fund the development of a marketing plan but it will not fund the actual marketing. According to the Director of Product Clubs and Partnerships, the elements of success for the Product Clubs are vision, committed partners, financial strength and a dedicated administrator (Ohman, 2001).

The Bay of Fundy Product Club is based on industries surrounding the Bay of Fundy, which lies between the provinces of Nova Scotia and New Brunswick. It is approximately 1000 km around the Bay of Fundy and most of the businesses which are involved in the tourism industry are small businesses. The main mission of the Bay of Fundy Product Club is to develop the Region as an excellent ecotourism destination. In developing the Club, the administrators decided not to try and attract members but chose to offer partnerships as the term has the impression of being more inclusionary (Young, 2001). One of the first phases of the development of the Product Club was to conduct research in developing an inventory of the various tourism businesses. A series of five maps was created that included Nature Interpretation Sites for the Bay of Fundy, Heritage and Museums Maps, Accommodation Inventory Report, Food and Beverage establishments (based on travel writers) and Nature Tour Operators (Young, 2001). Based on this research, the Bay was also divided into three main ecozones, which are directly related to themed tourist ecozones. These ecozones included Fundy Aquarium Ecozone, Sea Cliffs and Fossils Ecozone and World Highest Tides Ecozone (Young, 2001). Once the inventory was complete, the organization moved to develop a mission statement. The visioning process led to a focus on the elements of Sustainability and Conservation, Product Development and Marketing. In terms of Sustainability and Conservation, the organization is working towards having the Bay of Fundy established as a World

134

Table E.2 Product Clubs

Product Club	Description
Aboriginal Tourism Product Club	Partnership with 10 Tourism organizations in Quebec. The aim is to develop authentic tourism products and act as a catalyst for aboriginal cultural, heritage, ecotourism and soft adventure tourism. The club wants to improve Aboriginal tourism by creating a sustainable network of key stakeholders and obtaining research on market potential
Aboriginal Waterways Product Club	Group organizes packages along the Saskatchewan and Qu'Appelle River systems. Through these tours, Aboriginal heritage and culture is explored and learned while focusing on the precontact and fur trade eras.
Acadian Tourism Product Club	The Club wants to promote Acadian culture by developing new products, enhancing existing products, and developing new packages for tourists. Initial partners include the Société Nationale de l'Acadie, government agencies from New Brunswick, Nova Scotia and Prince Edward Island, Atlantic Canada Opportunities Agency, the Francophone federation of Newfoundland/ Labrador and Parks Canada.
Adventure, Outdoor and Ecotourism Product Club	Alliance of partners who develop and market adventure travel/ecotourism products with tourism operators. Looking to develop five to eight new adventure travel products in targeted areas as initial models and examining key factors to establish a tour operator/wholesaler in Quebec specializing in adventure travel/ecotourism.
Arts in the City Product Club	The Club aims to bridge the gap between the tourism sector and the arts community in Vancouver B.C. by increasing the amount of export-ready arts product through increased communication between arts and tourism businesses.
Atlantic Economuseum Network Product Club	This Club supports tourism product development at Economuseums throughout the Atlantic provinces.
Bay of Fundy Product Club	This Club joins tourism associations and economic development agencies in Nova Scotia and New Brunswick to position the area around the Bay of Fundy as a world class ecotourism destination. The club is conducting market research and product development.
Canadian Golf Tourism Alliance Product Club	The Club aims to increase the saleability of the golf product, to package information and to evaluate delivery mechanisms with a view to increase product and service levels. Web page provides links to Canada's 2000+ courses.
Conservation Lands Product Club	The aim is to develop a model for cooperative product development and sustainable ecotourism in urban fringe areas. The club originated in Ontario based on five Conservation Authorities, which are environmental management and environmental protection agencies.
Country Road Agri-Tourism Product Club	This Club wants to bridge the gap between tourism and agriculture-based services by conducting research and industry education leading to the creation of new agri-tourism packages. They also hope to join with the Cuisine, Wine and Culture in Canada Product Club as well as others. Founding partners include Manitoba Country Vacations Association, Manitoba Agriculture and Food, Manitoba Culture, Heritage and Tourism and regional tourism associations.
Cross-Country Ski Product Club	This Club is comprised of cross-country ski centres, tourism resorts and outdoor recreation centres in Quebec.
Cuisine, Wine and Culture in Canada Product Club	This group includes restaurants, wineries, chefs, growers, retailers, agri-tour operators and aims to educate visitors about all their products. The Club originated with Tastes of Niagara in Ontario and is attempting to expand to create synergies between the cuisine, wine and culture segments of Canada's tourism industry.

Product Club	Description
Ecotourism Product Club (Saskatchewan)	This Club joins the Canadian Biosphere Reserve Tourism Consortium (CBRTC) and Canada Biosphere Reserves Association (CBRA). It is hoping to expand to 10 biospheres in eight provinces by 2002. Attempting to sell their product internationally by using United Nations–World Biosphere Reserves designation as a recognition factor.
Festival Network Product Club	This Club brings festival organizers from all across Canada to develop product, unite the Canadian Festival sector and expand access to key marketplaces. The Club originated with Festival Network Ottawa (Ontario) and has expanded to 30 festivals and events which are linked through a web page.
Garden and Bloom Tours of Canada Product Club	Combining private, public and municipal sectors this club seeks to create market-ready tours with a theme of gardening, botany and horticulture that stretches from coast to coast. They hope to focus on the protection of the environment in rural and urban settings.
Greektown Product Club	Brings together 400 businesses in Toronto's Greektown to expand and strengthen cultural tourism using a combined effort of restaurants and stores.
Health and Wellness Product Club	This Club's vision is to promote Canada as a premier destination for health and wellness tourism. There are 21 partners, from stakeholders at the provincial and national levels. The Club is developing new export-ready health/wellness packages, based on knowledge of customers and markets.
Heritage Product Club	The Club's aim is to develop packages that allow tourist to learn about the French culture in Western and Northern Canada. The Club will act as a catalyst for alliances and partnerships between tour operators, DMOs (Destination Management Organizations) and the cultural and heritage communities in Western Canada.
Hostels Canada Product Club	This Club aims to join all hostels across Canada in a national network that promotes hostels. Partners also include transportation groups, travel agents and tour operators.
Independent Innkeepers Product Club	Club develops new packages for heritage inns throughout Ontario and focuses on community ecotourism and cultural products.
Lighthouse Product Club (Nova Scotia)	The Club utilizes lighthouses for international and domestic tourists, which are not in use in Atlantic Canada. There are 13 partners and 17 associate members, including three provincial governments, the Atlantic Canada Opportunities Agency (ACOA), attractions, tour operators and municipalities.
Northern Wilderness Adventure Product Club	This Club hopes to develop products and packages targeted towards adventure tourism in Canada's north. Members include tourism associations, transportation groups, food and beverage companies and First Nations tourism businesses.
Ontario East Adventure Product Club	This Club will aim to develop new packages, which focus on the regions' abundance of heritage associations in combination with waterway and adventure products. Members include resorts, whitewater-rafting companies, etc.
Product Club for Tourists with Special Needs	This Club is developing packages for people with special needs and restricted physical abilities. It originated in Quebec and it also assesses and lists accessible accommodations, attractions and restaurants.
Quebec Maritime Product Club	This Club brings all aspects of the tourism industry together to improve the small businesses in and around the eastern regions of Canada. It works as an international marketing organization for the tourist regions of the Bas-Saint Laurent, Gaspésie, Côte-Nord and Îles de la Madeleine.

Product Club	Description
Saskatchewan River Basin Product Club	This Club's aim is to package natural heritage and ecotourism products in and around the Saskatchewan River. It is also a network of partners committed to increasing stewardship of the river basin through development.
Ski and Snowboard Industry Product Club	Links the ski and snowboard industry and the tourism industry to make the Canadian product stronger and more competitive.
Sport Tourism Product Club	The aim of Sport Tourism is to make Canada more competitive when 'bidding' for international sports events. The Club will accomplish this by education and development of a competitive bidding template available to all members. Members include Visitor and Convention Bureaux.
The Great Canadian Fossil Trail Product Club	This Club hopes to create cultural and scientific partnerships linking paleontological sites with communities through education and the development of cross-sector partnerships, which will translate into community economic development. (British Columbia, Alberta, Saskatchewan)
Trail of the Great Bear Product Club	This Clubs brings 75 Canadian Members of the Trail of the Great Bear Region to promote touring, ecotourism and cultural/heritage products in the Rockies of Alberta and British Columbia. Members include operators in food and beverage, transportation, accommodation and soft adventure industry.
Trans Canada Trail Product Club	This is a national partnership that involves Trail Councils from every province and territory. This Club hopes to research, map and gather tourism data, which will be used in a series of trail guidebooks. These books will give access points, information about towns and villages nearby and historical and cultural features about the trail.

(Source: www.canadatourism.com/productclubs)

Biosphere Reserve. In terms of Product Development the Club is focusing on getting their products market ready. Finally with respect to Marketing, the Product Club undertook a very successful direct mail campaign, which was targeted at three major cities in the United States namely Atlanta, Tampa and Orlando. They have focused on target marketing and have developed an advertising partnership with the American Automobile Association (AAA) in the United States. The Bay of Fundy has come to the end of their first three-year mandate under the programme and is looking to move forward. The next steps include developing a new three-year business plan, remaining focused on target marketing in the US, and continuing to develop partnerships such as AAA or VIA Rail in Canada (Young, 2001). The steering committee for the group has proven to be an effective liaison to the industry (Young, 2001).

The formation of the Product Clubs has allowed the industry to conduct market research, which in turn can be used to generate marketing plans. One of the main mandates of the Hostels Canada Product Club is to 'create a profile of the hostelling industry by collecting detailed information on the spending habits of young travellers as well as pinpointing the main markets from which they originate' (Hostels Canada, 2001: 16). The Product Club membership is made up of hostel owners, tour companies, travel agencies, adventure operators and magazine publishers from across the country.

Conclusion

In attempting to attract additional tourists to Canada, the CTC has embraced partnerships and strategic alliances through the Product Club programme. The programme has grown to 31 Clubs involving over 250 partner organizations and more than 5000 associated members and businesses. The CTC builds its marketing programmes around product clusters including touring, history and culture, winter, cities and resorts and adventure and inside each cluster are a series of themes. The development of the Product Clubs is encouraged around these themes, following in part the suggestion of Seaton and Bennett (1996) that a country may present itself in different ways to different groups so that the destination becomes not one brand but many. The diversity of Product Clubs from the Aboriginal Waterways Product Club to the Ecotourism Product Club to the Heritage Product Club to the Sport Tourism Product Club to the Northern Wilderness Adventure Product Club, all represent a range of new products for tourists.

The development of the Product Clubs offers a number of challenges and opportunities, which can be illustrated by revisiting the *Four Cs of Strategic*

Alliances cited in Brouthers, Brouthers and Wilkinson (1995). By focusing on strategic alliances between small and medium-sized businesses, the Product Clubs allow innovation based on *complementary skills* of group members that may not have been possible for a small company to develop in its own. In the initial stages of a Product Club, there is new product development with the assistance of funding from the CTC. The background work to get the various projects up and running can be very intensive as was noted above in the Bay of Fundy Product Club, however, the hard work has paid off with a successful marketing compaign to selected US cities.

Co-operative cultures and *compatible goals* exist between the firms as they link up to develop new products and go after new markets. The potential for network development between a wide variety of stakeholders within the Product Clubs is very high. The CTC holds an annual meeting for Club directors, which further enhances the chances of communication between the Clubs. There are challenges which face the Product Clubs and firms need to take steps to ensure that *commensurate levels of risk* are present for all parties. Some of these challenges, in part, will come over the long term as the CTC funding ends for the Product Clubs at the end of three years. If the Product Club is to survive, it may mean that individual companies will need to contribute higher levels of both finance and administrative support. As Caffyn (2000) suggested in her Tourism Partnership Lifecycle Model, there is potential for tourism partnerships, as in all partnerships, to stagnate and efforts must be taken to secure a long-term strategy. Many of the Product Clubs have a very diverse membership and it will be important for the Club to maintain a common vision and common set of goals if it is to succeed. Brouthers, Brouthers and Wilkinson (1995) strongly indicate that when strategic alliances are created, companies need to select their partners carefully and this will become even more apparent at the end of the initial three-year funding period. As the number of Product Clubs increases and the original Clubs start to become independent from CTC funding, the Product Clubs will have to ensure that they have developed a sound, long-term marketing strategy so that Canada continues to gain both international and domestic tourists.

Bibliography

Batchelor, R. (1999) 'Strategic marketing of tourism destinations', in Vellas, F. and Bécherel, L. (eds). *The International Marketing of Travel and Tourism A Strategic Approach*. Basingstoke: Macmillan.
Bramwell, B. and Lane, B. (eds) (2000) *Tourism Collaboration and Partnerships: Politics, Practice and Sustainability*. Clevedon: Channel View Publications.

Brouthers, K. D., Brouthers, L. E. and Wilkinson, T. J. (1995) 'Strategic alliances: choose your partners', *Long Range Planning* 28 (3), 18–25.

Caffyn, A. (2000) 'Is there a tourism partnership lifecycle?', in Bramwell, B. and Lane, B. (eds) (2000) *Tourism Collaboration and Partnerships: Politics, Practice and Sustainability*. Clevedon: Channel View Publications, pp. 200–29.

Canadian Tourism Commission (CTC) (2000) *Product Clubs Building Canada's Tourism Industry*. Ottawa: Canadian Tourism Commission (brochure).

— (2001) 'Vision', *Communiqué* 5 (1), 2.

Crotts, J. C., Buhalis, D. and March, R. (eds) (2000) *Global Alliances in Tourism and Hospitality Management*. Oxford: Haworth Press.

Go, F. M. and Williams, A. P. (1993) 'Competing and cooperating in the changing tourism channel system', *Journal of Travel & Tourism Marketing* 2 (2/3), 224–9.

Goeldner, C. R., Ritchie, J. R. B. and McIntosh, R. (2000) *Tourism Principles, Practices, Philosophies*. (8th edn) New York: John Wiley and Sons.

Gulati, R. (1998) 'Alliances and networks', *Strategic Management Journal* 19, 293–317.

Hashimoto, A. and Telfer, D. J. (in press). 'Tourism Distribution Channels in Canada'. In E. Laws and D. Buhalis (eds). *Tourism Distribution Channels: Practice, Issues and Transformations*. London: Cassell Academic.

Hostels Canada Product Club (2001) *Communiqué* 5 (3), 16.

Katz, H. (2001) 'CTC "puts on the Crown"', *Communiqué* 5 (1), 1, 3.

Morgan, N. and Pritchard, A. (1998) *Tourism Promotion and Power: Creating Images, Creating Identities*. Chichester: John Wiley and Sons.

Ohman, T. (2000) 'Roll-out of new product clubs begins', *Communiqué* 4 (8), 1, 14.

— (2001) *Product Clubs do they work*? Paper presented at the National Winter Tourism Forum 2001, Niagara Falls.

Seaton, A. V. and Bennett, M. M. (1996) *Marketing Tourism Products: Concepts, Issues and Cases*. London: International Thomson Business Press.

Telfer, D. J. (2000) 'Tastes of Niagara: building strategic alliances between tourism and agriculture', *International Journal of Hospitality and Tourism Administration* 1 (1), 71–88.

— (2001) 'Strategic alliances along the Niagara wine route', *Tourism Management* 22 (1), 21–30.

Vellas, F. and Bécherel, L. (eds) (1999) *The International Marketing of Travel and Tourism: A Strategic Approach*. Basingstoke: Macmillian.

www.canadatourism.com/productclubs

Young, T. (2001) 'Bay of Fundy Product Club', Paper presented at the National Winter Tourism Forum, Niagara Falls.

139

F Satisfaction in Outdoor Recreation and Tourism Settings

Muzaffer Uysal and Francis P. Noe

Introduction

Customer satisfaction in select National Parks

A conceptual journey can take many routes but this one covers the results of case studies on the satisfaction perceptions of customers who are visitors to National Parks in the southeast region of the US. The parks typify some of the finest examples of natural ecosystems for the area, or commemorate historical, civil engineering and architectural feats. They include the Chattahoochee National Recreation Area, the Blue Ridge Parkway, Biscayne Bay National Park, Castillo de San Marcos National Monument and Forts, Moores Creek National Battlefield, the Virgin Islands National Park at St John, Cape Lookout National Seashore and Gulf Islands National Seashore. Figure F.1 shows the locations of the selected National Parks included in this review.

The parks are part of a contiguous subculture in the US, and attract foreign and domestic visitors who usually expect a more 'down-home-rural' unpretentious customer-service atmosphere. The specific park studies began twenty-one years ago and are still evolving and growing as we learn more about how to measure, understand, model and predict customer satisfaction.

Most tourists are content to be transient in their expectations. Yet, the parks share one thing in common, a certain interest and excitement sometimes bordering on fanaticism among some of the tourists. Two women, for example, return on the same day and at the same time each year, to photograph their favourite sites along the Blue Ridge Parkway. That is dedication to a travel experience, and requires a measure of customer loyalty, strengthened by service to the customer.

Figure F.1 Locations of the selected National Parks

Remember that National Parks are never described in mediocre terms. They are the 'Great', the 'Grand', the 'Big' and the 'Virgin'. They are frequently enormous in land mass and traverse multiple states like the 500-mile Blue Ridge Parkway. By all human comprehension, such tourist parks are rightly and appropriately grandiose in size and impact. To attract tourists and public support, however, they must achieve a level of customer satisfaction to match their designation. If that is not the case, then chances are they will cease to exist as a viable tourist enterprise. Tourists learn quickly by word of mouth, advertising and experience that there are alternatives to the Virgin Islands National Park, and the Great Smoky Mountains National Park. There are simply no guarantees for those national parks, since the international travel community offers grandiose experiences by other names. The key to survival for these enterprises is imparting an exceptional quality of customer service.

A theoretical model for measuring service satisfaction

Park managers of public outdoor areas need confirmation from the tourist that the facilities, services and programmes provided are generally satisfactory. Measuring quality and service is premised on what Manning (1985:6) refers to as 'evaluative communication between visitors and managers'. Developing effective ways of soliciting accurate and reliable feedback from the public about an outdoor recreational tourist experience presents certain measurement problems, one of which is properly limiting the definition of an outdoor recreational situation. As part of the proposed solution to that problem, these research projects attempted to sharpen scaling techniques by testing whether instrumental and expressive attributes, defined in detail below, are distinct behavioural indicators that are effective predictors of satisfaction.

The case studies in this chapter feature comparisons of the results of surveys previously gathered from tourists visiting National Parks and tries to explore how attributes in a tourist situation are specified. Two issues dominate this research, namely, identifying indicators or attributes of satisfaction and specifying a satisfaction model. In the process of conducting these park surveys, it became evident that the practical usefulness of the findings improves when data pertain to specific programme components, rather than complex global programmes or general issues (Rutman, 1977). In fact, Mandell (1989:174–200) argues that understanding different settings is critical for assessing how programmes and policies vary in effectiveness; that means evaluating specific details.

The problem of specification in measurement is essential to understanding an attitude of satisfaction. The measurement model adopted in the National Park surveys assumes a direct approach for determining satisfaction. The current model is specified in such a way that the scale items ask the respondent to make a series of judgements about their experience in terms of satisfaction. The action or behaviour is broken down first into component parts. Specific services, facilities, personnel and programmes are identified which facilitate achieving a pleasurable end.

Functional theorists, in part, emphasize actions to obtain specific ends that are more rationally defined. These are called 'instrumental action'. These facilitating service actions include detailed components of a tourist situation such as the available transportation and communication services, facilities providing rest, relief and refreshment, and provider roles offering direction and information. Instrumental attributes are means used by the tourist to achieve some desired end such as dining, driving, parking, etc., while the goal-oriented attributes are the psychological or social benefits derived by participating in a recreational goal such as fishing, swimming, sightseeing, taking a boat tour, etc.

Satisfaction is not only influenced by the above specific facilitating attributes but also by less concrete possibilities that are tourist goals bringing subjective rewards. Borrowing again from the functionalists, the term 'expressive action' refers to the internal states of respondents designating more subjective emotional responses. Csikszentmaehalyi (1981:332) comes closest to identifying leisure pursuits such as travel for pleasure as an expressive activity that provides immediate 'intrinsic rewards as opposed to delayed gratification'. In the strictest sense, expressiveness could be interpreted as the behavioural result of some subjective inner emotional state. Isa-Ahola (1980:231), too, stresses the importance of intrinsic rewards that are built into the activity, such as 'gratification in winning or losing a game, pursuit of happiness, and self-actualization'. Emphasis is directed to the psychological or subjective state as the respondents in the surveys interpret them. Expectations or actions defining the central purpose of the activity such as touring an historic fort, fishing, visiting a beach or participating in a river floating event are actions that are meant to gratify the tourist with positive reinforcement. In specifying scale attributes the concepts of instrumental and expressive are adapted to the tourist situation of touring a National Park.

But many satisfaction studies are more limiting in their analysis and stress either the expressive or instrumental dimensions of behaviour. A study by Lounsbury and Polik (1992) evaluates four expressive related needs adopted from Beards and Ragheb's leisure motivation scale relating to vacation behaviour. The intellectual, social, competence-mastery and stimulus avoidance attributes are measured in relationship to reported satisfaction. All four expressive attributes are positively related to satisfaction. In such cases, expressive attributes are commonly compared and evaluated with respect to each other. The reported satisfaction of residents, for example, adjacent to Moore Park in Metro Toronto is based more on a visual appreciation rather than actual recreational use (Bornstein, Milliken and Fitzgibbon, 1985). A sense of refuge symbolized in the visual experience of the landscape typography offers greater expressive satisfaction for adjacent residents than having to engage in physical activity such as walking or hiking that would lead to another but more active expressive experience.

Research studies also emphasize instrumental attributes, such as dealing with facility restrooms, fencing, lighting, shade or building conditions (Bartlett and Einert, 1992). These studies usually assess the facilities and services that park management directly control, such as the study by Vaske, Donnelly and Williamson (1991) monitoring the quality of service in a New Hampshire State Park stressing the instrumental dimension of satisfaction. Instrumental behaviour is important for understanding not only physical and contextual environmental conditions but also how role performances are managed between the service worker and the customer in a tourist situation. Successful management of those interactions in the service situation is 'crucial' for maximizing 'customer satisfaction' (Mahoney, 1987).

The instrumental and expressive attributes in the above recreation and tourist studies are distinguished by targeting for analysis a range of attributes in a situation. These concepts are not foreign to allied disciplines. For example, in marketing research, the interpretation of instrumental and expressive is very similar. Swan and Combs (1976) define instrumental performance as the means to an end or the evaluation of physical product, while the expressive attribute is the personal experience of the end in itself or the psychological interpretation of a product. Give this perspective, they assert that satisfaction is produced only through the expressive experience. In social-action theory, however, both concepts are treated as necessary for human action. Both engage different purposes with the instrumental being more cognitively oriented whereas the expressive is more emotional or feeling oriented. The evaluative mode of behaviour is more associated with expressive experiences within the context of social-action theory. In essence, Czepiel and Rosenberg (1977), also marketing experts, consider expressive experiences as behaviours which 'truly motivate and contribute to satisfaction', while the instrumental are maintenance attributes which, if absent, create dissatisfaction. In our testing of the expressive–instrumental model, it is reasonable to speculate that instrumental attributes also influence satisfaction along with the expressive given the fact that so few studies have tested this attribute model mix.

In short, expressive indicators involve core experiences representing the major intent of an act, in this case seeking a satisfactory outdoor experience in a park (swimming, sightseeing, camping, hiking a nature trail, touring a fort, floating a river, etc.).

Instrumental indicators serve as actions or behaviours towards facilitating that desired end (parking, rental services, restrooms, concession services, etc.). These distinctions are used to specifically define the case characteristics of a park or resort in a natural outdoor situation that possibly affect customer satisfaction.

Case studies of select southeast National Parks

To obtain tourist responses, a seasonally adjusted survey was used in all the cases except for the Chattahoochee River rafting festival where participants were contacted on the day of the event. In all cases, a cluster-sampling technique was used in randomly contacting park users during the morning and afternoon hours to determine a willingness to participate in the study. A single week was selected for the spring, summer and autumn. An attempt to sample the Blue Ridge in the winter failed because of the weather and too few visitors to justify the expense. At Castillo de San Marcos winter visitors were included in the survey because public-use data pointed to four distinct seasons of use. In randomly selecting a week for each season, only those weeks without holidays, festivals or local community promotions were selected to optimize sampling of a general park user rather than a specialized user. The park visitors were intercepted at entrance points following a random process, and if agreeable they received a mail questionnaire. A modified Dillman approach was utilized to insure adequate return rates. Acceptable response rates ranged from a low of 50 per cent for the Chattahoochee river-rafting event to a high of 76.7 per cent for the Blue Ridge Parkway. Most rates clustered around the high 60s or low 70s.

The review of park surveys provides the central core of information for these cases. The analysis of the data strictly focuses attention on how the expressive and instrumental attributes at each site affect customer satisfaction. Since that is the soul of these studies, a minimum of contextual and historical detail is deliberately kept in check. Enough information about the park cases is provided, but not so much that it would detract from the central message of this work.

There is also an underlying applied philosophy in how each of the case studies is formulated. The language in the surveys is site specific and asks the customers to evaluate what they come in contact with in their experience. Since all the parks contain multiple sites, only those with which the customer came in contact are measured. In that way, the programmes, facilities and services at each site can be measured on how successfully or poorly they are performing with regard to the customers' perceptions and expectations. As you might suspect, it is easier to change the instrumental attributes, while the expressive that identify the site for what it offers are less open to management intervention. With that in mind, the following eight cases are summarized. Findings are presented in roughly the same chronological order in which the studies took place beginning with the Chattahoochee river-rafting event.

Chattahoochee National Recreation Area

In 1978 the United States Congress authorized the establishment of a 48-mile National Recreation Area between Atlanta and Buford Dam in the State of Georgia. The river begins in the mountains of north Georgia and flows south to the Gulf of Mexico. Access points along the river allow for visitor input for tubing or rafting. The flow of the river is very placid and calm, and allows for a very leisurely and unhurried experience. Hiking or jogging trails along the river link some of the sites together. The park is ideal for family and individual day-use.

An annual event, a so-called Raft Race, attracted thousands of people but became so large, the logistics became unmanageable. The event was not a race, but actually a rite of spring and provided an occasion for a large social gathering for spectators as well as participants. The age of the spectator and participant customer tended to average in the mid-twenties. Over 50 per cent were unmarried, and about a third were active students. Income and occupation crossed all levels.

This river event at the Chattahoochee National Recreation Area outside Atlanta, Georgia provided the opportunity to test if understanding instrumental qualities increased the predictability of satisfaction as opposed to obtaining an assessment based solely on expressive qualities. Event festivities such as the partying, music and revelry among the rafters, however, accounts for most of the explained satisfaction. Since the expressive activity is the major function of the event, it is not surprising that it dominates the satisfaction of the partici-pants (Noe, 1987). High satisfaction is found only among the five expressive attributes.

Of the twenty-four attributes, highest dissatisfaction is found among the instrumental attributes with restroom facilities, parking availability, traffic to and from the event and food and beverage facilities leading the list.

Because the size of the sites could not safely and satisfactorily accom-modate the large numbers attending the event, it has since been cancelled. Those attending one of the last events of this kind at the river were generally satisfied (65 per cent) with the overall organization while 13.8 per cent were dissatisfied, with the remainder being neutral or uncommitted (Aveni, 1980). The results from the data confirmed the limitations of the instrumental facilities and services that could not be changed given the physical limitations of the sites and suburban communities. As a consequence, it assisted planners in making the decision to forgo any other scheduled events of this magnitude for the future.

Blue Ridge Parkway

The Park, Parkway and Recreation Study Act of 1936 began the process in the United States of bringing outdoor recreation to the entire country. This study opened the way for the creation of the Blue Ridge Parkway that connects Shenandoah National Park in the State of Virginia with the Great Smoky Mountains National Park in the States of Tennessee and North Carolina. At the time of its initial construction, the Parkway took advantage of America's love affair with the automobile and opened up a part of the US that is rich in the beauty of nature and local culture. Before the Parkway, many of these areas were not easily accessible to a customer market. The Parkway is noted for its scenic beauty, historical sites of a past agrarian way of life and outdoor recreation, including hiking and camping. By far the major attraction of the parkway is its numerous sightseeing experiences. It offers a wide selection through the differing seasons of the year in terms of vegetation and native wildlife scenes.

In evaluating the facilities, services and programmes along the Blue Ridge Parkway through Virginia and North Carolina certain attributes stand out. The most satisfying are the expressive character of the Parkway represented by an enjoyable driving and riding experience. This roadway opens up nature's beauty, a clean, litter-free road, a road adequately restricting commercial development, a road providing a quiet, visual experience, and a road with nicely designed guard rails, shoulders, bridges and tunnels. The least satisfying attributes are found among the instrumental characteristics. Services such as providing reasonable auto repair and fuel, emergency communication facilities and adequate directional signs, and sufficient camping facilities caused dissatisfaction among 10 per cent of Parkway visitors. While these failures focus management attention on human programmes that are subject to improvement, the majority of Parkway users are more interested in sightseeing, walking for pleasure, picnicking, outdoor photography, nature-walks and visiting fairs. Such activities are more comparable with the core purpose of the Parkway. More detailed findings leading to these and other results are found in the report by the Center for Public and Urban Research, GSU (1987).

Biscayne Bay National Park

The park site is located in south Florida near the city of Miami to the north. The park is water based and part of a larger natural recreation area. At the north end, the park is bordered by Key Biscayne, Chicken Key and Bill Braggs Cape State Park. The south border is Key Largo, John Pennekamp Coral Reef State Park and Key Largo Coral Reef Marine Sanctuary. On the west side, the park is bordered by the state of Florida and Biscayne Bay itself, while on the east a string of Keys runs north and south. There are major facilities and services located on the Keys. Further to the west, yet part of the south Florida ecosystem, is Everglades National Park and Big Cypress. The combined attractions offer the potential for a bay-to-marsh experience.

In evaluating tourists using Biscayne National Park in south Florida, the vast majority of the boating public agreed that the park offers a safe place for boating, access to water and outdoor recreation opportunities, a quiet visual experience and an enjoyable diving experience. The expressive attributes again emerge as dominant factors influencing satisfaction. On the negative side, instrumental factors again appear to have more of an effect on perceptions of dissatisfaction. Insufficient docking, lack of convenient restrooms, directional signs and navigational aids, inadequate shower facilities and crowding stood out as concerns for a minority of the tourists. Those experiencing problems are concerned with poor fishing, crowding, litter, dirty restrooms and showers, too many insects, bay pollution and reckless boat operators, reinforcing some of the evaluational perceptions.

The differences in perceptions seem, in part, to be a result of environmental attitudes, some favouring a more developed park as opposed to those tourists who want a more natural experience (Jurowski, Uysal, Williams and Noe, 1995). In that respect, tourist expectations tend to opt for more management intervention that would provide more ranger patrols, a more aggressive enforcement of safety rules, more regulation on boaters around diving areas, increasing designated diving and wildlife-viewing areas, and more intervention by providing more mooring sites, picnic facilities, toilets, parking facilities, navigational aids, pest control, and finally less commercial fishing in the confines of the National Park. Certainly, the results confirmed the problem tourists experience with the instrumental attributes that are further reconfirmed by how their expectations supported changes in those attributes to improve the situation.

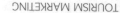 Castillo de San Marcos National Monument and Forts

This Historic Park is located in the city of St Augustine, Florida. There are two forts comprising this historic site, Castillo de San Marcos and Matanzas. They are part of a historic district that includes part of the city. The original fortifications date back to the Spanish influence and then later the English influence, and finally to their use by the US in the early part of the 1800s as points of defence along the eastern seaboard.

The ratings of the touring public are consistently high across all the four seasons of the Park. The expressive attributes associated with the ranger staff including their presentations, demonstrations and interpretative programmes at Castillo de San Marcos are ranked as excellent. The friendly, polite staff are further rated high because of their informal discussions with the public, and the quality of their formal presentations describing the history of the fort. The next highly rated set of attributes is also expressive in nature and highlights the appearance of the fort.

Conversely, the attributes that are least appreciated encompass instrumental factors that repeatedly appear in all four seasons of the year among different samples. The availability of parking, benches for resting and audio boxes are three instrumental attributes receiving poor ratings. However, an expressive attribute dealing with the appearance of the moat (an area easily despoiled by floating litter and the stagnant appearance of the shallow water) also received a poor rating. This is one of the few times in these studies of various National Park situations that a facility associated with an expressive attribute received negative ratings.

Similar results from the seasonal surveys at Fort Matanzas produced a familiar pattern of responses. Again, the expressive attributes such as the appearance of the fort and the grounds received high marks, as did the interpretative talk on the ferry to the fort; however, the types of exhibits at the fort, and availability or lack of information received less satisfactory rating. The instrumental factors such as the availability of parking and sufficient rest areas received even lower ratings.

The expectations of the tourists support their evaluations of the fort operations. They expect to be informed about the history and how people lived in the forts. They want to see displays of historic artifacts and costumes portraying the dress of the time. They also expect to be fully informed through interpretative talks by park rangers or by remote audio presentations. And finally, the visiting tourist expects a place to sit and rest. Clearly, these factors are easily under management control. What pleasantly surprised the tourists were the video presentations of light and sound, historical live reenactments of the period, antique cannon firings and a picnic area and snack bar in the fort. Although unexpected, these features received high favourable satisfaction ratings.

Virgin Islands National Park at St John

Located in the Caribbean, in the West Indies near Puerto Rico in the Atlantic Ocean, the Park covers approximately 20 square miles of which a little over 50 per cent is land based while the remainder is underwater and laced with coral reefs. Trunk Bay is billed as one of the ten most beautiful beaches in the world and there are other beach sites scattered around the island. The park offers outdoor recreation activities such as camping, hiking and boating, along with snorkelling, swimming and sunbathing.

150

In evaluating the facilities of the visitor centre at Cruz Bay, the expressive functions of the centre such as the informational displays and the informal staff interaction with the tourist received high marks. The tangible aspects such as being litter free and the landscaping were also valued. The instrumental attributes such as clean, odour-free restrooms, drinking water and refreshments, availability of seating for resting and directional signs are poorly rated. At Hawksnest and Trunk Bays, the highest ratings are associated with the beaches, the swimming and wading, the clean and sandy beach areas, the snorkelling and the helpfulness of the lifeguards. Again, the tourists poorly rated the instrumental attributes. At Cinnamon Bay, the beach, swimming area and covered picnic area are rated highly as expressive attributes. The small site museum received the poorest expressive attribute rating while restrooms, the poorest instrumental rating. The poor overall rating comes from a very small minority of the tourists since most of the instrumental services such as food and shopping options are provided by a concession operation that is itself perceived as offering good to excellent service.

Depending upon the type of tourist, support for the above ratings changes. The more consumptive, non-environmental-oriented tourist wants and expects an increase in signage, beach shelters, more pull-offs along the road to view scenery, information, picnic areas, toilet facilities, hiking trails, guided tours and more historic ruins to visit. The more conservation-oriented tourist expects fewer man-made structures, fewer people on the beaches, and more wildlife and native vegetation projects. Shifts in preference depend on type of attribute, but also the expectations of the type of tourist.

Moores Creek National Battlefield

Located near Wilmington, North Carolina, the historic site commemorates one of the earliest patriot victories of the American Revolutionary War. The visitor centre contains a museum with displays of period clothing, a weapons exhibit, a slide presentation explaining the battle and a gift shop. A system of trails permits tourists to view the sites of the battle, accompanied by interpretative displays, audio stations and monuments helping to explain what happened the day of the battle. The Park contains picnic areas with shelters and a special-events centre for local presentations or festival type programmes.

Quite unexpectedly an instrumental attribute, namely adequate parking, is found to be the top-ranked factor in assessing the battlefield and visitor centre. This is unusual given the previous dominance of expressive attributes in the other cases. However, the remaining top-rated attributes are expressive including a friendly and available staff for questions, absence of litter, the appearance of the grounds and monuments as well as the reconstructed bridge and history trail, the historical information, and the discussions, explanations and demonstration programmes. The ratings of the top-rated attributes are in the 90 per cent level.

The attributes evaluated poorly included the unavailability of benches for resting, not unlike the finding at Castillo de San Marcos. Other instrumental attributes rated on the poor-to-fair side are informational and directional signage. Two of the poor-to-fairly-poor-rated attributes included expressive attributes referring to the size and number of displays in the Park museum. In reviewing the perception of problems listed by the tourists, directional, informational and not enough information, the small size of the visitor centre housing the museum, dirty restrooms and litter are among the top instrumental attributes listed.

The expectations of the tourist public listed parking at the picnic area and the visitor centre as their first and second priority. This certainly explains why parking as an instrumental attribute ranked first in this case study. The remaining expectations are oriented to more expressive features such as expecting historic and special-event-programme information as well as artifact displays that serve to inform. But a place to sit and rest, not unlike the above forts case study, appears in the top ten most desired expectations. For the most part, the expressive and instrumental continue a similar pattern as in the above cases, save for parking (Floyd, 1993b).

 ## Cape Lookout National Seashore

The National Seashore is comprised of a long, thin chain of sandy islands on the North Carolina coast that range from Beaufort inlet in the southeast to Ocracoke in the northeast. The shore is a mix of bare, sandy, windswept beaches, and sparse, mixed vegetation and a dune system off the beach covered in sea oats and salt meadow grass. Behind that dune system is a large system of salt marshes that occupy the bay side. The seaside is a turtle nursery that includes the famed endangered Loggerhead. The seashore provides recreational activities from shelling, sunbathing, backpacking and primitive camping for the tourist. Along the coast, boating, fishing and sea kayaking are available. Cabins and campsites are available for more extended visits. The island chain is connected by ferries, and at the island's tip is Shackleford Banks and Cape Lookout lighthouse and keepers' quarters.

The rating of the attributes by the tourists at Shackleford finds that of the thirty characteristics listed, the top attributes are expressive. They include the swimming area, friendliness of the staff, birdwatching, camping, fishing, shell collecting, cast netting and overall appearance. The bottom-rated attributes tend to be instrumental dealing with the availability of waste containers, shade shelters, picnic tables, restrooms, and the drinking water and its quality. The rating of the Core Banks, Portsmouth Village, the Historic Lighthouse, and Keepers Quarters follows a similar pattern with the expressive receiving the highest ratings and the instrumental faring the poorest. Those faring the worst in the eyes of the tourists are insufficient waste and disposal containers, litter, cleanliness of the facilities, and finally a more biological irritant of too many insects.

The expectations of the tourists confirm their satisfaction ratings. The tourist expected and anticipated more restrooms, places with scenic vistas, and park information sources, and exhibits disappointment when these expectations are not met. Once again, however, the touring public was surprised by what they did not expect and such an experience adds positively to their feeling of satisfaction. These included such things as more beach rentals, people acting out how life at the lighthouse was conducted in the past, lifeguards and protected beaches, a place staging local events and a museum. The tourist data for this case study and review are found in a report by Floyd (1993a).

 ## Gulf Islands National Seashore

The seashore is located on the Mississippi Gulf Coast and is made up of barrier islands, sandy beaches, coastal marches and bayou. This study focuses on the tourists to Fort Massachusetts on Ship Island. This site offers the best opportunities for primitive camping, fishing, boating, swimming, picnicking, hiking and visiting an historic fort and ruins. The fort and water-based recreation opportunities are reached by private boat, or excursions that leave the communities of Gulfport and Biloxi. Today, these communities also play host to a large commercial gambling industry that is a subsidiary of the large Nevada corporations.

In evaluating the ratings of the visitors to the fort on the Mississippi Gulf Coast, the average overall rating of satisfaction indicates that 89.4 per cent of respondents rated the site good to excellent (Jurowski, Cumbow, Uysal, and Noe, 1995–6:59). The attributes that are the most outstanding again follow the expressive—instrumental pattern. The excursion boat rides presenting an interpretative programme about the Mississippi Sound and sea life, the tour of the fort, walking the island, the clean beaches and pier area, the swimming areas and the quality of water for swimming received the high expressive ratings. The lower ratings tend to be instrumental attributes such as the picnic tables, sales items, drinking water, shade and shelter areas, and restrooms. At the fort area, the outdoors and guardroom exhibits, although associated more with expressive attributes, also receive low ratings. However, they still represent the responses of a small portion of the touring public.

The effects of the instrumental and expressive attributes on satisfaction were analysed applying a LISREL path model to the variables so as to best select 'the richest and most parsimonious model ... to explain the satisfaction process' (Jurowski, Cumbow, Uysal, and Noe, 1995–6:56). In testing the efficacy of the various models, the final model resulting from this research implies

> that instrumental and expressive satisfiers work together to produce overall satisfaction. Marketing strategies must recognize that expressive expectations play an important role in the assessment of satisfaction while instrumental expectations alone are not nearly as important. However, overall satisfaction depends upon instrumental facilitators. Likewise, park managers concerned with the allocation of resources must be careful not to focus on either instrumental or expressive factors exclusively, in light of the interplay of these variables in influencing how park users evaluate their site experiences. (Jurowski, Cumbow, Uysal, and Noe, 1995–6:65)

In summarizing the above case findings, a pattern of expressive attributes takes the lead in providing satisfaction ratings while instrumental attributes seem to take the lead in providing corresponding dissatisfaction ratings. These attribute distinctions are not to be thought of as categorically distinct but rather as working together to reflect an overall evaluation. The last case study in this series has now begun the process of investigating the interaction between the expressive and instrumental attributes

Conclusion

This chapter primarily focused on satisfaction in outdoor recreation and tourism settings by providing examples from select National Parks in the southeast region of the United Sates. The review of the case studies reveals that there are several unique characteristics that can be attributed to the nature of the experience taking place in such areas, and specific settings. In its simplest form, the main elements of satisfaction – expressive and instrumental attributes – in outdoor recreation and tourism settings can be examined within the context of a tourism system representing two major components of the marketplace, namely, demand and supply.

The tourism system consists of an origin and a destination in its simplest form. An origin represents the demand side of tourism from which visitors come. A destination, on the other hand, refers to the supply side of tourism that may have a certain attractiveness power. The tourist and tourism attractions are the central aspects of the system. The transportation and information (marketing) components and resources at destinations are seen as 'linkages' which enable the tourist to make decisions concerning where to go, how long to stay, and what to do. These linkages, however, also enable the provider (public or private) through promotion, product and programme development and pricing strategies to directly affect the decisions of prospective tourists (Uysal 1998; Fesenmaier and Uysal 1990). The interaction between the two is reciprocal and affects the intensity of demand and visitation patterns and travel flows. Destinations go through different phases of development. So, the interaction between the market and destination will change over time in terms of the types of visitors attracted and their behavioural characteristics.

A tourist does not derive utility from possessing or consuming travel destinations; rather, the tourist derives utility from being in the particular destination for some period of time. The very existence of tourism depends on the availability of resources at the destination. The resources that attract tourists are numerous, though varied in distribution and degree of development and in the extent that they are known to the tourist market (Pearce, 1987). On the market side, producers of transport, accommodation, catering and enter-tainment services are involved with travel-marketing intermediaries such as tour operators and travel agents. On the supply side, leisure and recreational activities at destinations are the concern of the different types of tourism suppliers, including local and state agencies, private business owners, tourism destination organizations, and the providers of infrastructure and supporting services of tourism.

However, in order for a destination or site attribute to respond meaningfully to demand or to reinforce expressive factors, it must be perceived and valued. Important factors affecting this relationship between motivations and destination attributes are accessibility of the sites, reasons for travel, information about the site, destination and activities preferred by the tourist (Gunn, 1988; Smith, 1983). The interaction between demand and supply is essential for the recreation and tourism experience to take place.

Tourists form expectations of a destination based upon advertising and promotional campaigns, past experience, word of mouth that, in turn, may influence the demand for tourism destinations. The quality of the service and the quality of the facility and its perceived value also directly affect the quality of recreation and tourism experiences and thus the level of future demand. Further, the level of satisfaction that the tourist feels is also dependent upon the ability of the destination to deliver the type of experience which it has marketed as a function of its facilities and programmes (Fesenmaier and Uysal, 1991; Ryan, 1995).

The analogy drawn here has both theoretical and practical implications. Some expressive attributes are the behavioural results of inner emotional states. These attributes are the essence of travel motivation in the first place, representing the demand side of the equation. The responses to the demand side and/or expressive attributes, including benefits sought at the destinations would then naturally represent the supply side of travel experience. Therefore, the instrumental are maintenance attributes without which one may not achieve some degree of satisfaction on a measurement scale from the experience. It is clear from the case studies reported that instrumental attributes also influence satisfaction along with the expressive. Obviously, providers of services and/or Park Rangers are the ones who are likely to exert control over the content and scope of instrumental attributes in outdoor recreation and tourism settings. They are in charge of respondent changes in expectations, and then accordingly manage and monitor resource use and development so that any occurrence of disconfirmation is minimized. Since the case studies clearly support that both expressive and instrumental attributes of services and products collectively and complementarily influence satisfaction, the common variance that is explained by these two sets of attributes should be delineated. Providers of services and products need to make sure that they have the minimum level of desired performance of services and products, which may be considered critical in the psychological interpretation of such services or products. The degree to which managers control this commonality between instrumental performance and the psychological interpretation of such performance will eventually influence satisfaction and the corresponding development of successful programmes, facilities and management and monitoring mechanisms.

The case studies utilized in this review also suggest that satisfaction may show variation from site to site, or from attraction to attraction within one site, resulting in variations in the spatial distribution of visitation. This imperfect factor of immobility as a function of distribution of tourism-supply resources creates the comparative advantage of a particular location (Hoover and Giarratani, 1984). In this respect, location must be considered as a very special type of differentiation worthy of separate treatment (Smith, 1995). Spatial competition among tourist destinations revolves around maintaining repeat visitors and intensifying their use per visit in terms of number of nights and expenditures, converting the one-time visitors into repeat visitors, converting deferred demand into effective demand, and monitoring changes in potential demand until it is ripe for conversion into effective demand. Therefore, the place dependency of satisfaction should be of great concern in meeting the expectations of tourists. Situational and structural differentiation of products and services would pose additional challenges for providers to be more proactive in facilitating the enjoyment of product offerings. It is clear from the reviewed cases that in evaluating facilities, services and programmes, the most satisfying are the expressive character of the site(s) in question. However, it is important to remember that instrumental factors can have more of an effect on perceptions of dissatisfaction. Therefore, it is important to recognize that the existing attractions still have inherent constraints within which providers need to meet strategic management goals and satisfy visitor expectations.

The demand side of the equation harbours the notion of value that tourists attach to their leisure and recreation experiences. This value may take on either the perceived importance of service or benefit(s) to be received and the transaction value of the service being rendered. Hesket, Sasser and Schlesinger (1997) suggest that service value to most customers (or all customers) can be enhanced by increasing either results delivered or process quality, or both, while reducing either prices or service acquisition costs, or both. One can also mention a host of possible mediating variables (duration of experience, gender, ethnicity, seasonality, or personality type and the like) that may influence the intensity and the direction between expressive and instrumental attributes of products and services (Noe and Uysal, 1997). Managers and destination promoters must be aware of variations that may result from mediating variables in order to attract segments of tourists with differing expectations and provide the level and type of performance that would enhance rather than detract from the experience.

Monitoring visitors' satisfaction with facilities, programmes and services is important in maintaining a sustained and successful business. Monitoring should not only include pre-travel experience but also post-travel experience. The state of (dis)satisfaction can take place throughout the different phases of recreation and tourism experience, ranging from the pre-trip planning, anticipation and expectation stage to the on-site experience and to the post-trip reflective stage. The generation of consistent longitudinal data is essential in enhancing and managing tourists' experiences in outdoor recreation and tourism settings.

The quality and availability of tourism-supply resources are critical elements in meeting the needs of the ever-changing and growing tourism market. As Taylor (1980) suggests, if the goods and services required by the visitor are known, it is possible to list their availability in an area and determine how well the supply matches the demand. As a marketing tool, a supply–demand interaction system allows an area to be carefully matched with present and potential visitors. Tourism suppliers need to be knowledgeable about the expectations and needs of different tourist types so that appropriate goods and services can be delivered to sustain and increase demand for their destinations (Taylor, 1996). The development and modifications of tourism resources and products in accordance with changes in consumer preferences and expectations may ensure continuing success of visitor satisfaction and increased demand for travel and tourism. The existing physical tourism resources need to be augmented with careful planning and marketing of tourism products and services. The delivery of tourism goods and services onsite should be carried out in such a way that tourists' expectations can be confirmed so that the facilities meet the expressive and instrumental dispositions imposed by the visiting tourists

Bibliography

Aveni, A. (1980) 'Rambling Raft Race', Report Southeast Regional Office, National Park Service, Atlanta, Georgia.

Bartlett, P. and Einert, A. E. (1992) 'Analysis of the design function of an adult softball complex in a new public recreation park', *Journal of Park and Recreation Administration* 10 (1), 71–81.

Bornstein, G. Milliken, J. D. and Fitzgibbon, J. (1985) 'Moore Park: a study in visual and recreational preferences', major paper, University of Guelph, School of Landscape Architecture. Microfiche copy available: The Library Business Office, McLaughlin Library, University of Guelph, Ontario, Canada N1G 2WI.

Center for Public and Urban Research, GSU (1987) 'Blue Ridge Parkway', Report Southeast Regional Office, National Park Service. Atlanta, Georgia.

Csikszentmahalyi, M. (1981) 'Leisure and socialization', *Social Forces* 60 (2), 135–8.

Czepiel, J. A. and Rosenberg, L. J. (1977) 'The study of consumer satisfaction: assessing the "so what" question', in Hunt, K. H., *Conceptualizations and Measurement of Consumer Satisfaction and Dissatisfaction* (Report No. 77–103). Cambridge, Mass.: Marketing Science Institute.

Fesenmair, D. and Uysal, M. (1990) 'The tourism system: levels of economic and human behavior', in *Tourism and Leisure: Dynamics and Diversity*, Zeiger, J. B., and Caneday, L. M. (eds) Alexandria, V.A.: National Recreation and Park Association. pp. 27–35.

Floyd, M. (1993a) 'Recreation Research Survey of Cape Lookout National Seashore', Final report submitted to the National Park Service, Texas A & M University, College Station.

— (1993b) 'Recreation Research Survey of Moores Creek National Battlefield', Final report submitted to the National Park Service, Texas A & M University, College Station.

Gunn, C. A. (1988) *Tourism Planning*. 2nd edn. New York: Taylor and Francis.

Heskett, J. L., Sasser, W. E. and Schlesinger, L. A. (1997) *The Service Profit Chain*. New York: Free Press.

Hoover, Edgar M. and Giarratani, Frank (1984) *An Introduction to Regional Economics*. 3rd edn. New York: Alfred A. Knopf, Inc.

Iso-Ahola, S. E. (1980) *The Social Psychology of Leisure and Recreation*. Dubuque, Ariz.: William C. Brown.

Jurowski, C., Cumbow, M. W., Uysal, M. and Noe, F. P. (1995–6) 'The effects of instrumental and expressive factors on overall satisfaction in a park environment', *Journal of Environmental Systems* 24 (1), 47–67.

Jurowski, C., Uysal, M., Williams, D. and Noe, F. P. (1995) 'An examination of preferences and evaluations of visitors based on environmental attitudes: Biscayne Bay National Park', *Journal of Sustainable Tourism* 3 (2), 73–86.

Lounsbury, J. W. and Polik, J. R. (1992) 'Leisure needs and vacation satisfaction', *Leisure Sciences* 14 (2), 105–19.

Mahoney, E. D. (1987) 'Recreational marketing: the need for a new approach', *Visions in Leisure and Business* 5 (4), 53–71.

Mandell, M. (1989) 'Estimating the marketing effect of intervening variables in pooled cross-sectional and time series designs: model specification and estimation procedure', *Evaluation Review* 13 (2), 174–200.

Manning, R. E. (1985) *Studies in Outdoor Recreation*. Corvallis: Oregon State University Press.

Noe, F. P. (1987) 'Measurement specification and leisure satisfaction', *Leisure Science* 9, 163–72.

Noe, F. P. and Uysal, M. (1997) 'Evaluation of outdoor recreational settings: a problem of measuring user satisfaction', *Journal of Retailing and Consumer Services* 4 (4), 223–30.

Pearce, D. G. (1987) 'Toward a geography of tourism', *Annals of Tourism Research* 6 (3), 245–72.

Rutman, L. (1977) *Evaluation Research Methods: A Basic Guide*. Beverly Hills: Sage Publications.

Ryan, C. (1995) *Researching Tourist Satisfaction: Issues, Concepts, Problems*. Routledge, London.

Smith, L. J. S. (1983) *Recreation Geography*. London: Longman.

— (1995) *Tourism Analysis: a Handbook*. 2nd edn. London: Longman.

Swan, J. and Combs, L. (1976) 'Product performance and consumer satisfaction', *Journal of Marketing Research*, 40 (April), 25–33.

Taylor, D. G. (1980) 'How to match plant with demand: a matrix for marketing', *Tourism Management* 1 (1), 55–60.

— (1996) 'A new direction', in *Recent Advances in Tourism Marketing Research*. Fesenmaier, D. R., O'Leary, J. T. and Uysal, M. (eds) New York: Haworth Press, Inc., 253–63.

Uysal, M. (1998) 'The determinants of tourism demand: a theoretical perspective', in *The Economic Geography of Tourism*, Ioannides, D. and Debbage, K. (eds) London: Routledge, 79–95.

Vaske, J., Donnelly, M. and Williamson, B. N. (1991) 'Monitoring for quality control in state park management', *Journal of Park and Recreation Administration* 9 (2), 59–72.

G Don't Know, Don't Care: The Importance of Information for Visitors to the Great Barrier Reef

Gianna Moscardo

Introduction

The Great Barrier Reef (GBR) encompasses an area of nearly 350,000 square kilometres and stretches 1500 kilometres along the northeast coastline of Australia. The GBR is a world heritage area and contains more than 2900 individual coral reefs and 250 tropical islands. The GBR is also a major tourist and recreational attraction with more than 1.5 million people visiting each year with a commercial tour operator and more than 2 million local residents accessing the area using private boats. A major challenge for the GBR tourism sector is that of achieving sustainability both in terms of the environment and visitor demand for tourism products. This case study will examine the role of information for both managing negative environmental impacts in this region and for enhancing the quality of the visitor experience and thus contributing to visitor satisfaction.

Tourism and the Great Barrier Reef

While this area has always been an important tourist attraction, prior to 1982 use was limited because of the time required to travel to the reef from adjacent ports. In 1982 the introduction of large, high-speed catamarans changed the nature of GBR tourism dramatically. These new boats allowed tour operators to offer one day trips to the middle and outer reefs with greater comfort and convenience to larger groups of visitors. Growth following the introduction of this new technology was fast with annual growth rates in the first decade of approximately 30 per cent. In that decade the number of commercial reef tour operators increased tenfold and the number of sites accessed increased by 400 per cent with 35 times more visitors than before 1982. Not surprisingly there has been much concern by conservation groups and government agencies about the potential for negative environmental impacts.

In addition to these pressures to manage environmental impacts, reef tour operators are also faced with major competitive pressures. A large proportion of the visitors who arrive in the coastal regions adjacent to the GBR are international visitors. Australia is a large country and for the majority of domestic tourists who live in the southern capitals a visit to the reef region requires a four to six hour flight. Thus, for Australians, many international destinations are real alternatives to the GBR. It is not uncommon to find package deals to international destinations such as Bali or Hawaii offered to Australians that are comparable in prices and travelling times to those associated with travelling from the southern part of the country to the GBR region. Thus reef tour operators compete for all their clients with many other international tropical coastal destinations. There is also serious competition within the industry. The rapid growth of tourism in this region was not characterized by much diversity of tourism product. With some exceptions the most common occurrence has been the replication of a small number of basic types of operation. Table G.1 summarizes these basic patterns. The most dominant type of pattern has been that of the large catamaran day trip to a pontoon moored at a reef. There are a number of operational and environmental reasons for this lack of diversity in the basic structure of GBR tourism. Options are restricted by the nature and number of sites that operators are permitted to access, safety and weather considerations, and the locations of infrastructure to support operations.

In summary the tourism industry on the Great Barrier Reef faces some serious challenges to its sustainability both in terms of maintaining the quality of the environmental resources it depends upon, and in terms of providing visitors with quality experiences. A number of different mechanisms or options exist to meet these challenges. In the case of minimizing environmental impacts these can include exclusion from sensitive areas, restrictions of certain activities, regulation of activities, and operator and visitor education. In the case of competitive pressure the options include maximizing the uniqueness of the settings visited to differentiate between products and the provision of quality service. All of these options require a good understanding of the nature of reef tourism and its consequences to both the reef and its visitors.

Table G.1 Summary of basic patterns of Great Barrier Reef tourism operations

Day trips – larger boats	Day trips – smaller boats	Island day trips	Dive trips – overnight
Usually large catamaran	Variety of vessel types	Variety of vessel types	Smaller vessels
Capacity usually >100 passengers	Capacity usually <50	Capacity can vary	Capacity usually <40
Travel to single site (perhaps with enroute short stop). Usually a large pontoon moored at a reef	Travel to more than one site	Provide transport to one or more islands	Travel to one or more reef sites
Provide snorkelling equipment and platforms for access for snorkellers	Provide snorkelling equipment. Access to water directly from boat	Sometimes snorkelling equipment is available	Often part of a learn to dive course
Offer glass-bottom boat and/or semi-submersible tours of the reef	Sometimes offer boomnetting	Resort activities available on some islands for visitors	Sometimes opportunities for close contact with marine wildlife
Marine biologists give talks and take guided snorkel tours	Sometimes have marine biologists for talks and tours	Some opportunity for guided walks	Some talks and environmental information
Opportunities for SCUBA diving	Opportunities for SCUBA diving	Resorts may offer SCUBA diving	Diving is main activity

Understanding reef visitor satisfaction

The Cooperative Research Centre for the Great Barrier Reef World Heritage Area, known as CRC Reef, provides strategic scientific information, education and training to enhance reef-based industry and management of the Great Barrier Reef World Heritage Area. As part of its programme of research it includes regular surveys of reef visitors using commercial reef tour operations. These surveys have been conducted annually since 1994 and currently the survey data set consists of 6903 completed surveys. The surveys have been conducted in six languages with 54 different reef operations working from major ports and islands along the entire length of the coast adjacent to the Great Barrier Reef. These commercial reef operations included a variety of sizes and types of boats, and lengths and purposes of the trip. People were surveyed on sailing day trips, overnight cruises, large and small day trip boats, diving trips, and island day trips.

This survey was designed to cover two major sets of variables. The first set included questions describing patterns of reef visitation and activity participation, modes of travel, socio-demographic characteristics and satisfaction. The second set included those variables that have been identified in previous research as likely to influence or predict the patterns of use. These included travel motivations and previous experience with the region and other similar locations. All the questions included in the survey will be covered in the results section and details on the generation of the questions will be given where relevant (see Moscardo, 1999b for more details on the methods used).

Table G.2 Measures of reef visitor satisfaction

Overall enjoyment of the reef trip	Mean Score = 8.5 out of 10 (Standard Deviation = 1.6)	91% gave a score of 7 or higher
Satisfaction with		
Staff friendliness	Mean score = 8.3 (SD=1.8)	84% gave a score of 7 or higher
Staff knowledge	Mean score = 8.0 (SD=1.9)	80% gave a score of 7 or higher
Range of activities available	Mean score = 7.7 (SD=2.0)	77% gave a score of 7 or higher
Value for money	Mean score = 7.2 (SD=2.3)	69% gave a score of 7 or higher
Amount of information provided	Mean score = 7.1 (SD=2.3)	63% gave a score of 7 or higher
Quality of information provided	Mean Score = 7.0 (SD=2.3)	64% gave a score of 7 or higher
Would you take another reef tour if you visited this region again?	No Don't know Probably Definitely	9% 18% 33% 40%
Would you recommend a reef tour to friends or relatives?	No Don't know Probably Definitely	1% 4% 22% 73%

Reef visitor satisfaction was measured in four ways and the overall results of these four questions are given in Table G.2. The four types of question were

• An overall enjoyment rating from 0 meaning not at all enjoyable, to 10 meaning very enjoyable.
• Ratings of satisfaction with key aspects of the service provided on the same scale as used for overall enjoyment.
• Whether or not people would repeat a visit to the Great Barrier Reef in the future.
• Whether or not people would recommend a visit to the Great Barrier Reef in the future.

Four different types of question were used to cover all the possible options as suggested in the literature on measuring tourist satisfaction (Noe, 1999). As would be expected all four measures were significantly correlated with each other. The most important two measures for the reef tour operators, however, were those relating to repeat business and likelihood of recommendation. Thus these two variables were combined to create a single behavioural measure of visitor satisfaction. The results of this were as follows.

- 3% of the sample would neither repeat nor recommend a reef trip to others
- 12% of the visitors would repeat a reef trip but not recommend it to others
- 40% of the visitors would recommend a reef trip to others but were not sure they would do one again themselves
- 45% would both definitely repeat and recommend a reef trip

The next stage of the research involved a series of analyses using a variety of statistical analysis techniques to determine what factors were associated with the decisions to repeat and/or recommend a reef trip. The first important finding was that the only differences between those who would definitely repeat and recommend and those who would recommend but might not repeat were that the latter group were older, more likely to be international visitors and more likely to have less time available for holidays. In other words, the major difference between these two groups was that of opportunity to repeat a reef trip. Therefore they were combined for the rest of the analyses. The three resulting groups of visitors can be profiled as follows.

Those who would neither repeat nor recommend a reef trip were

- generally younger than the others
- more likely to have visited other coral reefs
- more likely to give staff a lower rating for their knowledge
- more likely to come from Asia
- the least likely to have had information about the reef before they started their reef tour
- the most likely to suggest more information as an improvement to reef operations.

Those who would repeat but not recommend a tour were

- more likely to be local residents
- more likely to travel regularly to the GBR
- generally motivated by the opportunity to relax in a pleasant natural environment
- the most likely to suggest more activities and more educational activities as improvements to reef operations.

Those who would recommend and repeat if possible were

- less likely to have been to other coral reefs
- more likely to give staff a higher rating for their knowledge
- more likely to have used several sources for reef information before visiting
- generally motivated to experience nature and see the beauty of the GBR
- more likely to engage in more of the activities available
- more likely to have seen marine wildlife
- more likely to talk about an educational activity as their best experience.

Overall it seemed that satisfaction was associated with experience and information provision. Those visitors who had more information before their reef tour and who experienced knowledgeable staff and enjoyable educational activities were more likely to say that they would both repeat a reef trip and recommend it to others.

Reef visitor understanding of environmental impacts

Another series of research studies within the CRC Reef Program has concentrated on understanding visitor and resident perceptions of the environmental status and potential threats to the well-being of the Great Barrier Reef. These studies have focused on evaluating existing and proposed educational programmes and conducting national and regional telephone surveys (see Green et al., 1999, for more details of these specific projects).

One of the telephone surveys focused on visitor's understanding of the specific activities and events that could threaten the environmental health of the GBR. Of the 1600 people who completed the survey, 1319 had visited the GBR. These visitors were asked to describe their most recent trip and the answers to these questions indicated that 36 per cent had visited with a commercial reef tour operation and 64 per cent had been independent visitors using either ferries or private vessels. One of the requirements of a permit to operate a commercial tour business within the Great Barrier Reef Marine Park is that operators provide some educational services to visitors. The aim of these activities is to explain basic aspects of the reef environment and its protection and how visitors should behave to minimize their own impacts on the GBR. Thus the 36 per cent of the visitor sample who had been on their most recent trip with a commercial operation would have been at least exposed to some sort of environmental information.

A number of comparisons were made between the responses of the commercial tour visitors and the independent visitors to various questions about the nature of the Great Barrier Reef and threats to its environment. These comparisons indicated that

1 The commercial tour visitors who had been exposed to educational activities were more likely to describe the reef using words associated with its World Heritage status (89 per cent versus 81 per cent of the independent visitors). These words included fragile, threatened, in need of care, unique, diverse and important to the whole world.

2 Independent visitors were more likely to state that some of their own personal actions were likely to have a negative environmental impact on the reef (14 per cent versus 8 per cent).

3. Commercial tour visitors were more likely to rate the potential negative impact of uncontrolled tourist activities as very large (23 per cent versus 17 per cent of the independent visitors).

4 Commercial tour visitors were more likely to give specific answers to an open-ended question about serious threats to the reef environment (64 per cent versus 56 per cent of the independent visitors). The commercial visitors were also more likely to list specific tourist activities and tourism development issues associated with negative environmental impacts (25 per cent versus 17 per cent).

In all cases these differences were statistically significant based on chi-square analyses. Overall it appears that visitors who were likely to have been exposed to some educational activities knew more about tourist behaviours likely to threaten the reef environment, to rate these more seriously, and to describe the reef using words related to its World Heritage status. They were also less likely to report engaging in damaging behaviours. While the evidence was not strong, the consistent pattern of results supports the conclusion that educational activities can inform and influence tourist behaviour in a positive fashion.

Information and service quality management

The results reported in the previous sections highlight the importance of information for visitor satisfaction and for encouraging visitor appreciation and minimal-impact behaviour. The results also suggest some ways in which this information can be used to enhance service quality that are consistent with three of the five categories listed by Gyimothy (1999).

Facilitation of choice

In this category are information products or services that can assist visitors to make better choices about what they will do and where they will go. Visitor satisfaction is enhanced through better matching of visitors to the activities and destinations available.

Several studies of reef visitor satisfaction found that one key problem visitors had was organizing their time while at the reef (Green, 1997). It seemed that visitors often did not know what was available until they arrived at their reef destination and that they lacked sufficient information on the time required

Gyimothy (1999) argues that a sense of discovery is related to the activities.

can also assist in lessening the negative environmental impacts of individual about minimal-impact behaviours. Information on minimal-impact behaviour cept of discovery needs also to be linked to the importance of educating visitors experience offered. For sustainable tourism in nature-based settings this con-tuaries and zoos, for example, education is the major component of the guided walks and tours, self-guided trails, ecotours, art galleries, fauna sanc-are either important components of the experience or are the experience. In experiences. In many tourism and recreation settings education and learning This refers to the importance learning and discovery can play in visitor

Facilitation of discovery

social system.

the place they are visiting and can encourage visitors to feel part of a larger municate effectively with visitors can assist visitors to feel as if they understand are critical factors in visitor satisfaction. Knowledgeable staff who can com-the reef visitor satisfaction studies show that staff friendliness and knowledge local residents and to have pleasant social encounters with staff. The results of The examples given for this category include opportunities to meet and mix with

Facilitation of integration

or stroller for the reef trip?
• How easy would it be for our visitors to find out if a baby would be better in a backpack
• Do we have an introduction activity to prepare visitors for their experience?
• Is there a uniform system of signs?
• Do we have a good map to help visitors find their way around?

information services in this category include

Some questions that tour operators can ask themselves to evaluate their relaxation (ibid.).

higher levels of satisfaction with their reef experience and greater feelings of given out as brochures indicated that visitors who used the schedules expressed suggested activity schedules (ibid.). An evaluation of some proposed schedules One proposed solution to this problem was the development and distribution of had missed opportunities to make the most of their time in this environment. many people feeling that they did not make good use of their time and that they for participation in various activities. These two information gaps resulted in encouragement of visitors to be mindful, a concept that has been explored in some detail by Moscardo (1999a). Mindfulness is encouraged by providing variety in the educational activities offered, by making personal connections to visitors and encouraging active participation, and by using clear structures such as themes and stories to organize information (ibid.).

Communication and educational activities can be varied in a number of ways such as

- where they are conducted (interpretive talks on the boat are very different from those given on the beach)
- when they are conducted (beach walks at night are very different from those conducted in the day)
- the level of physical effort required
- the level of mental effort required (an interactive activity where visitors have to answer questions is a different experience from sitting listening to a marine biology talk)
- who they are with
- the themes they pursue (a fishy glass-bottom boat tour of a reef is different from a tour of the same area which concentrates on corals and sponges).

Opportunities for interaction or participation can also encourage a sense of discovery. Getting involved in an activity, rather than observing someone else, encourages a sense of control as most activities require decisions and choices. Getting involved can also build personal connections. Marine interpreters can encourage visitor participation in a number of ways. They can ask the visitors questions and give them the clues to help them find the answers. Visitors can be asked to assist in the preparation of interpretive activities or in aspects of marine research.

Even the most mindful marine visitor will not be able to gain an understanding of their environment if they cannot understand the information being provided. Using themes and telling stories are much more effective than listing facts. Anecdotes work better than abstract principles and metaphors and analogies work better than statistics. Anecdotes, metaphors and stories bring the information back to the personal experience of the visitor. According to Wurman, 'facts are only meaningful when they relate to a concept that you can grasp' (1989:172).

In addition to the categories listed above Gyimothy (1999) includes facilitation of access and facilitation of basic needs as part of tourism service provision. The facilitation of access refers to the provision of infrastructure and facilities to allow tourists to visit sites and attractions. The facilitation of basic needs refers to important basics such as accommodation and food. While the examples given in this category do not include the use of information, it could be argued that safety is a basic need and good safety information is part of the facilitation of basic needs.

Summary

Providing visitors with information is a common activity in tourism. The situations range from basic safety messages and simple directions through to complex explanations of the cultural or evolutionary history of a place. Giving visitors knowledge is particularly important for activities such as guided tours, visitor information centres, museums, art galleries, zoos, the presentation of historic buildings and sites, and visitor education programmes in National Parks and other protected environments. The information reported in this case study on the satisfaction and understanding of visitors to the Great Barrier Reef highlights the importance of information for service quality management. It also suggests that greater attention be given by tourism managers to ensuring that they are providing the right information to their clients in the most effective way.

Bibliography

Green, D. (1997) *The Development and Evaluation of Activity Schedules for Tourists on One-Day Commercial Reef Trips*. CRC Reef Research Centre Technical Report No. 18. Townsville: CRC Reef Research Centre.

Green, D., Moscardo, G., Greenwood, T., Pearce, P., Arthur, M., Clarke, A. and Woods, B. (1999) *Understanding Public Perceptions of the Great Barrier Reef and its Management*, CRC Reef Research Centre Technical Report No. 29. Townsville: CRC Reef Research Centre.

Gyimothy, S. (1999) 'Visitors' perceptions of holiday experiences and service providers: an exploratory study', *Journal of Travel and Tourism Marketing* 8 (2), 57–74.

Moscardo, G. (1999a) *Making Visitors Mindful: Principles for Creating Quality Sustainable Visitor Experiences through Effective Communication*. Champaign, Ill.: Sagamore Publishing.

— (1999b) 'Supporting ecologically sustainable tourism on the Great Barrier Reef', in Molly, J. and Davies, J. (eds.) *Tourism and Hospitality: Delighting the Senses*. Canberra: Bureau of Tourism Research, 236–53.

Noe, F. (1999) *Tourist Service Satisfaction*. Champaign, Ill.: Sagamore Publishing.

Wurman, R. S. (1989) *Information Anxiety*. New York: Doubleday.

H Managing a Heritage Site for Visitor Satisfaction

Elmar Sauerwein and Harald Pechlaner

Introduction and overview

Traditionally, museums in Austria have not relied upon marketing techniques to draw customers. Several difficulties contribute to this. Firstly, there is no national marketing plan, and current administrative arrangements vary tremendously. Secondly, many museologists regard themselves as professionals whose true work is the care of artifacts. They view management and its techniques as an intrusion on their real work. A third hindrance is the fear that active promotion of public museum services will result in excessive demand and inadequate funds. In developing a marketing strategy, museums need to predict and anticipate 'customer' needs. A client-centred philosophy needs to be adopted in which users participate in both the definition of requirements and the evaluation of the organization's offerings.

The authors present a customer satisfaction management programme developed for an alpine open-air museum exhibiting traditional farms. It is situated in South Tyrol (Italy) and is managed by public authorities.

This museum is part of a pilot programme of the South Tyrolean Tourism Management, which wants to establish South Tyrol as a cultural destination. The reasons for this goal are obvious and well-known throughout tourism (Silberberg, 1995):

- Cultural tourists earn more money and spend more money on vacation
- Cultural tourists spend more time in an area while on vacation
- Cultural tourists tend to stay in higher rated hotels
- Cultural tourists tend to shop more

Description of the museum

Figure H.1 The museum in Dietenheim
(Courtesy Museum of Dietenheim)

The museum of Tyrolese Popular Art in Dietenheim was founded in 1981. It consists of 27 buildings (farms, mill, lodges, etc.), which give an extensive overview of the way of living of former generations in the Tyrol. The museum in Dietenheim now attracts 70,000 visitors per annum, but in 1995 it had 100,000 visitors. This reduction motivated the management to participate in a pilot project. The reasons for this reduction can be found in the currency appreciation of the Italian Lira against the Austrian Schilling in the last years[1], and in the expansion of other leisure sites in South Tyrol.

- The museum tries to enhance the understanding of the former way of living by special events like sheep-shearing, yarning wool, grain milling, etc. The target groups for these activities are mainly coach tourists and school classes.

[1] The recent introduction of the ECU (€) as the common currency in Europe will avert this problem. (Editor)

- Guided tours are free of charge and are offered several times a day in different languages (German, Italian, English)
- Many objects (buildings and tools) are described in detail. In the main buildings video and audio resources are provided. Some displays include a simulation model, which can be used for a small fee.
- There are several rest areas, and each building has benches nearby. Benches are also provided in the area between the buildings.
- There is a museum restaurant located near the entrance/exit of the museum. But guests can consume drinks and food they have brought with them. After the museum visit the bowling alley can be used free of charge.
- There is no formal children's playground, but the area between the buildings is intended to act as a playground.
- The museum shop contains print, audio and video souvenirs about the museum and South Tyrol. Puzzles and plays are sold, too.
- The museum's personnel have very little contact with visitors except the cashier.

Theoretical blackground

Customer satisfaction is a basic element of marketing museums. Satisfaction serves as an important basis for customer retention, word-of-mouth recommendations and any complaining behaviour. Price elasticities are reduced, cost of transactions and of attracting new customers are reduced. Thus, it has a strong effect on profitability (Fornell, 1992; Anderson, Fornell and Lehmann, 1994; Reichheld, 1996), and plays an important role in the formulation of marketing strategies (Matzler, Sauerwein and Pechlaner, 2000). Services and technologies available to museums and other entertainment facilities have made it easier to imitate products and services. It is therefore increasingly difficult to rely on features alone for differentiation from competitors. In order to establish products and services that guarantee a high level of customer satisfaction we first need to fully understand the relevant attributes.

Relevant attributes can be classified in three categories according to the Kano model of customer satisfaction (Matzler, Sauerwein and Pechlaner, 2000):

1 *basic factors:* minimum requirements that cause dissatisfaction if not fulfilled but do not lead to customer satisfaction if fulfilled or exceeded. The fulfilment of basic requirements is a necessary, but not sufficient, condition for satisfaction.
2 *performance factors:* lead to satisfaction if fulfilled or exceeded and lead to dissatisfaction if not fulfilled. Thus, they can cause both satisfaction and dissatisfaction.
3 *excitement factors:* factors that increase customer satisfaction if delivered but do not cause dissatisfaction if they are not delivered or if their performance is perceived to be below expectations.

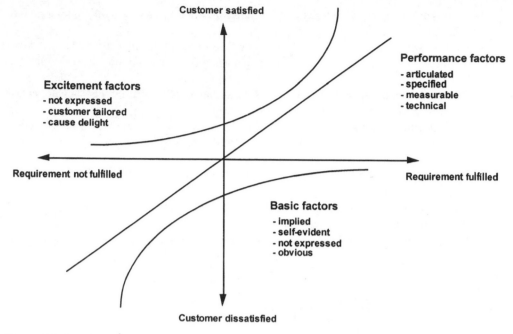

Customer satisfied

Excitement factors
- not expressed
- customer tailored
- cause delight

Performance factors
- articulated
- specified
- measurable
- technical

Requirement not fulfilled

Requirement fulfilled

Basic factors
- implied
- self-evident
- not expressed
- obvious

Customer dissatisfied

Figure H.2 Kano's model of customer satisfaction
(Sauerwein, 2000)

Hence, the managerial strategy should be as follows: basic factors have to be fulfilled to an expected standard; performance factors should be competitive in their fulfilment; finally, excitement factors should be included to distinguish the product/service from the competition and excite the customers.

Excitement factors in particular lead to increased customer loyalty and recommendation. Just consider these statistics (SPSS, 2001):

- Only 5 per cent of all customers complain
- On average a person with a problem tells eight people about the problem
- Satisfied customers tell five people about their positive treatment
- Cost of acquiring a new customer is five times higher than keeping current customers

These well-known facts underline the importance of satisfying customers in order to retain them with your company. Ensuring their satisfaction is vital for a business in order to reach its long-term objectives.

The case study intends to show how a cultural enterprise can identify these relevant attributes of its service for the customer, classify it as one of the aforementioned factors, measure the satisfaction and importance of these attributes and the overall satisfaction. Analysing a service into attributes and classifying these allows the museum to identify clearly what can be done to improve value.

172

As changes and initiatives are implemented in the organization, the customer satisfaction index score may be monitored as a way of evaluating the initiatives. But an important part of assessing satisfaction is not only determining the average satisfaction with a specific feature or overall satisfaction. Dissatisfied customers often withhold information and you need to correct malfunctions of the services.

The process of customer satisfaction management includes the following steps (Matzler et al., 1996)

- Getting the voice of the customer
- Constructing the questionnaire
- Administering the interviews
- Evaluation and interpretation
- Consequences and action plan

Getting the 'voice of the customer'

There are several ways to get the voice of your customer. Commonly the following are used (Rickard, 1996; Naumann and Giel, 1995)

- **Customer councils**
  Councils are employed to bring together a group of customers so that one can better understand future needs, what the museum is doing right and, by far the most important, identify critical areas in which improvements can be made. These councils consist of tourist guides, tourists, teachers.
- **Focus groups**
  This traditional market research process is used to understand customer requirements and/or problems in a specific area. It is employed twice a year.
- **Executive communication exchange**
  Top management is brought together with the customers in order to focus on issues customers want to discuss, including their future needs. This is done especially for travel agents, school teachers and customers of cultural departments of the local government.
- **Surveys**
  These surveys provide input about how customers rate the museums and can be used for internal and external benchmarking reasons. A survey is the main instrument used in the customer satisfaction programme of the two museums.
- **Customer queries and complaints**
  These instruments provide additional sources of input that identify specific areas and opportunities for improvement. There is a praise/complaint box at the exit of the museums. Furthermore, every complaint or suggestion is to be written down on a complaint form at the cash desk. Complaint forms can be completed on-screen, too, and this is accessible to all employees. Once a customer raises an issue, the employee taking the complaint owns it until it is resolved.

- **Market research**
Market research is done by analysing secondary market studies about trends in leisure behaviour and attitudes.
- **Benchmarking, analysis of competitors**
In order to compare with other open air museums the top management regularly visits other museums, conferences and analyses newspapers. Market research studies are also bought.

Each one of these instruments provides helpful insights into customer requirements. Understanding the voice of the customer enables the service development process to begin, using the customer's requirements as the basis on which to design and develop new service offerings.

Construction of the questionnaire

We used focus group interviews to determine product and service requirements, assuming that group-dynamic effects enable a greater number of more diversified customer needs to be discovered. Customer interviews are useful for registering visible product requirements and customer problems, but when investigating potential *new* and *latent* product requirements they are usually insufficient. In particular, attractive requirements are not expressed by the customer, as these are features he does not expect. These features can be determined by asking the customers for problems they have in using the product/service. Another method used in this case was interviews with experts from other museums and leisure sites. Lead User analyses were conducted with travel agents and travel guides. Regular customers were invited to invent-the-future focus groups.

This resulted in the following list of requirements:

- special programmes
- documentation
- food/refreshments
- children's playground
- description of exhibits
- orientation
- personnel/staff
- rest areas
- museum shop
- interactivity
- guided tours

Customers were asked to rate each requirement on importance and satisfaction. The 7-point scale ranged from very important to absolutely unimportant and very satisfied to very unsatisfied. Furthermore they were asked to express their overall satisfaction with the museum. In order to assess loyalty, the customers were asked whether they would come back for another visit and whether they would recommend the museum to others.

The customers were also asked to give open-ended comments on every requirement in order to get weak and strong points.

Administering the interviews

A standardized questionnaire reduces the influence of the interviewer, the return rate is very high and if there are comprehension difficulties, the interviewer can explain. Sometimes the questionnaire had to be explained by the interviewers. The questionnaire was administered to 400 customers of Dietenheim from April to October, the peak season. There was a severe problem with the identification of the characteristics of the population in question. Up to that time Dietenheim had no data about its customers whatsoever. In order to determine the population, data was taken in the first two weeks of April. The data taken consisted of age, gender, nationality and differentiated between single tourists and coach tourists. On this data the first 100 customers were interviewed in April and May. In the second and third weeks of June this procedure was repeated. These two weeks were chosen because they were the beginning of the school holidays in Germany and the Netherlands, from where the majority of the tourists in South Tyrol come.

Evaluation and interpretation

Method

Vavra (1997) introduces an analytical procedure for the identification of factors. By comparing the explicit, stated importance and implicit, or derived, importance of customer satisfaction criteria one can classify service requirements in three categories.

The customer is asked to assess the importance of a set of attributes on a scale from 1 to 7 (very unimportant – very important). This is the self-stated importance. The revealed importance is derived from the correlation coefficient of the satisfaction for a certain requirement with overall satisfaction.

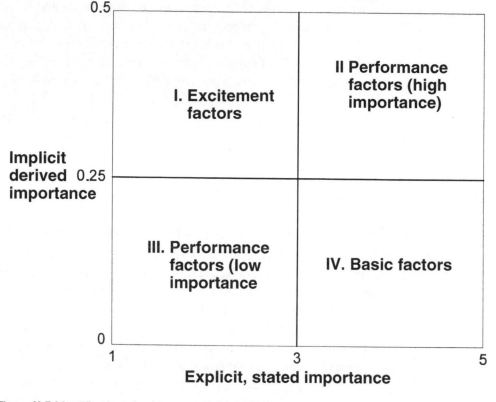

Figure H.3 Identification of customer satisfaction factors
(Source: Matzler, Sauerwein and Pechlaner, 2000, adapted from Vavra, 1997, §. 385)

The precise positioning of the quadrant boundaries is somewhat arbitrary. In this case the arithmetic mean of explicit and implicit derived importances was used.

These measurements are used as coordinates for plotting individual attributes on an importance grid, self-stated importances on the horizontal axis, derived importances on the vertical axis.

Through combining both measurements, four quadrants can be identified:

I Attributes in quadrant I can be considered as the Excitement factors. They are not so important for the customer, but have a great indirect impact on overall satisfaction.

II Quadrant II attributes are Performance factors (high importance). Attributes where direct and indirect importance are identical can be classified as one-dimensionals.

III Quadrant III attributes are Performance factors (low importance). The same can be said of these attributes as for high importance factors, but they are of lower importance to the customer.

IV Quadrant IV attributes are Basic factors. These attributes are considered very important by the customer, but have only low impact on overall satisfaction.

Results

Three requirements turned out to be excitement factors: special events, museum shops and interactive displays. Special events have the highest impact on overall satisfaction. Not surprisingly, the description of exhibits and other documentation turn out to be basic factors. Refreshments and a children's play area are performance factors of lower importance, whereas rest areas, guided tours, orientation and staff make up performance factors of high importance.

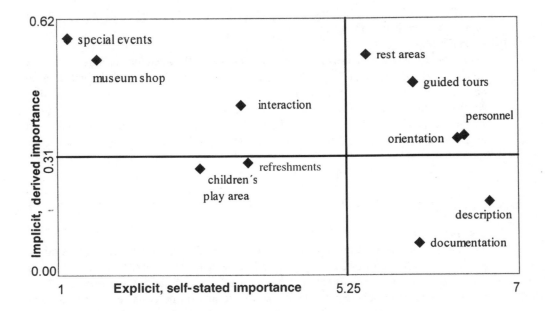

Figure H.4 Examination of the importance/performance-relationship

Consequences and action plan

Excitement factors

- **Special events**
Special events constitute the attraction with the highest implicit importance. Comparing the programme with other museums and leisure sites in the vicinity indicates a clear lack.
During the administering of the questionnaire, the museum counted visitors to special

events which it had not done before. The increase in visitor numbers was significant. In addition, the satisfaction of these customers was significantly higher than that of normal visitors. Thus, the museum achieves two goals by arranging special events: an increase in customer satisfaction and an increase in visitor numbers. Special events have the advantage of attracting specific regular customers.

The goal set for the next year was to increase the number of special events to one per month, and, in addition, the museum intends to organize special exhibitions twice a year.

- **Interaction**

Generally, there is consensus (Tobelem, 1997) about the need to involve the visitor in order to enhance his satisfaction. This case study confirms these findings. Having a demonstrator without involving the visitor does not have the same effect. This is valid especially for school classes. The museum set a target of a 40 per cent increase in interactive exhibits to be fulfilled within a year. Activities proposed include, for example, candle making, corn milling, etc.

- **Museum shop**

There should be more products with direct reference to the museum for sale. A merchandizing line will be developed. Postcards and information about the museum are not sufficient. Handicrafts will soon be sold in the shop. Additionally, local farmers will sell their products on certain days near the museum shop. This farmer's point of sale will act as a draw to the museum for the locals. Once a month the museum plans to organize a big farmers' market with reduced entry fee to the museum to draw local people to the museum.

Basic Factors

- **Documentation**

Free information leaflets are very scarce and kept in the museum shop. There is no information at the entrance of the museum. Some visitors suggested that the museum should provide some basic material containing information about the museum at the cashier, for example, a map with the different buildings and other basic information. This would ensure that customers would be able to take home a souvenir of the museum.

- **Description of exhibits**

The design of the description is mixed. Older descriptions are mixed with newer ones. It is intended to standardize descriptions within the next two years. The two-year horizon was adopted because quite a lot of historical research is necessary. The descriptions will follow a certain structure containing basic information for the fast reader and secondary information for the more interested reader (especially older people). The type size has to be convenient for older customers. There should also be seats for older people to give them the opportunity to sit down and read in more comfort.

Performance factors of low priority

- **Children's playground**

There is no children's playground in Dietenheim. The museum management considered the premises between the buildings as a playground for children. Customers criticized the absence of swings, slides and sand-pits. The typical behaviour of children as observed is that they attach great importance to having breaks and playing in a playground. Children are a very important group of customers (with their parents). There is fierce competition between leisure sites for children. The museum management plans to erect a supervised playground, giving parents the opportunity to relax, too.

- **Refreshments**

Currently, the refreshment provision consists of a restaurant. The satisfaction with this restaurant is relatively low compared to other features. Repeatedly customers criticized the lack of local food. Instead of offering sandwiches, chips, hamburgers and other 'international' food, the restaurant should offer local specialities (e.g. tyrolese dumplings) to give visitors the opportunity of experiencing the local culture through its food. In focus groups, domestic customers expressed their willingness to use the restaurant without visiting the museum, just to eat traditional food. The construction of a separate entrance will enable this.

Performance factors of high priority

- **Orientation**

Satisfaction with the orientation system was relatively low. Some customers had difficulties orientating themselves in the museum area. The design of orientation signs was different from the design of the exhibit descriptions and led to further confusion among visitors. Repeatedly, customers demanded more and better signs.

- **Staff**

There are very few contacts between staff and visitors, except at the cash desk and in the restaurant. The concept of the museum demands a self-contained visit. Other contacts with staff occur when special events or demonstrations are conducted. The satisfaction score for the friendliness of the restaurant staff posed a problem. The management is trying to resolve this problem by organizing a customer orientation workshop for this staff. The workshop will then be conducted for the other staff at a later stage, too.

- **Rest areas**

As the area of the museum is quite big, being able to sit down and rest between buildings or in the buildings is of importance to customers. The ability to rest and relax is directly related to the number and quality of benches. The number of benches is considered to be too low and has to be increased. Additionally, there will be rest areas in the buildings themselves. This measure will enhance visitors' experience of the historical buildings.

- **Guided tours**

Guided tours are conducted regularly at Dietenheim free of charge. The tours are held in different languages: German, Italian and English. The tours in English are for Dutch visitors, due to the lack of a Dutch-speaking guide. The management plans to include guided tours in packages for hotels and/or travel agents near the museum. Such packages would include a guided tour, some sort of demonstration and a meal. These packages will start soon.

Further measures to be taken

- **Tools and utensils**

  Visitors criticized the lack of typical everyday objects in the buildings. They complained about this lack because they felt these objects would enhance the appreciation of the way of life of former generations. The museum has a large stock of these objects not yet on display, because the museum lacks the manpower to catalogue the items. In the summer, the museum management wants to employ two history students to index the items and to work out descriptions.

- **Multimedia presentation**

  The museum management intends to develop multimedia presentations in the buildings to enhance the experience. This should incorporate interactive elements, too.

- **Illumination**

  Lighting in the buildings is very dim. The management claims that this is authentic for the period, but could be convinced to introduce additional light sources. Older people especially complained about not being able to read the descriptions and not being able to make out the details of the furniture.

- **Computerized cash desk**

  Due to the lack of a computerized till it was very difficult to identify quantitative and qualitative customer characteristics. This system is not only devised to facilitate the process of accounting, but also to identify visitor frequencies.

- **Signposts**

  There are too few signposts in the vicinity of the museum and visitors had difficulty finding it. This was identified in the preliminary focus groups. The evaluation team joined several customers on their way to the museum in order to identify the misleading or missing signposts.

- **Marketing**

  Customers complaining about the lack of signposts also mentioned insufficient advertisements. The museum management will correct this by providing leaflets and other information to hotels and guesthouses. Guesthouses are very important, because they provide their guests with personal advice about where to visit, and are therefore especially influential.

- **Internet**

  The museum is not present on the world wide web. Examples were given to the management about how the museum could approach the construction of its own website. The most far-reaching idea is to construct a virtual museum (see http://www.virtuellesmuseum.at/vm/english/home/index.htm as an example.) A simpler version provides basic information on the museum and what it has to offer. A mailing list of hotels, travel agents and pupils could be created. When presented with these propositions the management stressed a severe problem concerning the qualifications of their employees: very few of them are accustomed to working with computers.

- **Other minor measures**

  In the areas between the buildings smoker areas were set up. Space in the museum shop was used to create a baby room. The frequency of garden maintenance was increased following customer complaints.

Towards a cultural destination management in South Tyrol

The interdependence of culture and tourism has already been pointed out earlier in this text. But although they agree on the necessity for the preservation of cultural heritage, national politics and the destination tourist policies are still not aware of its real potential for locals as well as guests. Destinations are products or sets of products and/or services regarded as critical in the decision to visit an area for a holiday stay (Bieger, 1998). It goes without saying that heritage forms a crucial element of destinations and represents the chance to release potential for sustainable tourism on the condition that the cultural infrastructure is preserved and maintained (Inskeep, 1991).

Guests define a personal value chain for their stay. Hence, a new challenge of offering an appropriate system of values in a variety of user-friendly elements must be accepted by the destination management and museum management. This means that the variety of individual performance (productivity) offers has to be integrated, more strongly than ever, into a cooperative whole (Bieger, 1998). As the example of a destination's and a museum site's service chain in Figure H.5 shows, there are numerous elements of the chain that can and should be provided in cooperation.

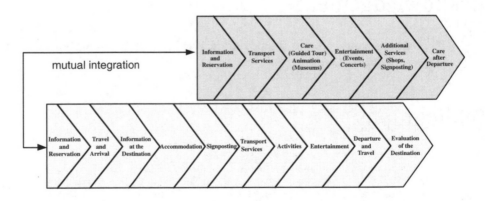

Figure H.5 Integration of destinations and cultural heritage sites
(Based on Pechlaner, 2000)

These efforts should result in the establishment of a knowledge base and an environment where destinations, heritage sites and other elements act as

learning organizations or networks practising and facilitating a mutual acquisition and sharing of information and core competencies in order to develop new
potential for a sustainable destination.

Future outlook

There are some strategies for museums to deploy in order to meet the approach
'What can I do for you?' (Silberberg, 1995).

- Museums can help hotels develop weekend escape packages to overcome a common
  problem of high occupancy during the week and low occupancy at weekends.
- They can help convention planners who need convenient destinations and activities for
  delegates' or spouses' programmes.
- They can describe their admission ticket as a full-day pass to encourage visitors to come
  and go during the day to shop, dine at restaurants in the area or visit other attractions.
  They can close their own restaurants, most of which lose money anyway, and instead
  encourage visitors to dine at local restaurants.
- They can seek trade-offs with town-centre merchants and property owners. That is,
  heritage groups receive free or low-cost space in return for sponsorship of performances
  or special exhibitions during retail promotions, special events or festivals.
- They can develop operating schedules that coordinate as much as practical with common
  retail hours.

Acknowledgement

The authors would like to thank Harald Wohlfart for his valuable work in the
support of the project

Bibliography

Anderson, E. W., Fornell, C., Lehmann, D. R. (1994) 'Customer satisfaction, market share, and
  profitability: findings from Sweden', *Journal of Marketing* 58 (July), 53–66.
Brandt, R. D. (1987) 'A Procedure for identifying value-enhancing service components using
  customer satisfaction survey Data', in Surprenant, C. (ed.) *Add Value to Your Service*. Chicago, Ill.:
  American Marketing Association, pp. 61–65.
Bieger, T. (1998) 'Reengineering destination marketing organizations – the case of Switzerland',
  Paper to the TRC-Meeting, 15–18 May, Brijuni, Croatia.
Fornell, C. (1992) 'A national customer satisfaction barometer: the Swedish experience', *Journal of
  Marketing* 55 (January), 6–21.
Hayes, B. (1997) *Measuring Customer Satisfaction: Survey Design, Use, and Statistical Analysis
  Methods*, 2nd edn. Milwaukee, Wis.: ASQ Quality Press.
Inskeep, E. (1991) *Tourism Planning – An Integrated and Sustainable Development Approach*. New
  York: Van Nostrand Reinhold.

Matzler, K., Hinterhuber, H., Bailom, F. and Sauerwein, E. (1996) 'How to delight your customers', *Journal of Product & Brand Management* 5 (2), 6–18.

Naumann, E. and Giel, K. (1995) *Customer Satisfaction and Measurement*. Milwaukee, Wis.: ASQ Quality Press.

Pechlaner, H. (2000) 'Cultural heritage and destination management in the Mediterranean', *Thunderbird International Business Review*, 42 (4), 409–26.

Reichheld, F. F. (1996) *The Loyalty Effect*. Boston: Harvard Business School Press.

Rickard, N. E. (1996) 'Xerox puts the Customer first', in: Bounds, G. (ed.), *Cases in Quality*, Chicago, Ill.: Irwin, pp. 250–63.

Sauerwein, E. (2000) *Das Kano-Modell der Kundenzufriedenheit – Reliabilität und Validität einer Methode zur Klassifizierung von Produkteigenschaften*. Wiesbaden: Gabler.

Sauerwein, E., Matzler, K., Pechlaner, H. (2000) 'Factor structure of Customer satisfaction – theory, measurements, implications', in *Hotel 2000*. 15th Biennial Congress, Opatja, 25–28 Oct 2000, pp. 267–79.

Silberberg, T. (1995) 'Cultural tourism and business opportunities for museums and heritage sites', in *Tourism Management* 16 (5), 361–65.

SPSS (2001) 'Using satisfaction survey to achieve a competitive advantage' http://www.spss.com/registration/index.cfm?WP_ID=21.

Tobelem, J.-M. (1997) 'The marketing approach in museums', *Museum Management and Curatorship* 16 (4), 337–54.

Vavra, T. G. (1997) *Improving Your Measurement of Customer Satisfaction: a Guide to Creating, Conducting, Analyzing, and Reporting Customer Satisfaction Measurement Program*. Milwaukee, Wis: Stout.

183

1
Marketing Australia to Koreans: Confused Signals or Shrewd Strategy?

Bruce Prideaux

Introduction

The purpose of this chapter is to illustrate the role of NTOs (National Tourist Organizations) in international marketing using the strategies adopted by various Australian national and state government tourist offices to market Australia and regions within Australia in the Korean market. Compared to the normal structure of a single representative NTO, Australia's tourism marketing in Korea is divided between national and state sponsored tourism offices. The difficulties imposed by this approach to marketing are examined in this chapter. For the purpose of this chapter destinations are defined on both a national scale as well as on a smaller regional scale. In its simplest form, a destination may be defined as 'the focus of facilities and services designed to meet the needs of the tourist' (Cooper et al., 1998:102). Scale is therefore determined by the size of the area being described and may be as large as a nation or at the other end of the spectrum, a much smaller area, even down to city size. Thus Australia can be defined as a destination as can each individual state of Australia, Queensland for example. On a smaller scale discrete regions within each state (the Gold Coast located in Queensland for example) may also be described as a destination. The concept of Australia as a destination versus individual states as destinations lies at the core of the manner in which Australia is represented in overseas markets by the Australian Tourist Commission (the national NTO) and various state government funded State Tourist Offices (STOs). As a consequence, any confusion in overseas markets over Australia as a destination versus individual states as destinations may be seen as an outcome of the manner in which Australia is marketed.

Marketing Australia overseas – from federation to present

Australia's overseas promotion is built on a unique partnership between the Australian Tourist Commission (ATC) and State Tourism Offices that are operated by all Australian states, as well as promotional activities funded by the private sector. For example, in Korea, Australia is represented by the ATC at NTO level and Tourism Queensland (TQ) at STO level. Until 1998 Tourism Victoria also maintained a representative office in Seoul, however, this function is now undertaken by the Victoria Tourism Office representative based in Taiwan. Similar strategies have been adopted by other STOs. In addition a number of Regional Tourism Authorities (RTAs), including the Gold Coast Tourism Bureau, also actively market in Korea but without the aid of their own representative office. The structure of Australia's overseas marketing is a product of the federal model of government that was adopted by Australia. This model of overseas representation by a mix of NTOs and STOs is relatively uncommon with Canada and the United Kingdom being two other examples.

Prior to 1901 the then six self-governing colonies in Australia were directly responsible to the Colonial Office in London. There was no Australian government or nation although this changed in 1901 when the six colonies federated surrendering some of their powers to the new national government, the Commonwealth of Australia. Under the terms of federation individual states remained sovereign while the new Commonwealth government could only exercise those powers surrendered to it by the states. This concept of state sovereignty remains the basis for government in Australia and has allowed the present situation where states are constitutionally entitled to operate STOs in overseas markets, often in competition with other STOs and the ATC.

As a consequence of these constitutional arrangements a strong central–periphery tendency has emerged and created tensions in Australia where the centre has long been shared between Sydney, the state capital of New South Wales, and Melbourne, the state capital of Victoria. The remaining states of South Australia, Tasmania, Queensland, Western Australia and the self-governing Northern Territory constitute the periphery. The continental size of the nation and the concentration of population in the states of New South Wales and Victoria further exacerbate these tensions. The concentration of international airline services through Sydney and to a lesser extent Melbourne also adds to the centre–periphery structure of Australia's tourism industry. For states on the periphery, the difficulty has long been to attract direct airline services from overseas generating regions. Thus airports such as Brisbane and Cairns, which both service large tourism destinations, have to compete with Sydney and Melbourne for airline services. However, the preference of many airlines is to hub services through Sydney and Melbourne, thereby directing traffic away from cities located in the periphery. The absence of strong charter airlines, the lack of demand for high-yield business travel to non-Sydney/Melbourne destinations and low demand for airfreight services in cities in the periphery has entrenched the preference of airlines to hub through Sydney and Melbourne. Low margins on services that predominately cater for relatively low-yield leisure travel are reasons recently cited by Qantas for deletion of direct services to Canada, Osaka and Shanghai in 2001 and in previous years to Malaysia and Korea.

To overcome centralist tendencies that have been evident from colonial times, states have adopted a defensive strategy which has encouraged the maintenance of STO representation in major overseas markets. The significance of direct origin–destination air services in demonstrated by the changes that occurred in the structure of Korean visitation to Australia in the period following the Asian Financial Crisis period. The Crisis, which commenced in Thailand in July 1997 and quickly spread to Korea and Indonesia, occurred when foreign investors lost confidence in the currencies of the countries involved (Prideaux, 2000). The subsequent flight of capital and severe economic downturn caused outbound tourism from the affected countries to collapse. In the case of Korea the number of outbound tourists to Australia (i.e. tourists inbound to Australia) fell dramatically as illustrated by Figure I.1. Prior to the crisis the Australia–Korea route was serviced by five airlines (Qantas, Korean Air, Ansett, Asiana and Air New Zealand) with direct services to Brisbane, Cairns and Sydney with plans announced to introduce direct services to Melbourne. After the Crisis, Qantas, Ansett and Air New Zealand discontinued direct flights, Cairns was deleted as a port and services to Brisbane were substantially reduced. Qantas retained a token presence by code sharing services with Asiana. Recent increases in the number of Koreans visiting Australia has not attracted airlines back into the market and as a result of reduced competition, airline prices are relatively high compared to other air routes of comparable length.

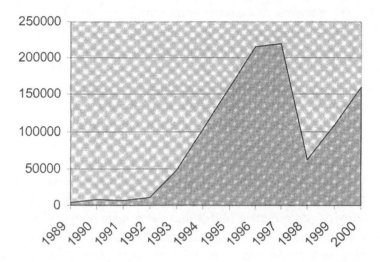

Korean Visitors

Figure I.1 Korean inbound visitors to Australia 1989–2000
(Source: ATC, 2000a)

Australian Tourist Commission

The origins of the ATC can be traced back to the establishment of the Australian National Travel Association (ANTA) in 1929 with a charter to represent the full spectrum of interests in national travel promotion (Davidson and Spearritt, 2000). Prior to the establishment of the ANTA each state in the Commonwealth had established its own tourism bureau, often under the control of state railway departments. A number of the state bureaux actively promoted their state tourism industries in overseas markets as well as domestically. Apparently suspicious that the larger states of Victoria and New South Wales would be the major beneficiaries of promotion funded by the ANTA, each state has retained its own tourism bureau to undertake domestic and in some cases international promotion.

Following a review of its structure and tasks in 1964, the ANTA was subsequently disbanded and a new organization, the Australian Tourist Commission (ATC), was launched in 1967. The original charter of the Commission excluded development and planning functions, exclusions that continue to the present. Planning and development, where undertaken, are assigned to other government agencies. STOs continued to operate overseas offices partly over concerns that the larger states would dominate inbound tourism. The ATC was given responsibility for overseas promotion with domestic promotion being left entirely to STOs. To overcome friction that occasionally developed between the ATC and STOs operating in overseas marketing the Partnership Australia Program was established in 1993 to coordinate the activities of the ATC and STOs. In 2001 the programme was replaced with a new programme, Destination Australia Marketing Alliance (DAMA), which clearly delineated functions and responsibilities that the ATC and STOs would operate under when represented in the same overseas market. While the primary objective of DAMA and its predecessor, Partnership Australia, is to increase the effectiveness of marketing efforts by reducing potential confusion in the marketplace, the continued dual approach to marketing reflects a residual suspicion by STOs that a completely centralized approach to marketing would disadvantage individual states.

The current role of the ATC is to undertake destination marketing, often in conjunction with state tourism offices and the private sector. Blunn (1988:47) stated that the Commonwealth Government's view of the role of the ATC was to 'sell Australia as a destination in its own right, with product specific marketing being the prime responsibility of the industry'. This view continues to describe the government's thinking about the role of the ATC. The operation of the ATC is defined by an outcome that is achieved through a series of three objectives ascribed to it by the Commonwealth Government. Outcome Indicators and Output Indicators measure the Commission's performance in each objective. The Commission's stated outcome is 'The number of visitors to Australia from overseas will increase and the benefits will be maximised, including benefits from employment, while Australia will be protected from adverse environmental and social impacts from international tourism.' The Commission's objectives, as set out in the ATC Act of the Commonwealth of Australia, are (ATC 2000a:6)

1 To increase the number of visitors to Australia from overseas,
2 To maximize the benefits to Australia from overseas visitors,
3 To ensure that Australia is protected from adverse environmental and social impacts of international tourism.

While objective three indicates a proactive, perhaps even regulatory function, the Commission does not have legislative authority to protect Australia from adverse environmental and social impacts that might arise from international tourism. In the Commission's 1999/2000 Annual Report only token mention was given to this objective and there was no mention of specific policies implemented to achieve this objective.

The Federal Government provides substantial funding for the ATC, although an independent Board of Directors governs the organization. Currently, the ATC maintains 12 overseas offices including an office in Korea.

Funding for 2000 (ATC, 2000a) amounted to AUD$137.4 million, consisting of AUD$90 contributed by the Commonwealth Government and AUD$46 million contributed by the private sector for joint marketing compaigns. In 1999/2000 the Commission incurred a small operating deficit of AUD$1.4 million. To undertake its marketing functions, the Commission employs approximately 200 staff, 116 of whom were based overseas in 2000. To achieve its objectives the Commission has invested considerable resources into the building and main-tenance of Brand Australia as the cornerstone of its marketing programmes. Activities and programmes that promote Brand Australia include a very suc-cessful visiting journalists programme, electronic and print media advertising, websites, issuing travellers guides, helplines, displays, travel industries mar-kets and fairs, travel agent training and funding of a range of marketing activities. The success of these programmes is illustrated by the Commission's estimate that the 1999/2000 Visiting Journalist Program generated more than AUD$1.3 billion in stories about Australia in the international media. For example, the ATC sponsored trips to Australia by 196 US journalists whose generated print and electronic stories about Australia's tourism industry would have cost an estimated AUD$256 million if paid for by the Commission (ATC, 2000a). Similarly, 379 Asian journalists visited Australia under the Visiting Journalist Program generating an estimated AUD$111 million in stories in print and electronic media. Korean journalists generated an estimated AUD$36 mil-lion in print and television publicity. The Commission is also actively involved in market research that is made available to the private sector. In its promo-tional activities the ATC concentrates on promoting image rather than specific products, although the Commission does sponsor a series of events where Australian firms are encouraged to market their own products. Examples include ITB (Berlin), the major annual trade fare for the international travel industry in Europe, and the Australian Tourism Exchange.

Structure of the Korean outbound industry

Overseas travel is still a relatively new experience for many Koreans, the final barriers to overseas travels by Korean nationals only having been removed in 1989. The Korean travel industry is described by the ATC (2000b) as being price driven and extremely competitive, with consumers requiring 'value-for-money' packages. Most Koreans prefer to travel overseas as members of tour groups although the numbers of independent travellers are increasing, particularly in the youth market where backpacking is becoming increasingly popular.

Following a shake out in the number of companies involved in selling overseas travel in the aftermath of the Asian Financial Crisis, the Korean travel industry has become more professional with many unscrupulous operators exiting the industry. Consumers were given greater protection in 1998 when the government introduced the relatively expensive and compulsory 'Consumer Protection Guarantee Bond' for all General and Overseas Travel Agencies. Only these agencies now have the right to advertise outbound package. However, consumers remain very price conscious and as a long-haul destination Australia has to compete with Europe and North America for a share of the Korean market. Compared to the relatively low prices of tickets to Europe and North America, travel to Australia is relatively expensive, a consequence of the duo-poly enjoyed on the Korea to Australia route by Asiana and Korean Air, compared to the intense competition on many other Asian and European services.

Although there is no formal distinction between wholesalers and retailers in Korea three major operators control a significant part of the outbound market through their bulk allocation of airline seats particularly during the high season (ATC, 2000b). Products packaged by these companies are retailed through General Travel Agents, which handle both inbound and outbound travel, and Overseas Travel Agencies which handle only outbound travel. Consumers are able to book through travel agencies as well as directly with the wholesale companies.

Marketing Australia in the Korean market

Korea unexpectedly emerged as a major source market for Australia's tourism industry rising from 32nd overall position in 1982 to sixth in 1996 before falling to 9th in 1999. Rapid growth continued until the Asian Financial Crisis engulfed Korea in November 1997 at which point all outbound travel fell substantially. Following recovery from the Crisis by mid-1999 outbound travel again grew rapidly with Australia being a major beneficiary. By 2000 rapid growth in Korean inbound tourism resulted in Korea becoming the eighth largest source for tourists with strong indications that its significance would continue to grow in the future. Figure I.1 illustrates the growth in Korean inbound tourism to Australia in the period 1989 to 2000.

Bilateral tourism between Australia and Korea is lopsided with Australia enjoying a highly favourable tourism surplus with few Australian leisure travellers visiting Korea. The surprising aspect of the bilateral relationship is that there are few substantial links of a personal, cultural or historic nature linking the two nations. One of the contributing factors to the success that Australia has enjoyed in the development of Korea as a source market must be attributed to the success of Australian marketing campaigns.

The ATC (ATC 2000) has identified a number of target segments in Korea including:

- Honeymooner/Young Office lady who make up approximately 9 per cent of total outbound and 35 per cent of Korean arrivals in Australia.
- Young families who account for approximately 7 per cent of total outbound and 13 per cent of Korean arrivals in Australia.
- Mature Age/Silvers who make up approximately 15 per cent of total outbound and 20 per cent of Korean arrivals in Australia.
- Backpackers who are a growing segment representing approximately 10 per cent of all outbound Koreans and 20 per cent of arrivals in Australia.
- Education Travel which accounts for approximately 3 per cent of outbound from Korea but 10 per cent of Korean arrivals in Australia.

Koreans wishing to visit Australia have access to relatively restricted itinerates focused primarily on Brisbane/Gold Coast, Sydney and Melbourne. Itinerates are constrained by the lack of competition between airlines, use of only two entry ports (Brisbane and Sydney), the high cost of domestic travel in Australia because of the relatively long distances between major areas of tourist interest, and the preference for low-cost tour packages by Korean consumers. Packages are usually five to six nights in length and normally include two destinations in Australia. The distribution of Koreans between the major eastern states of Queensland, New South Wales and Victoria is illustrated in Figure I.2 that shows state market share of bed nights for the period 1989 to 1999.

Yet within Australia's destination-marketing strategies there are a number of contradictions. After the initial success of the Australian Tourist Commission in marketing Australia as a destination, a number of state tourism offices began to actively campaign in the Korean market promoting their state tourism industries in opposition to the national image promoted by the ATC. First, Tourism Queensland established a representative office in Seoul later followed by Tourism Victoria although the Victoria office was withdrawn in the wake of the rapid decline in all Korean outbound tourism in the months following the impact of the Asian Financial Crisis. The situation that emerged had some potential for confusion in the mind of Korean consumers as well as the travel trade. Paralleling the destination marketing campaigns, organized and substantially funded by the ATC, were campaigns designed to promote individual Australian states as destinations in their own right. This is a unique situation brought about by Australia's federal system of governance discussed previously.

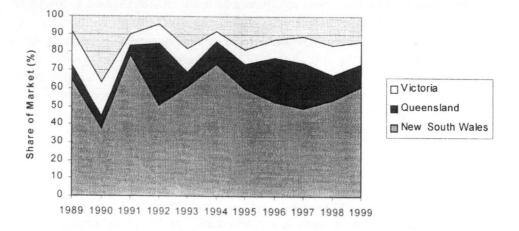

Figure I.2 Share of Korean market by state, 1989–1999
(Source: ATC 2000a)

The Australian Tourist Commission in Korea

The ATC commenced its activities in Korea in 1992 achieving a number of firsts, including the establishment of the first NTO in Korea and the first use of television to promote an overseas destination. For the ATC the opening of a Seoul representative office and investment in marketing was a calculated gamble, particularly as there were no direct flights between the two countries at that time. Initially staffed by two Korean staff and later expanded to three, the office was upgraded to an official ATC office with staff becoming ATC employees rather than contractors in 1997.

Capitalizing on its position as the first NTO into Korea, the ATC invested considerable funds (approximately AUD$2 million annually) in running a number of tactical campaigns that included use of print and electronic media. The aim of these activities was to build an image of Australia that would appeal to the Korean market and that would capitalize on the research reported on in the 1992 (ATC, 1993) market survey. The success of the ATC's activities is evident in the rapid growth achieved in the period 1992 to 1997.

As part of its marketing activities the ATC regularly undertakes extensive market segmentation studies (ATC, 1993) and in 1992 identified a number of primary and secondary markets in Korea. The primary target group were identified as Koreans aged over 30 who have a monthly income of 1.5 million Won or higher. The honeymoon market was identified as a major secondary market. To tap these markets the ATC employed a strategy based on television and print advertising aimed at convincing consumers that Australia was a highly desirable destination to visit. The ATC effectively utilized television commencing with the television commercial 'Make friends with Australia' in 1992. This was followed in subsequent years by further campaigns incorporating both television and print material. In 1996 tactical campaigns were developed to create new market segments including ski, golf, backpacker and honeymoon tourists. Marketing was scaled back after the Asian Financial Crisis although limited promotional campaigns using electronic media continue. Surprisingly, the resumption of economic growth has not encouraged the ATC or STOs to resume the more expansive format of promotion employed prior to 1997 even though the Korean market recorded very high growth rates (see Figure I.1).

The emphasis placed by the Korean Government on enhancing the overall level of computer literacy of the Korean public is well demonstrated in the increasing use of the Internet by Korean consumers for searching for travel information and for purchase of travel products. While the ATC has developed a comprehensive website that delivered 35,671 pages (ATC, 2000b) to Internet users in Korea in 1999, a Korean language site has yet to be developed.

In contrast to the large promotional budgets prior to 1997 the post Asian Financial Crisis budget allocations have been small at about AUD$0.8 million in 2000–1. Emphasis is now given to educating the travel trade on Australian products, sponsoring visiting Korean journalists to visit Australia and limited participation in travel shows in contrast to the expensive media campaigns previously directed at the consumer. In a sense, the Commission is living off the goodwill generated prior to 1997–8 without developing new programmes to maintain the long-term sustainability of the Korean market. While Australia is still regarded as Korean's most desired destination and a major destination for honeymooners (ATC, 2000a), failure to reinvest in the market may have negative impacts in the future, forcing STOs to step up marketing activity to support established state destinations such as Cairns and the Gold Coast which, in contrast to Sydney, can be described as being located in the periphery. In the long term a defensive strategy to retain market share, if adopted by STOs, could lead to a weakening of the strength of Brand Australia with the National brand perhaps becoming weaker than the State brands. The fragmentation of branding in these circumstances could be anticipated to have a long-term detrimental impact on the Korean consumer and travel trade.

Tourism Queensland

Tourism Queensland (TQ) is a semi-government Commission established by the Queensland State Government to undertake a wide range of tourism-related activities on behalf of the state government and the state tourism industry. Direct government funding for all marketing activities undertaken by TQ in 1999/2000 amounted to AUD$47.3 million (TQ, 2000). A number of tasks have been given to Tourism Queensland including promotion, policy advice to government and commercial activities centred on tour packaging and tour wholesaling and retailing, although commercial operations are largely restricted to domestic markets.

To undertake international marketing TQ has established an International Marketing Department that controls offices in nine countries including Korea. Total spending on international promotion and marketing in 1999/2000 was AUD$12.4 million with forty-three full-time staff members based in Queensland and overseas directly supporting international marketing. The scope of activities undertaken by TQ in international marketing includes:

- Provision of advice and introduction to international travel agents
- Publication of guides on international markets
- Publication of Tourism Queensland brochures that include specific products
- Offering subsidized rates at most international trade shows
- Participation in travel roadshows
- Development of Queensland products in emerging markets
- Arrangement of familiarization visits by journalists and buyers to Queensland
- Training in Queensland products
- Assistance in the development of inbound itineraries and products for international distribution.

In Korea, TQ's budget has fallen from AUD$0.8 million (1996) prior to the Asian Financial Crisis when it maintained an office with three staff to AUD$0.23 million and one staff member in 2001. In 2001 TQ operated out of the same office as the ATC and because of its very small budget restricted activities to collecting market intelligence, arranging familiarization visits to Queensland, distributing promotional material, representing Queensland at travel and consumer shows and trade training. Considerable reliance was placed on the Partnership Australia Program with the ATC to maximize Queensland's presence in the Korean market.

Discussion and conclusion

The size of Australia and the diversity of its tourism products are factors that lie behind the competition between states and between states and the national tourism office in the promotion of tourism products. While it is entirely logical to argue that Queensland offers a different tourism product from that offered by domestic rivals in Tasmania or Victoria, competition between STOs and the ATC appears to some degree counterproductive particularly as the majority of Koreans visit Queensland for at least part of their trip. Given the current construction of air services between the two nations, Korean visitors have limited options for visiting states other than Queensland, Victoria and New South Wales, particularly as most Koreans travel in tightly organized tour groups with an average length of stay that rarely exceeds six days.

While from the ATC's perspective, the granting of sole responsibility for destination marketing would offer considerable appeal, the TQ perspective is at the opposite end of the spectrum. Given the dominance of Sydney as the primary Australian airline hub and the relatively high cost of flying tour groups from Sydney to destinations in periphery areas such as Cairns, the need to encourage direct access to Korea and similar origin markets is obvious. In this sense TQ has a primary role of competing with other states and principally Sydney for access to overseas markets via direct airline services. The quid pro quo to encouraging direct air services, given the potential for low-yield predominantly leisure services, is for state NTOs to direct substantial resources into destination marketing in origin countries.

It is unlikely that the current situation where STOs operate in the same markets as the ATC will change unless Sydney were to lose its role as the national hub, which is unlikely. As a consequence there remains the need for the ATC to continue to cooperate with STOs through the Partnership Australia (now DAMA). The scaling back of ATC and NTO promotion during a period of rapid growth is a major concern for the Australian tourism industry. Without substantial new investment in marketing to continually strengthen consumer perceptions of Australia as a desirable destination, other nations prepared to invest more heavily in marketing may siphon potential visitors away from Australia to competing destinations.

In all markets where the ATC shares promotional responsibility with STOs it is apparent that the Destination Australia Marketing Alliance programme should continue to build a strong Brand Australia with the STOs retaining responsibility for tactical marketing of products. It is also obvious that the ATC needs to ensure that Sydney is not given an unfair advantage because of its role as the national hub. Perhaps there is a need for the ATC to become more vigorous in attempting to encourage airlines to operate direct flights to destinations on the periphery in Queensland as well as in other states.

It is clear from observations made in this chapter that NTOs and STOs fulfil important roles in brand development and building market share. In countries that recognize the tourism industry as a serious export industry it is apparent that the belief expressed by economic rationalists that governments should abrogate responsibility for marketing is misplaced. As the battle for the tourism dollar intensifies globally, it is likely that an information-hungry public will continue to demand the type of information traditionally supplied by NTOs while the tourism industry will continue to look to the leadership that NTOs can provide in brand development and marketing support. It is also apparent that destination marketing by NTOs remains a long-term commitment that should be maintained despite interruptions that may be caused by events that include the Asian Financial Crisis, political crises and natural disasters.

Acknowledgements

I would like to acknowledge the assistance given by officers of the Australian Tourist Commission and Tourism Queensland in preparing this chapter.

Bibliography

Australian Tourism Commission (ATC) (1993) *Market Segmentation Studies*. Sydney: Australian Tourism Commission.

— (2000a) *Annual Report 1999/2000*. Sydney: Australian Tourist Commission.

— (2000b) *Profile: Your Marketing Guide to North Asia, China, Hong Kong, Korea, Philippines, Taiwan*. Sydney: Australian Tourism Commission.

Blunn, A. S. (1988) 'The role of governments: a government point of view', in *The Roles of Government in the Development of Tourism as an Economic Resource*, ed. McSwan, D. Seminar Series No. 1. Townsville: Centre for Studies in Travel and Tourism, James Cook University, pp. 43–52.

Cooper, C., Fletcher, J., Gilbert, D., Shepherd, R. and Wanhill, S. (1998) *Tourism Principles and Practice*. Harlow: Longman.

Davidson, J. and Spearitt, P. (2000) *Holiday Business in Australia since 1870*. Melbourne: Melbourne University Press.

Prideaux, B. (2000) 'The Asian financial crisis and the tourism industry – lessons for the future, *Current Issues in Tourism* 2 (4), 279–93.

Tourism Queensland (TQ) (2000) *Annual Report 1999/2000*. Brisbane: Tourism Queensland.

J Branding the Gold Coast for Domestic and International Tourism Markets

Noel Scott

Introduction

This chapter examines how branding of the Gold Coast, Australia was carried out. The concept of 'branding' products and services has become a very common marketing practice. Branding has developed to such a level that brand names are sometimes more valuable than the products or services they represent. In 1994 the most valued brand was Coca-Cola, worth an estimated US$36 billion dollars to its owners (Upshaw, 1995). The simple rationale underlying the concept of branding is that a product's image is as important as a product's physical attributes. Creating the right image can mean the difference between success and failure of a new product. It provides information about a product or a destination the customers have not used or visited previously. While we may not have travelled on The Orient Express or visited Las Vegas, we know a lot about them and this influences our choice to buy. Developing and managing a destination brand is a complex task and requires the input and support of destination stakeholders as well as support from research and marketing specialists.

The Gold Coast

Queensland, Australia is a major holiday destination for both international and domestic holiday visitors. Within Queensland, there are five established tourism destinations (see Figure J.1), each with its own character. The longest established and largest of these destinations is the Gold Coast, located in the South East corner of the State.

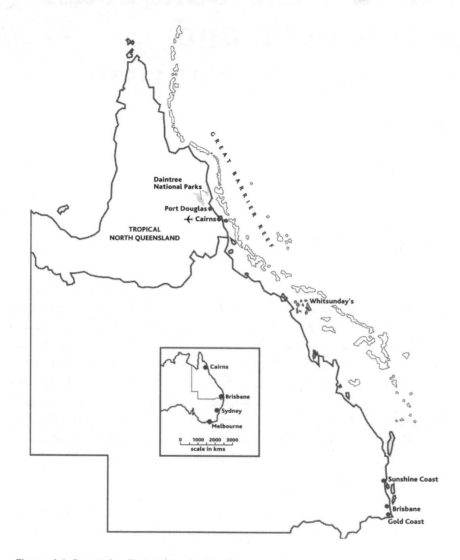

Figure J.1 Queensland's tourism destinations

Tourism destinations can be classified on a development continuum from undeveloped to developed. An undeveloped destination will contain little or no commercial tourist infrastructure, accommodation that is restricted in quantity and quality, poor transportation links and few international holiday visitors. On the other hand, the Gold Coast is a fully developed destination with a range of accommodation options (five star international hotels to budget accommodation, apartments and holiday houses – over 100,000 beds are available) and sophisticated attractions.

Natural attractions include 40 km of white sandy beaches as well as a subtropical hinterland area while man-made attractions include three theme Parks – Warner Brothers Movie World, Sea World and Dreamworld – a Casino, and several large shopping centres with outlets ranging from up-market labels to seconds stores. An international airport is located in Brisbane, capital of Queensland, less than an hour away by car or train and a domestic airport is located within the Gold Coast City area.

Gold Coast Attractions

The top five attractions that come to mind for domestic travellers when thinking about the Gold Coast are

- Sea World (mentioned by 33%)
- The beaches (29%)
- Movie World (28%)
- Theme parks in general (20%)
- Dreamworld (20%)

While recent visitors who have been in the past three years are more likely to mention other attractions such as Conrad Casino (18%) and shopping (12%), non-visitors have a narrow view which does not extend past the beaches and theme parks (see, Tourism Queensland, 1997).

Tourism is the main economic activity on the Gold Coast and supports a population of around 400,000 people. The Gold Coast population is growing at around 4 per cent per year while tourism activity is increasing at about 6 per cent p.a.

Market segments

Just as there is a spectrum of holiday destination from undeveloped to developed and different types of activities and sights, there are also different types of visitors that may wish to go to those destinations. The task of a brand manager is to ensure that the right information about a destination is communicated to the right people. In order to do this it is necessary to match the activities and features of the destination to those segments of the market for which these are most attractive. Targeting the right market segment means that promotional expenditure is not used to advertise to people who are not likely to be interested in visiting the destination.

The visitor markets for the Gold Coast may be divided into domestic and international segments. An audit of the characteristics of visitors conducted as part of the branding exercise for the Gold Coast highlighted the importance of the domestic segments as shown in Figure 2. Domestic holiday-makers are the principal market segment for the Gold Coast, accounting for 62 per cent of visitor nights at the destination. However, the review also noted that the international market (15%) was growing at five times the average for interstate visitor nights (3%), with intrastate (1%) lagging behind at a third of the inter-state growth rate over the past ten years.

The domestic market may be further divided into Queenslanders and interstate visitors (primarily from the Eastern Australian States of New South Wales and Victoria). The New Zealand market is also important and similar to the interstate market in terms of access and holiday benefits desired. The international market is primarily drawn from Asia and includes Japan, Singapore, Hong Kong, Korea and Taiwan. The potential market for the Gold Coast is primarily determined by cost and distance variables. However, the actual market achieved and the scale of tourism on the Gold Coast is a reflection of the development and marketing over many years. Much of this development has been the result of the actions of tourism entrepreneurs (Russell and Faulkner, 1999). A number of niche markets are also important for the Gold Coast, including sports events (Indycar racing) and Schoolies week (where around 50,000 year-twelve students gather to party and celebrate on the Coast after completing their examinations).

Some seasonality was noted in the Gold Coast market with the January Christmas holiday period having higher occupancy than the May low season as shown in Figure 3.

Organization of Gold Coast tourism and key stakeholders

The natural and built environment planning and marketing functions for the Gold Coast are separate. The planning function resides primarily in the hands of the Gold Coast City Council and individual developers along with a number of specific interest groups such as the Surfers Paradise City Heart Association (SPCHA). The Gold Coast City Council is responsible for upkeep and management of beaches and public areas and has a regulatory role in new construction

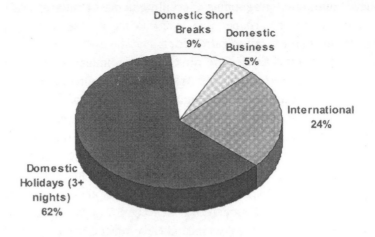

Figure J.2 Size of origin markets (visitor nights 1995)
(Source: Tourism Queensland, 1997)

	January 1996 PEAK	May 1996 LOW
Hotel/Motel Room Occupancy	85%	69%
Hotel/Motel Average Room Rate	$119	$109
Holiday Unit Occupancy	81%	41%
Holiday Unit Average Rate	$82	$61

Figure J.3 Seasonal demand for accommodation – Gold Coast
(Source: Australian Bureau of Statistics, 1996)

activity. Retail business activity is coordinated through local organizations such as SPCHA. The planning objectives of the Gold Coast City Council must balance the perceived tourism needs of the Coast as a whole along with those of the local community and business in particular locations.

Tourism marketing functions are centralized with the Gold Coast Tourism Bureau (GCTB) having overall responsible for cooperative marketing activities for its members. The Gold Coast City Council provided over a million dollars of funding for the GCTB in 1997 with other funding coming from a 700-strong membership base. The GCTB's objectives are to increase the economic contribution of tourism to the local economy and this is achieved through a variety of individual marketing programmes, including domestic television advertising, travel trade promotions, cooperative overseas marketing, visiting journalist tours and travel agent familiarization trips.

These marketing activities are conducted in conjunction with a variety of other organizations including the Australian Tourism Commission (ATC), responsible for marketing of Australia in international markets, Tourism Queensland (TQ), the State Tourism Promotion Office for Queensland, responsible for the marketing of Queensland as a tourism destination, as well as tourism operators on the Gold Coast. The GCTB has a staff of nine people.

TQ has a small marketing team dedicated to the marketing of the Gold Coast which performs a variety of promotional tasks and in addition operates two self-funded commercial operations, SUNLOVER (a wholesaler of Queensland holiday product) and the Queensland Government Travel Centres (a chain of retail travel agents). These operations provide access to the tourism distribution systems for a wider variety of 'product' than otherwise would be available as well as performing an information provision role for potential visitors to Queensland. The Australian Tourism Commission also conducts marketing of Australia and the Gold Coast in international markets. Finally, individual operators of tourism product conduct both cooperative and stand-alone promotion and marketing programmes directed at attracting their own preferred segments. These functions are shown in Table J.1.

Table J.1 Role of tourism promotion organizations

	Role	Marketing functions
Australian Tourist Commission	Destinational marketing of Australia overseas	Promotion Marketing planning and coordination
Queensland Tourist and Travel Corporation	Destinational marketing of Queensland and its destinations domestically and overseas	Promotion State marketing planning and coordination
Gold Coast Tourism Bureau	Destinational marketing of the Gold Coast domestically and overseas	Promotion Regional marketing planning and coordination
Industry operators	Development and promotion of individual holiday components	All marketing functions

Branding as a marketing task

Clearly there are a number of stakeholders involved in marketing the Gold Coast. The combined spending of these organizations on their marketing activities involves many millions of dollars a year. This expenditure may be spread over 100 or more individual marketing activities. Central to the development of a Gold Coast brand in 1997 was the realization that coordinated marketing activity would increase the effectiveness of the expenditure. A number of authors have discussed destination marketing (Ashworth and Goodall, 1990; Buhalis, 2000; Calantone and Mazanec, 1991; Kotler, Heider and Rein 1993) and while the costs of this activity are often recognized, there is little discussion of means to improve performance.

Branding is one such means of increasing efficiency of marketing and is appropriate for destinations that seek to create destination awareness (knowledge of the destination) and destination image (a positive image of the destination) within a consumer market. The aim of a branding programme is to create brand equity. Increasing brand equity means that an increasing percentage of a particular market is both aware of a brand and favourably disposed to buy it compared to alternative brands. Keller (1993) identified six key elements that enhance brand awareness and facilitate the formation of strong brand associations in the mind of the consumer. These are brand name, logo, symbols, character, packaging and slogan. Branding is more than a new advertising slogan, it involves the development of a whole 'personality' with which a consumer can relate.

The advantages of a well-designed branding programme are that they allow a consistent attractive consumer message about a destination to be clearly communicated. It provides a coordination mechanism, as all involved in the branding programme are working together to the same objective. It also increases marketing efficiency in a number of ways. For example a branding programme will often involve the development of standard photographic images that convey specific messages about the destination. These images may then be made available to destination operators at a reduced cost to encourage their use. Cooperative marketing programmes involving these images may be organized at reduced prices due to bulk purchase of advertising space. A well-coordinated brand programme means that the stakeholders speak with one voice, obtain economies of scale in advertising and reduce confusion in the consumer's mind.

Developing a branding programme

In 1995, TQ reviewed its tourism marketing programmes and developed an innovative 'product portfolio' strategy focusing on the five major destination regions in the State. Prior to the adoption of this strategy, Queensland was promoted using a generic 'sun and sand' image with little differentiation between regions. The advantage of a product portfolio strategy is that it provides a greater range of tourism opportunities to the marketplace and allows each region to develop target markets, a destination brand and hence improve promotional efficiency. Such a strategy is logical for Queensland as its five main destinations encompass significantly different tourist experiences, from the Gold Coast's cosmopolitan beaches in the south to the world-class Great Barrier Reef and Daintree Rainforest around Cairns in the north of the State.

The primary aim of this product portfolio strategy was to develop 'destinational images' or brands within an overall portfolio for the State. This approach was found to be extremely attractive to regionally based tourism operators compared to an approach based on 'branding' of the State as a whole as it provides a sense of ownership for the destinations' marketing and encourages contribution to cooperative marketing programmes. The destination 'branding' process began in 1996 and initially involved assembling a stakeholder group drawn from operators in the destination as well as staff from the GCTB and TQ. The branding process involved the following steps.

- Market research (market audit, focus groups and in-depth interviews)
- Portfolio analysis
- Identification of target markets and a distinctive positioning for each destination
- Development of a joint marketing strategy
- Development of appropriate communication messages for the new creative campaign
- Implementation, tracking and review.

Figure J.4 illustrates the general process of destination branding.

Destinations as products

The decision to use a branding approach involves the recognition that destinations may be treated for marketing purposes as products just as Coca Cola or toothpaste are products. This means that the rules of mass communication and advertising can be applied to tourism destination marketing in the same way that they are applied for other products.

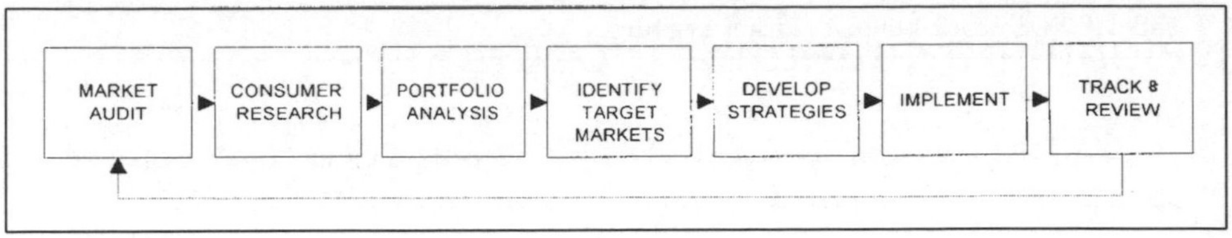

Figure J.4 Destination branding process

The tourism product – the holiday at a destination – is an amalgam of several products and services, the individual components of which are usually supplied by different organizations. Private companies that are often in fierce competition with one another supply most tourist accommodation, transportation and other services. In this respect tourism destinations are probably unique (Ashworth and Goodall, 1990) because the organizations promoting tourist destinations are not responsible for the management of the services they are marketing, and only indirectly profit from the success of the promotion.

Domestic target markets

In order to effectively develop target markets, the domestic holiday market was segmented into a number of distinct potential markets. The segmentation method chosen involved a combination of origin, life cycle and income. While a variety of segmentation methods are available this design was chosen to provide a method of segmentation which both reflects tourist behaviour and meets the marketing requirements of TQ and the GCTB, yet may also be easily adopted by all operators in their own market planning activities.

The segmentation criteria used involved

- four origin types, long-haul international, short-haul international, +400 km domestic market and the local market (people located less than 400 km from the region)
- Life-cycle types (singles, couples, pre-school families, school-aged families and older singles)
- Incomes, defined as household incomes with two types (above and below AU$50,000).

These segmentation criteria emphasized the effects of distance, time availability and affordability of travel. The criteria also distinguished between the travel patterns of families with children of school age and those with only pre-school children. This was understandably related to travel outside school holiday times. Further segmenting the household life cycle segments into higher (minimum AU$50,000 household income) and lower income categories created

Table J.2 Domestic holiday market segments

Household segment	Definition	Total population (000s)	% travelling away from home for at least 3 nights	Average no. of trips per year
1. Young singles	Head of household is single and under 45.	1616	72	2.4
2. Young couples	Couple with head of household less than 45 years with no dependent children.	1013	75	2.0
3. Pre school families	Head of household under 65 years with dependent children *all* under six years of age.	1231	63	1.8
4. School families	Head of household under 65 years with *at least one* dependent child between six and fifteen years of age.	4399	66	2.0
5. Mid-life households	Head of household aged between 45 and 64 years with no dependent children at home.	3959	64	2.0
6. Older households	Head of household aged 65 or older or retired.	2103	50	1.8

(Source: Roy Morgan Research, 1997).
[The data (Year to March 1996) refers to number of persons travelling for holidays of three nights or more not volume of visits over the year.]

twelve substantial and measurable holiday travel markets. Importantly, these market segments can also be targeted for media buying. This means that advertising spending can be channelled into television, radio or print media such that these specific segments are more likely to be exposed to the advertising.

Domestic target market and positioning

Based on these segments and the performance of the Gold Coast as shown in Figure J.6, stakeholders on the Gold Coast decided to maintain and grow three specific segments: high income young couples, school-aged families and mid-life households. These corresponded to the major existing market segments for the Gold Coast. In addition, a number of niche markets were identified outside the general segmentation scheme. These included the golfing visitor, events tourism and nature-based adventure travel. However, it was considered that the return from mass-media marketing to these groups did not justify the expenditure and that targeted promotional activity and magazine advertising was a better way of reaching these segments.

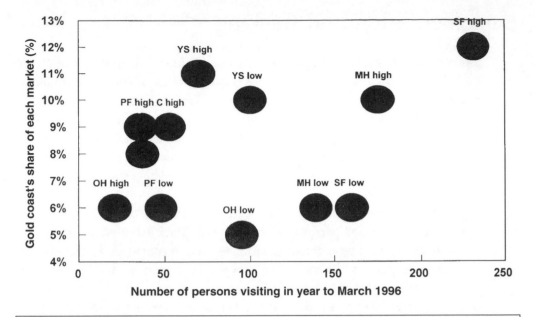

Figure J.5 Gold Coast domestic holiday segments and targets
(Source: Roy Morgan Research, 1997).
The data (years to March 1996) refers to number of persons travelling for holidays of three nights or more not volume of visits over the year.]

Given this choice of target markets, the positioning of the Gold Coast relative to its domestic competitors could be determined. As a result of commissioned quantitative and qualitative market research, stakeholders decided to position the Gold Coast in domestic markets based on 'beachside fun and entertainment'. Such a positioning was both competitive in the targeted segments as well as complementary to other Queensland destination brands, providing cohesion to TQ's overall portfolio strategy. The positioning of the destination was encapsulated in the advertising theme-line: 'The Ever Changing Always Amazing Gold Coast!' The Gold Coast brand personality is encapsulated in the words carefree, fun, friendly, active, entertaining, warm and confident. This positioning can be contrasted with that developed for another of Queensland's developed destinations: Tropical North Queensland. For this destination the positioning was based on 'big nature' with a domestic market tag line 'where rainforest meets the reef'.

Implementation and tracking

The next step in the branding process is implementation. As is shown in Figure J.6, the value of a branding exercise lies in part with the ability of the brand to draw stakeholders together so that a common 'face' is presented to the customer. In order to support this unity, a number of specific promotional tools were developed including a logo, recommended type style and a colour scheme for use in advertisements. Additionally, a number of recommended images were produced as a result of a professional photo-shoot. These images were available for use by stakeholders.

These promotional tools communicate the attributes of the region including the tone, style and personality of the brand. Their use in stand-alone and cooperative marketing programmes achieves greater consumer awareness and interest. Rossiter and Percy (1996) have argued that tourism is a high-involvement transformational product and as such requires highly emotional involving advertising treatments. Such advertising however also should address key concerns such as cost or availability. As such, most advertisements included information on the cost of a holiday package. Wholesalers and retailer travel

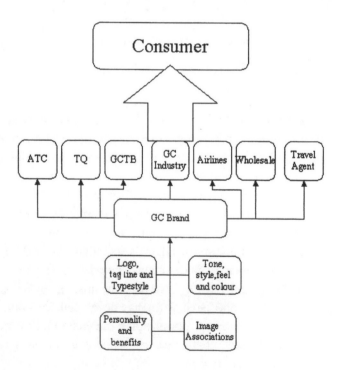

Figure J.6 Branding coordination roles

companies used these promotional tools to ensure their programmes reflect the brand and were able to adapt prices to reflect their own offering. Collateral guides including bromide sheets, top sheet fliers, sample advertising copy and layouts were also made available by TQ to members of the Gold Coast Tourism Bureau.

Using this promotional material, a number of cooperative advertising programmes were coordinated between stakeholders. These focused on the target markets identified and involved television, radio and print advertising. Television advertising was best for image development while press was best for price specials and informational advertising.

International target market and positioning

A similar planning process was used to develop a brand for use in the international markets. Analysis of the international markets to the Gold Coast indicated the importance of the Japanese market. In 1996, Japanese travellers provided approximately 40 per cent of visitors to the Gold Coast. In comparison, the next largest market was Korea providing 10 per cent of visitors. Japanese visitors also were a high-spending market.

As a result, TQ and stakeholders conducted a detailed situation analysis that involved a review of existing secondary research. Table J.3 shows the four main segments of the Japanese market and is based on research by the Japanese Travel Bureau (JTB). It demonstrates that the Gold Coast attracts a similar Japanese market to Australia as a whole but that both Australia and the Gold Coast were missing out on the over-50s Japanese overseas-traveller market. As a result of this and other analysis the two existing market segments for the Gold Coast (Young women and Honeymooners) were nominated as target markets and a new one – the New 50s – was also targeted. The New 50s are known in the west as baby-boomers, a market segment that is expected to grow in the future due to the ageing of the Japanese population.

Market research conducted in Japan is expensive and the budget for the development of the brand did not allow dedicated market research. Instead existing research from the Australian Tourist Commission (ATC) was reanalysed and for each market, the main benefits sought from holidays were determined. For example the 'Young woman' segment felt the benefit of a holiday in Australia was feeling free from restriction and enjoying activities such as scuba diving and horse-riding. Honeymooners saw Australia as a holiday destination mostly because they felt they could forget their worries and go home refreshed.

Table J.3 Japanese segments and ranking

Segment	Outbound	Australia	Gold Coast
Young women	1	1	1
Honeymooners	1	1	1
Families	2	2	2
New 50s	1	3	3

Attractiveness rating: 1-High 2-Moderate 3-Low
(Source: Tourism Queensland, 1997)

Based on this research, a position was adopted based on 'free-spirited nature'. The positioning adopted was similar to that adopted for Australia as a whole by the ATC, not least because this allowed the Gold Coast to benefit from advertising conducted by the ATC in Japan. A number of specific cooperative marketing programmes were developed for the Gold Coast using collateral material based on the brand developed. Other initiatives included the development of tourism wholesaler and retailer promotional material.

Discussion and conclusions

The Gold Coast successfully developed marketing programmes for both the Japanese and Australian markets using a similar planning approach. This method provided a systematic means of segmenting, prioritizing and targeting potential visitors. While the segmentation method was different, the overall approach to developing a marketing plan was similar. One essential prerequisite for this approach to work is cohesion between stakeholder groups. Tourism operators are often reluctant to discuss these with perceived competitors within a destination. Additionally, selection and prioritization of target markets required a significant improvement in cooperative behaviour and involved substantial destinational politics.

However, once the development of a mutually supportive advertising campaign has been developed within the context provided by a clear brand image, the majority of stakeholders are keen to continue the programme. In tourism destinations this often requires time to achieve and often the cohesion is in response to adverse market conditions. Ideally, however, the approach should be adopted proactively prior to any significant downturn in the market.

In the absence of a programme such as described here, the diversity of market segments that are targeted by different stakeholders often complicates identification of common target markets for a destination. One useful approach is to base the decisions on research in the origin markets that allows the needs of the consumer to be clearly identified. This means that the choices amongst market segments are based on information rather than opinion.

Destination branding efforts should be viewed as long-term investments requiring sustained effort during a three-to-five-year period. If a change in image is being considered then this time period should be increased. For the Gold Coast, the aim of this branding process was not to reposition or develop a new image but to ensure consistency amongst the marketing efforts of the diverse operators in the destination. Additionally, the planning process allowed the prioritization of new markets, facilitating coordinated market development activities across National, State and destination tourism authorities.

The benefits of this approach are apparent in increases in marketing expenditure targeting new market segments and a resulting increase in desti-nation awareness amongst those segments targeted. An additional and perhaps most important result is a better appreciation of the nature of the tourism markets on the Gold Coast by all operators, and a more analytical approach to marketing.

Bibliography

Australian Bureau of Statistics (1996) 'Tourist Accommodation Queensland', Canberra: ABS.

Ashworth, G., and Goodall, B. (eds) (1990) *Marketing Tourism Places*. London: Routledge.

Buhalis, D. (2000) 'Marketing the competitive destination of the future', *Tourism Management* 21, 97–116.

Calantone, R. J. and Mazanec, J. A. (1991) 'Marketing management and tourism', *Annals of Tourism Research* 18 (1), 101–19.

Keller, K. (1993) 'Conceptualising, Measuring, and Managing Customer-Based Brand Equity', *Journal of Marketing* 57 (January 1993), 1–22.

Kotler, P., Haider, D. H., and Rein, I. 1993, *Marketing Places*. New York: Free Press.

Roy Morgan Research (1997) *Roy Morgan Holiday Tracking Survey*.

Russell, R. and Faulkner, B. (1999) 'Movers and shakers: chaos makers in tourism development', *Tourism Management* 20 (4), 411–23.

Rossiter, J. R. and Percy, L. (1996) *Advertising Communication and Promotion Management*. (2nd edn). Sydney: McGraw Hill.

Tourism Queensland (1997) 'Branding the Gold Coast'. Unpublished report.

Upshaw, L. 1995, *Building Brand Identity*. New York: John Wiley & Sons.

K Seaside Town Regeneration: Herne Bay and Whitstable

Barbara Le Pelley, Brian Human and Michelle Grant

Introduction

This case study examines the two adjoining, but fiercely independent towns of Herne Bay and Whitstable located to the south east of London on the East Kent coast and the role adopted by the public sector in stimulating their regeneration.

Recognition of the contribution of tourism marketing in each town has achieved a holistic and inclusive approach to regeneration, a process described by Kotler, Haider and Rein (1993) as strategic place marketing. Central to this approach is that a place's potential depends not so much on its location, climate and natural resources as it does on its human skill, energy, values and organization. Another fundamental concept important to this approach is the value of identity and sense of place in sustainable destination regeneration and management (Urry, 1995).

Critical to the success for both towns has been achieving a package of solutions that are tailored to meet the needs of the place and its people and which reinforce local distinctiveness.

Structure of the case study

It is important to look at the particular circumstances of Herne Bay and Whitstable in relation to tourism trends in seaside resorts and their regional context. This provides the framework in which we undertake a critical analysis of each town that looks at:

- **History**
  For place marketing to be successful it is important to understand the physical, economic and social background of a place and its people.
- **Regeneration issues**
  This looks at the economic, physical and social problems faced in each town and the inter-relationship between them.
- **Marketing opportunities**
  A key starting point is to identify characteristics and features that present tourism marketing potential.
- **The process of regeneration**
  This looks at how regeneration was achieved in relation to delivery structures and mechanisms, projects and partners involved from both the public and private sectors.
- **Achievements**
  Finally, this looks at what has been achieved to date and the contribution individual projects and processes have made to the marketing potential of each town.

Herne Bay and Whitstable have embraced a similar strategic approach but this has translated into very different processes, projects and outcomes in each case. Therefore, we also examine these similarities and differences and the lessons which can be learnt for place marketing in other destinations.

Resort tourism in the twentieth century

During the 1970s many traditional seaside resorts in Britain experienced a severe downturn in tourism. The speed and extent of decline was brought about by a combination of factors (Shaw and Williams, 1997; Urry, 1995).

Central to the problem was that the marketplace was changing more quickly than the capacity of seaside resorts to respond. The rapid development of tourism resorts in southern Europe during the 1970s offered tourists guaranteed sun and value for money. Real disposable income was rising steadily and this, combined with rising lifestyle expectations, further spurred the trend for British people to take their main holiday overseas. British resorts could not compete on price or value for money with the large package tour companies.

Visitor numbers began to decline in British resorts and the large base of predominantly independently run serviced accommodation could not afford to undertake necessary improvements to meet changing visitor expectations and the more stringent requirements of new fire–safety legislation. Bedstock exceeded demand creating a combination of closures in holiday establishments, further decline in facilities and a shift from holiday lettings to social security tenancies. A cycle of decline began and many British seaside resorts reached the downward arc on the destination life cycle (Butler, 1980).

As the profile of tourism in the UK moved away from long holidays to short breaks and day visits, seaside resorts were left with large Victorian and Edwardian purpose-built hotels for which few alternative uses could be found. Some redundant holiday accommodation was converted for residential use creating a new, often retired, population. New residents were not necessarily supportive of reviving tourism and retired people generated less community tax revenue. This reduced the potential for local authority investment.

Access for many purpose-built nineteenth-century resorts was developed around the railway. Poor road access meant many resorts were unable to compete within the rapidly changing marketplace where leisure travel was predominantly car borne. Existing resident communities were isolated from job opportunities elsewhere and many moved away leaving a population of retired people and the socially disenfranchised.

During the 1980s many resorts sought to address these issues. Some resorts led successful regeneration initiatives where new niche markets could be identified such as conference tourism. However, other resorts were less successful. Much of the failure to turn around the fortunes of resorts related to the lack of rigorous analysis and understanding of wider local issues and the tendency to adopt off-the-peg solutions. Frequently, problems were narrowly defined as 'tourism specific' and a 'tourism-only' approach was adopted.

Herne Bay and Whitstable were administered as separate jurisdictions until 1974, when local government reorganization in the UK brought them under the administrative control of Canterbury City Council, which became the local authority for the wider area. In 1974 both towns were suffering the effects of the severe UK economic depression with unemployment standing at 27.5 per cent, more than twice the national average. They were heavily dependent on manufacturing industries, which had suffered badly in the recession and their other main economic sector, tourism, had been in decline for a number of years. Tourism in Herne Bay and Whitstable was suffering the same fate as other resorts in East Kent.

Both towns also suffered from poor road and rail communications and were so peripheral to the mainstream of economic activity that the likelihood of private sector investment was extremely remote. Any form of economic regeneration would be heavily reliant on the public sector.

The regional context – public sector initiatives

Kent has an extensive and long-established tourism industry. In addition to Herne Bay and Whitstable, traditional resorts around the coast include Margate,

Broadstairs, Ramsgate and Folkestone. All have struggled to maintain the value of tourism in the past 30 years, while heritage tourism has expanded in towns like Canterbury, Rochester, Chatham and Deal. Dover remains a major port of entry for overseas visitors and the Channel Tunnel, with the Eurostar Terminal at Ashford, is adding significantly to the influx of international visitors. Regeneration in Herne Bay and Whitstable needed to address local issues but also to find marketing solutions that could deliver a distinctive experience to their competitors in neighbouring resorts.

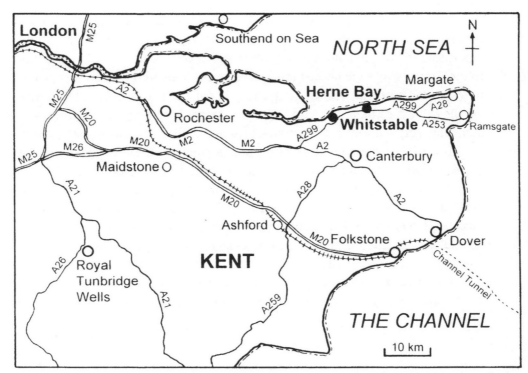

Figure K.1 Herne Bay and Whitstable regional setting

In 1982, Canterbury City Council undertook an assessment of the role it could play in economic development within its area. Tourism-related recommendations were to undertake

- a study of the recreational potential of the District with a focus on the issues for short-term private accommodation and the potential of leisure development on the land between Whitstable and Herne Bay
- an economic study of the potential of Whitstable harbour
- a regional tourism, leisure and recreation strategy

- a programme of land acquisition and preparation for future industrial, commercial and leisure development
- a programme of work schemes for amenity improvement.

A Tourism, Publicity and Economic Development Unit (TPEDU) was set up to attract new investment to the coastal towns but was singularly unsuccessful. The Thanet Way (the main access road to East Kent) had yet to be improved, development sites required basic infrastructure works and the sites competed with the thriving city of Canterbury.

In the mid-1980s an economic study of Kent was undertaken as part of the preparatory work for the Channel Tunnel. One aspect the Kent Impact Study examined was the economic impact on tourism. It concluded that enhancements to the Thanet Way were needed to improve accessibility to the resort towns and to lessen the potential negative impact of tourist traffic bypassing these areas via the M20. The Thanet Way was upgraded to a dual carriageway of motorway standard. This reduced journey times between London and the coastal towns but also reduced the number of direct access points to these towns along the route. A distinctive image became critical to avoid being bypassed.

The study also recommended that a development agency be set up for the area. The East Kent Initiative was established to attract inward investment and included a specific tourism marketing division, Discover East Kent.

In 1986 a study commissioned by Canterbury City Council to explore the potential to regenerate Herne Bay and Whitstable through leisure uses concluded that there was little potential for private investment. It appeared that only public-sector funding could achieve a turn around in the fortunes of both towns.

The impact of changes in population

The population of both towns grew rapidly between 1911 and 1951 mirroring the growth in tourism. Even after tourism began to decline the populations continued to grow (see Table K.1). By the 1970s, both towns functioned primarily as dormitory towns for Canterbury and London. While this increased the population it changed the social fabric and sense of place. The economic impact was a leakage of spend away from the place of residence to the place of work. As significant was the change in the profile of the population towards older residents. At 1991 nearly 25 per cent of the population of each town was in the 60–79 age-cohort and a further 7.4 per cent and 6.2 per cent in Herne Bay and Whitstable respectively were aged over 80.

Table K.1 Changes in population in Herne Bay and Whitstable

Year	Herne Bay Population	% change	Whitstable Population	% change
1911	7,180	–	7,982	–
1951	18,348	155	17,459	118
1971	23,660	29	24,530	40.5
1981	27,800	17.4	27,060	10.3
1991	32,770	17.8	29,490	8.9

(Source: Walton, 1997 and 'Profile' Population, Canterbury City Council)

Herne Bay

History

Herne Bay originally developed from a sheltered landing stage for small coastal craft trading between the northeast of England, Kent and London. The old town was established between the late 1700s and the 1820s around the Ship Inn, close to the landing stage. Most of the present town was laid out to a plan prepared in 1833 by Samuel Hacker of Canterbury, when a new formal street pattern was established, based upon three squares – Hanover, Brunswick and Oxenden – running east to west parallel with the sea front. The old town amalgamated with the new in the late nineteenth century when Herne Bay became a popular seaside resort, principally after the construction of the railway link with London. The town is located some 14.5 km north of Canterbury and its development resulted in two focal points, the High Street and the seafront promenade. This physical separation of the two visitor areas remains today, providing a marketing challenge to create a single tourism destination that combines the seafront and town centre.

Today, some individual houses and parts of terraces such as Marine Parade date from the 1830s. The clock tower was built on the promenade in 1837, the year of Queen Victoria's accession. The architecture is typical of the period but there are no buildings of outstanding merit.

The resort was based on mass transport by paddle steamer and trains from London. Herne Bay offered visitors seven miles of north facing shingle beach and good bathing conditions. In its first decades travellers from London heading for Dover took a boat to the pier at Herne Bay and continued their journey by coach, creating day and overnight visitors. The arrival of the railways killed off this trade but Herne Bay quickly evolved into a fashionable watering place, though it was always a modest size resort.

In its heyday, from 1900 to the late 1930s, families came for the whole summer staying in small guesthouses scattered around the town. There was one railway hotel and several large convalescent homes. After the Second World War additional accommodation was developed, principally large unsightly caravan parks laid out before the introduction of planning laws. In recent years there has been a conscious effort to improve these parks and several have been replaced by housing.

The decline in the traditional holiday market left Herne Bay with a vandal ridden and depressing seafront and few employment opportunities. The introduction of more rigorous fire regulations led to the closure of many of the smaller hotels and guest houses. Alternative uses for redundant holiday accommodation included residential homes for the aged and hostels for benefit claimants. These uses were not compatible with developing a new and positive tourism marketing image.

Regeneration issues

By the late 1970s the economy of Herne Bay was dominated by very small businesses operating at breakeven. Tourism had not only declined but the profile of visitors had changed from holiday-makers staying for two weeks to day visitors and self-catering holidays at caravan parks. The spend profile of these markets tends to be relatively low. Tourism activity focused around man-made activities, primarily amusement arcades on the seafront and self-contained caravan parks. As a result, visitors had largely sidelined town centre operators.

The seafront was run down and the town centre was suffering from urban decay and a lack of investment by the public and private sector. Limited distinctive heritage created no obvious opportunities that Herne Bay could use as a basis on which to develop strategic place marketing. At the same time it was critical to modernize the image of the resort without losing sight of its roots, not only as a means to attract new visitors but also to attract wider inward investment opportunities.

There was a lack of entrepreneurship within the business community and an unrealistic expectation remained that a single external source of funding would turn round the fortunes of the town. This created inertia and a dependency culture.

The key challenge for Herne Bay was how to bring about regeneration with no apparent access to large-scale private-sector investment. Regeneration and investment was needed to effect sustainable change quickly and to capture the imagination and support of the local community.

Marketing opportunities

Herne Bay appeared to have no unique selling point. Marketing opportunities such as proximity to large population catchments and an extensive seafront were insufficiently distinct and were shared with many neighbouring resorts. As we illustrate in the next section, Herne Bay did not commence regeneration with a clear vision of the future but developed a market niche over time and through trial and error. Arguably, the lack of an identified visitor marketing opportunity at the outset resulted in a broader based regeneration strategy.

Process of regeneration

Initially, the local authority concentrated on the town centre. A pedestrian scheme was undertaken for Mortimer Street (at that time a decaying secondary shopping street but now the main focus for shopping in the town). Shortly after a Town Centre Management Scheme (TCM) was established in 1991 as a partnership by the Local and County Councils, the Herne Bay Chamber of Commerce and the local Hotels and Guest House Association. However, the TCM was primarily a public-sector-led initiative with marginal local financial contributions.

The TCM attempted to revitalize the shopping and business image of Herne Bay and delivered a successful festival for two consecutive years. However, it did not deliver sufficient investment in new business opportunities to win ongoing local support. Arguably, an 'off-the-peg' approach had been adopted with insufficient funds to realize the scale and type of investment needed to overcome years of neglect. The objectives of the TCM covered a wide range of small-scale self-help business improvements, rather than a major investment scheme.

At the same time local expectations of the scheme were unrealistically high. Local businesses did not recognize that they needed to participate in the process by changing their attitudes and business practices to reflect changing circumstances.

Local focus groups to discuss a long-term approach produced ideas that were not welcomed by Herne Bay businesses at that time. Again, the emphasis was on a software approach achievable within limited budgets. Ideas included longer opening hours for shops, improving shop-front design and window displays and introducing customer care. With regret, it was decided that the TCM should be wound up and the Manager was employed by the local authority to refocus his priorities exclusively on an events calendar.

A more dynamic and fundamental project was required to trigger local confidence and engender attitudes that would deliver meaningful change.

An unlikely opportunity arose in 1990 when it was discovered the sea wall was about to collapse and needed urgent replacement. A cost–benefit analysis was required to secure Ministry of Agriculture Fisheries and Food (MAFF) funding for these repairs. Four options were developed.

- Rebuild the wall on its existing alignment – this would raise it by two metres and completely cut off the view of the sea.
- Build a new sea wall further out to sea – this would have raised the wall even higher and the impact of cutting off Herne Bay would be visually greater.
- Create a series of rock groins and a large beach – Herne Bay's relationship with the sea would be badly damaged and swimming more difficult.
- Create an offshore reef to break the force of the waves, remove the existing sea wall, replace the seafront gardens and create a new harbour and car park – this was the only option that would enable the town to retain its seafront.

A public exhibition generated overwhelming support for the most innovative scheme that retained the seafront. Reinstatement of Herne Bay's seafront gardens, which had been concreted over for many years, was regarded as a significant opportunity to enhance the environment and attract more visitors, but funding was needed for the more innovative elements of the scheme. The MAFF grant would only cover sea-defence work.

The six East Kent Districts (Canterbury, Dover, Ashford, Shepway, Thanet and Swale) had recently become eligible for an experimental European funding project (Interreg) to find out whether it was possible to develop a cross-border economic initiative that straddled a maritime boundary. The districts would be eligible to seek funding for economic regeneration projects, provided they were part of a package planned and developed jointly with a French town in the Nord Pas de Calais. By creating a seaside regeneration partnership with Wimereux in northern France, Herne Bay was able to access £3 million Interreg funding. The funding package included the seafront scheme, all-weather leisure facilities in the town centre (a swimming pool and cinema), a new museum and tourist information centre (TIC) on the seafront and renovation of a Victorian town centre park.

The town also secured National Lottery funding to repair and upgrade the Central Bandstand (a building of local and architectural interest in the seafront Conservation Area) as a seaside visitor attraction with TIC facilities.

Achievements

The regeneration of the seafront at Herne Bay achieved a 70 per cent increase in day visitors in the winter and a 20 per cent increase during the summer. Perhaps more significantly, new confidence developed within the local community. This new confidence is evident in facelifts undertaken to seafront properties and year-round opening hours of seafront businesses. The success has been to recreate a traditional seaside town promenade in a modern context. Traditional ice-cream parlours and fish and chip shops sit comfortably next to an attractive landscaped promenade with sculptures and flower displays. High maintenance service standards ensure a quality image prevails and the gardens provide safe play areas for children as well as areas for quiet contemplation. The tradition of providing seafront parking has been maintained and has been designed to minimize visual impact and congestion. However, the ability to park along the promenade may discourage some visitors from venturing away from the seafront and into the town centre.

The Events Coordinator has been critical in maintaining a lively atmosphere that encourages repeat visits. He organizes a year-long programme of events in Herne Bay, including a highly successful festival and provides a point of contact for coordinating the promotional activities of businesses. A highlight of the year is a specially commissioned seafront sculpture, which is constructed on the beach from combustible materials and explodes with fireworks, as the culmination of the festival. Investment in personal property and in local businesses has flowed from the confidence in Herne Bay engendered by the project, though further town centre investment is still needed. The poor physical links between the seafront and town centre suggest that the economic benefits of the regeneration have yet to be fully realized in the town as a whole.

Whitstable

History

Whitstable is an ancient town built on the site of two ancient barrows and was well known to the Romans for its oysters. The town lies about seven miles from Canterbury and has a varied history of smuggling, fishing, sea salt and the copperas industry (a dye made of local seaweed). It also boasts the first passenger railway line in the world developed by Stevenson to link Canterbury to Whitstable harbour and known as the Crab and Winkle line.

Whitstable is situated at the mouth of the Swale Estuary and the constant threat from flooding resulted in the layout of the old town. Three sea walls were built in response to this threat, the first at Middle Wall, which dates back to 1583. In the eighteenth and nineteenth centuries Whitstable grew into a busy fishing town and port. It became the foremost oyster-producing town in the country. After the decline of the oyster-fishery industry and following the First World War, the economic fortunes of Whitstable took a downturn. Nonetheless it retains the distinctive character of a small fishing and sailing town.

The parish church dates originally from the eleventh and twelfth centuries. The old harbour, rebuilt in 1832, was the port of departure for the first steamboat sailing from Britain to Australia in 1837. The highly critical architectural historian, Pevsner, remarks in his guide to North and East Kent 'There is no sense in perambulating Whitstable' (Newman 1969: 477), though he does make references to the distinctive Island and Middle Wall with their eighteenth- and nineteenth-century weatherboard cottages and the unusual tarred and weatherboarded 'Beach Stores'. Today the town is characterized by its small old houses and narrow streets, which provide an attractive physical backdrop against which to develop marketing opportunities.

Whitstable has always been described as a 'town that turned its back on the sea'. It was never a seaside resort though tourism was developed latterly and, like Herne Bay, there are a number of pre-planning-law caravan parks on the outskirts of the town. The beach is relatively small. There were also some large hotels located at Tankerton, a suburb on the outskirts of Whitstable that offers safe bathing.

Regeneration issues

The need for regeneration in Whitstable arose because of a loss of traditional industries of which tourism comprised only one part. Tourism was a contributor to, rather than the main cause of, decline in Whitstable.

The key challenge for Whitstable was how to capitalize on its local distinctiveness and heritage potential. A study carried out in 1986 recommended a new identity for Whitstable based around its main asset, heritage, in particular the oyster industry. The report also recommended creating opportunities for maritime leisure pursuits. These three strands became the focus for regeneration.

Despite economic difficulties Whitstable benefited from an active local community willing to become involved in local partnerships and had a number of talented entrepreneurs. This provided the local capacity to bring about change and to create a cohesive place-marketing strategy for Whitstable.

Marketing opportunities

The products with marketing potential were the physical and cultural heritage of the town, its oyster industry and the suitability of the coast for maritime leisure activities. The marketing opportunity related to each of these three products appeals to a similar visitor market profile.

The lifestyle trend towards an appreciation of fine cuisine and eating out and also for watersports tends to appeal predominantly to the ABC1 socio-economic groups. This group tends to have a high disposable income and, therefore, is more likely to take second holidays and short breaks. They also tend to have a greater interest in heritage. Whitstable presented a destination with the ability to offer a combination of complementary products in one place accessible by the large population catchment of London and the south east.

Additional but linked marketing opportunities arose from wider lifestyle trends. During the 1990s there was a move towards concern about health and lifestyle balance. This has led to two polarized approaches: a move towards self-development and to seek recuperation for short periods of time as a contrast to everyday living and a move to permanently change lifestyles, seeking out alternatives that are driven more by personal fulfilment than financial gain. The ABC1 socio-economic groups tend to be more able to make these lifestyle choices because of greater financial flexibility. Whitstable offers Londoners the opportunity to purchase second homes in a peaceful, historic town as a contrast to the Monday–Friday existence in London. At the same time the breathtaking sunsets above the Isle of Sheppey have been an attraction to artists for many years and a resident artist community has gradually evolved within the town.

Process of regeneration

A series of partnerships and initiatives were set up that attracted grant aid because of the town's heritage potential and distinctive local architecture. There are four key schemes.

- **Whitstable General Improvement Area (GIA)**
Using GIA funds and Environmental Health grants, Whitstable was able to improve an area of nineteenth-century housing immediately adjacent to the High Street. The scheme upgraded buildings, created town centre parking, pedestrianized some streets and created a children's play area and landscaping. This project was operational in the mid-1980s and ended when central government ceased the GIA scheme towards the end of the 1980s.
- **Whitstable Improvement Trust**
An ongoing scheme set up in 1984 as a public/private partnership. It tapped into funding from the Civic Trust and Kent County Council to carry out environmental and physical

improvement works, e.g. sensitive repair to historic buildings, design and installation of interpretation panels and street furniture and renovation of open spaces.

- **Whitstable Regeneration Partnership**
A public/private partnership set up in 1997 to develop a vision for the town using European, Lottery and SRB (Single Regeneration Budget) funding to deliver projects. The partnership comprises many of the smaller companies and organizations. A Whitstable Worker has been employed to help develop the artistic and maritime strengths of Whitstable. A national lottery grant was awarded in 2000 to develop an arts centre in the town.

- **Whitstable Artists Cooperative**
An ongoing partnership of resident artists set up in the mid-1980s, supported by South East Arts, to develop and promote public art in Whitstable.

Each initiative has received funding or support from Canterbury City Council.

Two local entrepreneurs have been central to the regeneration process. The owner of the Royal Native Oyster Stores, who also owns several local pubs, a hotel and a builder's merchants, recognized the potential to promote seafood and create a gourmet reputation for the town as a major business opportunity. Successful promotion of the Whitstable oyster has made the town a popular day-visitor destination for Londoners, principally to buy fresh shellfish. An annual Oyster Festival creates a promotional opportunity for the town and reinforces key marketing messages. The conversion of the original Oyster Stores into a restaurant and avant-garde cinema complemented the gourmet and artistic reputation the town was already developing. This, and its proximity to London, has resulted in Whitstable becoming a fashionable place for London's young professionals to visit and to purchase and restore local cottages as second homes. These changes have been fundamental to the overall success of the regeneration, but they have been the focus for some tensions in the town as some residents express concern about way the town is adjusting to the needs of incoming residents and visitors (illustrating the continuing relevance of the 'irridex' model described by Doxey, 1975).

A second entrepreneur has developed several business parks and starter units and a hotel alongside the A299 Thanet Way. These developments have considerably contributed to creating new jobs and economic activity in the town and immediate area.

Achievements

Recent changes have respected the historic sense of place and encouraged change that maintains a strong individuality. The town now has a new and highly visible identity as an artists' quarter and as a day-visit destination for heritage (and shellfish!) seekers.

The use of attractive blue and white street furniture, interpretation and street art has created a low-key upgrade to the seafront in keeping with the scale and artist-quarter atmosphere of the town. The conversion of the historic Oyster Court on the seafront into a gourmet seafood restaurant reinforces authenticity and builds on the unique oyster heritage of Whitstable.

The proposed arts centre in the town centre will create a link with waterfront activity. The town centre has gradually witnessed a change in shop use with a move from traditional independent food and household retailing towards special-interest independent retailers. This change reflects the interests of the artist community and the increase in visitors, though Whitstable like Herne Bay still retains a tradition of small independent general-purpose shops.

Similarities and differences between the towns

In both Herne Bay and Whitstable regeneration is a response to the problems of economic and environmental decline that have characterized many British resorts since the 1960s. However, behind this shared challenge there are fundamental differences between their respective starting points and present positions. The processes and inputs that have been necessary to achieve the present level of regeneration have both similarities and differences.

As has been shown above, Herne Bay and Whitstable are distinctly different towns, each with its own identity and sense of place. Herne Bay is a seaside resort with a history of tourism, but little distinctive heritage on which to hang regeneration. A key part of the regeneration strategy has been to make the best of what it has by restoring the traditional resort identity and reinvigorating the sense of place as a friendly, happy-go-lucky town for relaxing by the sea. Whitstable, on the other hand, is a historic fishing town that benefits from a strong heritage potential and attractive physical infrastructure. It selected tourism as one element in its regeneration strategy, thereby developing a new, hybrid resort identity and a sense of place embodying twentieth-century lifestyle values with a vernacular setting. In effect Herne Bay has returned to its roots while Whitstable has reinvented itself. However, in both cases identity, sense of place and local distinctiveness have steered the regeneration, guiding action towards locally appropriate solutions that ensure integrity is maintained and strengthened.

A fundamental difference between the process of regeneration in the two towns is the way change has been catalysed and progressed. The erosion of the sea wall at Herne Bay presented an opportunity to access significant funding to achieve a big-bang approach to regeneration. Without the impetus provided by that development it is arguable that the regeneration would not have happened, or at best would have happened in a less successful, piecemeal way. However, Whitstable has used an incremental approach, smaller-scale funding opportunities and local ideas and enthusiasm, an approach that reflects partly necessity and partly the culture of the town.

Public sector support from central Government and the County and District Councils has been an important catalyst for action in both towns. Support has come in kind, but also crucially in hard cash, including Lottery, European and Single Regeneration Budget funding. This involvement has been more direct in Herne Bay than in Whitstable where several intermediary agencies, e.g. the Whitstable Improvement Trust, have played a significant role. However, in both cases partnerships have been important. This has included vital endorsement and support from the local community, both by individuals and the voluntary sector. The business community has also been part of the partnership approach, though not particularly strongly engaged with the public sector. In Whitstable the role of two local entrepreneurs has been important, a level of personal involvement that has not been seen in Herne Bay. In summary, a key difference between the towns is that local community and private sector support has been a driver in Whitstable, while local community input has taken a more supportive role in a largely public-sector driven approach in Herne Bay.

Lessons of success

The regeneration problems faced by seaside resorts are not unique. Resorts share many issues faced by other types of towns and cities that have experienced a decline in traditional industries: these places show there is no point in trying to rely on the old industries, new directions have to be sought. The same applies to resorts that cannot afford to look only at tourism solutions to their problems. Given tourism trends in Britain, e.g. the move away from long holidays to short breaks and the increase of day trips, realistically tourism is likely to be only part of the solution.

An important starting point to developing a regeneration strategy is to understand the history of the resort and the dynamics of how and why it came to need regeneration. This involves understanding local culture and attitudes as much as knowing what economic and physical changes have taken place. The likelihood of successful regeneration is increased enormously by tapping into and promoting a strong identity and a unique sense of place. Herne Bay and Whitstable have avoided standard, off-the-shelf solutions or the development of inappropriate major new attractions. Both towns discovered that having the right mix of products is vital to achieving economically sustainable development. And by developing distinctive products they complement each other, rather than competing, despite their nearness. This fits well with the process described by Gordon and Goodall (1993).

Approaches in Herne Bay and Whitstable have respected the history of each town but have not been afraid to move on and introduce new ideas. Whitstable has been particularly successful in recognizing broader social and cultural trends and using them to good effect. The revitalization of the oyster industry and the development of arts and crafts there illustrate how new activities can be developed, activities that are industries in their own right, but are also complementary to tourism. Moreover, seaside regeneration should take a holistic approach embracing the whole town, not just the seafront, and Whitstable has been particularly successful in taking a town-wide approach. It has also tried to adjust sensitively to community tensions produced by change.

Success is also about process as well as projects. In Herne Bay a move from a TCM-led approach to physical regeneration of the seafront illustrates a confidence to change direction when required and a determination to deliver success. Both towns have shown the benefits of widespread community engagement and the strengths of different types of partnership. This has been important to the success of the resort regeneration and has the added advantage of building community capacity, which can then be used to tackle other issues on a broader front. This is significant for the future: whilst both towns have made significant progress, they are not yet out of intensive care. Recently, both towns have jointly received £1 million from the UK Single Regeneration Budget to continue the regeneration by focusing on community development in their two most deprived town centre electoral wards. It is important to recognize the long timescale and commitment needed to produce and maintain results.

Bibliography

Butler, R. W. (1980) 'The concept of a tourism area cycle of evolution: implications for the management of resources', *The Canadian Geographer* 24, 5–12.

Doxey, G. V. (1975) 'A causation theory of visitor-resident irritants, methodology and research inferences'. The Impact of Tourism, sixth annual conference. *Proceedings of the Travel Research Association, San Diego*, 195–98.

Gordon, I and Goodall, B (1993) 'Resort cycles and development processes', *Built Environment* 1 (18), 41–56.

Haider, D. and Rein, I. (1993) *Marketing Places*. New York: Free press.

Newman, J. (1969) *The Buildings of England*, ed. Nikolaus Pevsner, *North East and East Kent*. London: Penguin.

Shaw, G. and Williams, A. (1997) *The Rise and Fall of British Coastal Resorts*. London: Pinter.

Urry, J. (1995) *Consuming Places*. London: Routledge.

Walton, J. K. (1997) 'The seaside resorts of England and Wales 1900–1950, growth, diffusion and the experience of new forms of coastal tourism', in Shaw, G. and Williams, A. *The Rise and Fall of British Coastal Resorts*. London: Pinter.

L Investigating Consumer Choice in the E-Commerce Era: A Travel and Tourism Perspective

Ronnie Ballantyne

Introduction

The number of households with access to personal computers in the United Kingdom (UK) has risen dramatically in recent years. There are now approximately 11 million people within the UK using the Internet from their home. Essentially, advances in microchip mainframe technology have redefined the role and boundaries of the personal computer (PC). Previously the PC was used as a word processor and spreadsheet calculator, today the PC is viewed as a portal to the World Wide Web (WWW or Web) offering consumers access to information and more importantly from a marketing perspective an alternative method to traditional shopping channels.

Nevertheless, it is only very recently that the WWW has become user friendly via the introduction of browsers (or search engines) such as Netscape. Originally the Web was restricted to those who were computer literate, now thanks to browsers this barrier to use has been markedly reduced and as a consequence Internet shopping now offers a genuine alternative to more traditional methods. In today's market both computer novices and experts can now search the World Wide Web with relative ease.

The travel market – on line

The London Business School forecast that by 2009 some 60 per cent of all transactions with banks, travel agents and airlines will be online. If we consider the European online travel market as a whole, it is projected that this market will grow from $2.9 billion in 2000 to $10.9 billion in 2002. This accelerated projected growth can be attributed to many factors. Predominantly the improvement of bill-paying mechanisms and increased consumer confidence as security measures and privacy over payments has instilled more trust in Internet shopping in general. In terms of market share within the European online travel market the Airline websites and tour operators commanded 28 and 27 per cent of market share respectively. Online travel agencies followed closely controlling 26 per cent; railways 9 per cent; hotels 7 per cent; and car rental companies 3 per cent.

Air travel accounted for $5 billion of a total of $7 billion spent on the Internet in 1999, out-grossing all other products combined. Moreover, at present in America only 4 per cent of flight reservations are made online, in Europe it is approaching 1 per cent. Clearly the air-travel market offers much potential for Internet trade, nevertheless we must consider why growth in this sector is so small. The rationale for this appears to be that at present air travellers are predominately utilizing the Internet to browse for information before reverting back to more traditional methods when booking. Elements such as recommendation, trust, knowledge, advice and personal care provided by travel agents are clearly still very much valued by consumers.

Moreover, it must be noted that the majority of Internet flight sales can be attributed to simple 'point-to-point' flights, e.g. Glasgow–London–Glasgow. Low-cost airlines such as Easyjet and Ryanair, which predominantly provide this type of product attribute 90 per cent of ticket sales online (Cyberatlas, 2001). Consumers then appear confident when booking this type of flight but are reluctant when it comes to more complex itineraries – e.g. what happens if they make a mistake when entering details? Furthermore, when it comes to point-to-point flights the audience is most likely looking for cheap last minute deals. In contrast when the consumer has a complicated itinerary it is likely that they are prepared to spend a considerable amount of money and wish to benefit from the advice and the security provided by using a traditional travel agent. In effect someone else takes on the responsibility, and the perceived risk in the purchase decision is reduced. In addition consumers are likely to want the personal touch and the assurance that they are being provided with all possible options.

The nature of the consumer purchase decision

Two main factors are redefining the nature of the Consumer Purchase Decision within travel and tourism: the World Wide Web and increased product choice

The number of travel and tourism brands available has proliferated. This coupled with increasingly fierce competition and recent advances in Internet technology and e-commerce has presented consumers with a very daunting and sometimes complicated task: *Choice*. Within the travel and tourism marketplace consumers are now faced with a multitude of product offerings. Essentially consumers now face the phenomenon of *overchoice* with a vast array of brands competing for their attention and money, e.g. ATM, Thompson, Going Places; and within air travel the situation is similar, e.g. Go, Easyjet, Ryanair. The ability then to understand and predict choice is one of the most challenging areas within marketing and can be seen as the cornerstone for the successful implementation of the marketing philosophy.

E-commerce offers many potential benefits for both business and consumer. From the business perspective the potential audience is huge, offering increased and enhanced product visibility. Moreover there is economic benefit as costs are lowered over business supply and demand chains. Specifically, large savings can be made on marketing and distribution costs: for example, through utilizing computerized reservation systems the cost of printing and sending out documents is removed. Furthermore, opportunity exists to redefine the very nature of business/client relations and to explore other business directions at limited cost to the provider. Companies can learn more about customers and build up a profile of travel needs and preferences so they can package offers tailored to their individual need. This will lead ultimately to the development of HiTech Management Information Systems.

We must also remember that the Web is unlike other traditional marketing channels. Unlike traditional sources of communication such as print or television advertising where communication is one way, i.e. from the business to the consumer, the Web allows for high levels of *interactivity*, i.e. two way communication between the business and the consumer in real time. Through this interactivity consumers are then placed in a better position to identify and compare choice alternatives and hopefully this will ultimately lead to greater satisfaction on the part of the consumers as they are able to identify those brands which best suit their needs and wants.

From the consumer's perspective, the Web offers a vehicle on which to undertake detailed information searches on competing brands, leading to brand evaluation and, ultimately, to online shopping. Moreover, there is an economic incentive in terms of lower prices for the consumer. Other attractions include convenience, wider choice, home delivery and access to more information. Furthermore, the arrival of the Internet is also timely in terms of today's social trends. Increasingly consumers are adopting varied lifestyles very different from the traditional 9–5 working week and as a consequence the Internet offers increased convenience.

From one perspective, then, e-commerce potentially offers increased convenience for the consumer. However, in contrast, it can be argued that in reality e-commerce may not make shopping easier for consumers, in fact it may complicate the issue even more, adding to the *overchoice* phenomenon. As cited previously the present diversity of product choices is simply staggering and is set to increase. Consumers face a bewildering array of product options.

From a marketing point of view, it is then paramount to gain an understanding of consumers' decision-making processes within e-commerce. From this understanding marketers are in a better position to develop and maintain appropriate marketing mix strategies. Specifically, this understanding will lead to the design of better websites and lay the foundations for building better relationships with customers.

Understanding consumer decision-making

Traditionally after consumers recognize a need or desire for a particular product they will actively seek out information to identify potential routes to satisfy their need or desire. Consumers will firstly exhaust all decision-relevant information which is held in memory, e.g. which airline did I use the last time? If they feel that they need more decision-relevant information they will source it from the external environment, e.g. advertising, recommendation of others or, indeed, the Internet. Having identified several different products which they feel will satisfy their needs, consumers will then evaluate between these products to identify their preferred brand, leading to choice. Consumers will ultimately undertake a post-purchase evaluation in which they evaluate whether or not the brand fell below, lived up to or even surpassed their expectations. This information is then retained for future decision-making, e.g. a brand which surpassed the consumer's expectations is very likely to be considered for purchase again in the future.

The above process is often referred as the IP or Information Processing model and is illustrated in Figure L.1.

Although the above model seems logical and has found much support from both academics and practitioners alike, there are limitations, for example it does

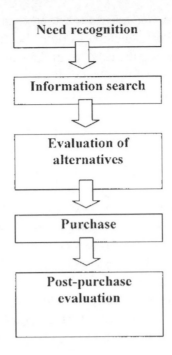

Figure L.1 Model of consumer decision-making
(Adapted from Engel, Blackwell and Miniard, 1993)

not allow for the current phenomenon of overchoice and the possibilities of information overload. It is often implicitly assumed that the more information consumers are presented with the *better* purchase decision they will make. In reality, as several empirical studies have proved, this is not the case; yes, consumers will perform better up to a point when more information is presented to them but each consumer will have a threshold, once this threshold is surpassed consumers become confused and will not make better choices (Miller, 1956).

In response to this, more recent research on consumer choice suggests that, in order to cope with this phenomenon of *overchoice* and potential information overload, consumers adopt screening or phased decision rules to simplify their decision-making whilst minimizing cognitive effort. Initially consumers will *Group* or *Chunk* brands together to simplify the decision-making process. In terms of process it is firstly hypothesized that consumers adopt phasing or screening strategies via the use of simple decision rules or heuristics to eliminate 'flawed' options thus creating a downsized set of brands normally referred to as the *Consideration Set* (the subset of brands from which choice is made, normally comprising three to six brands). Secondly, consumers identify a focal or preferred brand from the *consideration set* using more complex and elaborate decision-making strategies (e.g. see Gensch, 1987; Nedungadi 1990; Shocker et al. 1991). Furthermore, consumer motivation combined with resources such as time and cognitive processing ability may be limited in the real purchase situation thus highlighting the need for the consumer to simplify their decision-making processes and again providing further support to suggest that this is how consumer choice takes place in reality.

As suggested above, consumers will create a downsized choice set restricting their 'evaluation process' to those brands within the reduced set thus lessening cognitive effort. Several varying definitions of the consideration set currently exist, e.g. brands that a consumer will consider buying in the near future (Roberts and Lattin, 1991) or the subset of brands that are scrutinized carefully on a particular choice occasion (Kardes et al., 1993). Although several definitions exist a core element resides in each: the notion that the consideration set consists of *the relevant subset of brands from which ultimate choice is made* (Brown and Wilt, 1992).

The marketing implications are clear. Firstly brands must gain entry into the consumers consideration set, secondly they must become the preferred alternative and finally brands must have enduring appeal to maintain consideration set membership over time.

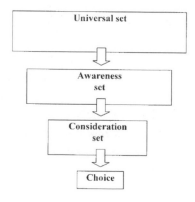

Figure L.2 A Common typology of consumer decision-making
(Adapted from Shocker et al. 1991)

This common typology of consumer decision-making then assumes a tiered multistage decision model, funnelling down the total number of brands leading to choice. Within the model the total number of brands available, the *universal set*, is firstly divided up into those brands which the consumer is aware of or has some knowledge of, the *awareness set*, consumers then further divide the awareness set into the *consideration set* and (non-consideration set). It is from the consideration set that the final choice is made. Traditionally consumers are thought to adopt utility maximization models to estimate choice. Utility maximization models are derived from basic economic theory. In simple terms it is postulated that the consumer uses all relevant information and then chooses the brand which they perceive to have the maximum brand utility. Brand utility can be described as the overall attractiveness of the brand (Gensch, 1987; Brown and Wilt, 1992; Bronnenberg and Vanhonacker, 1996; Roberts and Lattin, 1997).

Other recent research suggests that those brands which portray the correct image or personality are likely to become the preferred alternative from the consideration set. This is achieved by encouraging consumers to interpret the attributes of the brand with attributes with which the consumer aspires to (Sirgy, 1982; Doyle, 1990; Aaker and Fornier, 1995). This approach may indeed be closer to what happens in reality given the potential lack of consumer resources such as time, motivation and cognitive processing ability.

Furthermore, substantial empirical studies do support that this screening approach is utilized by consumers in many real-world brand-choice situations, indicating that this approach is not restricted to particular product types or choice scenarios. Given that the Internet is an obvious source of brand information and brand comparison for travel and tourism related products, gaining an understanding of how this process applies to Internet shoppers presents many practical benefits to marketing decision-makers when it comes to the design and delivery of marketing strategy.

Stewart Travel

Stewart Travel is a medium-sized independent travel agent located on the west coast of Scotland. The business was formed in 1972 by Mr William Stewart and has two outlets in prominent locations in Prestwick and Troon. The business offers a wide portfolio of products ranging from cruises, flights, package deals and business travel. For Stewart Travel the Internet is now viewed as a necessary component within the company's marketing mix. The Stewart Travel Internet site can be visited at www.Stewarttravel.co.uk.

Stewart Travel consider the Internet as an obvious source of brand information and brand comparison for tourism and travel related products. Having said this, the business recognizes that the web is only one potential source of product/brand information and consequently does not view the web in isolation but as an integral component of their overall marketing mix programme which must complement and reinforce the other marketing mix variables.

In effect Stewart Travel recognize that consumers will still utilize other information sources including their own personal experience or prior knowledge; recommendation from others and other traditional communicators such as print and television advertising as well as the Internet. Moreover, in many instances it may be these traditional sources of marketing communications which prompt a search on the Internet. Given this, Stewart Travel use many conventional forms of promotion including mailshots, telesales, local advertising, sponsorship and they also target local firms with a late-holiday information fact-sheet to generate interest and awareness and to prompt further information search by directing consumers to their Internet site.

The Stewart Travel Internet site immediately attempts to instil confidence in the consumer, citing the amount of experience which the company has and the attention which the company pays to the individual. For example on the home page it cites, 'What better to distinguish Stewart Travel from the rest than a reputation for attention to the individual?' Furthermore, membership of internationally recognized tourism authorities is also used to instil consumer confidence and trust. ABTA, IATA and ATOL brand logos are highly visible.

The Stewart Travel Internet site is an easy to use format, but interestingly at present the Stewart Travel site does not allow consumers to book online. Stewart Travel feel that at present only simple products such as point-to-point flights will be booked online and as the majority of Stewart Travel products are complex their Internet site is used primarily to generate awareness in the marketplace and also to encourage personal contact from the consumer.

Stewart Travel's perception of the products which it markets is also very interesting, this is clearly illusrated by the company copy line – 'Don't trust your dreams to just anyone.' This copy line appears on all communications and illustrates that the company perceives its product range as complex high-involvement products which are not necessarily suited to web trading. However, it must be noted that the interactivity element of the Internet is not overlooked, consumers can use 'Holiday Search' to specify desired destinations, departure and return dates and preferred airports to generate availability information.

Stewart Travel is also a member of the Advantage Consortium and Mr Stewart sits on the board of Directors. The consortium website can be visited at advantage4travel.com and consists of some 900 offices. Given the greater variety of products on offer from the Consortium, their web page is generating between between 2000 to 2500 hits per day and is attracting major advertising. The Advantage website offers the visitor the opportunity to identify the Consortium member physically nearest to the consumer by asking consumers to enter the first three letters of their postcode – on doing this consumers in the west coast of Scotland will be presented with a list of offices, including Stewart Travel. Consumers can then click on Stewart Travel and via a hyperlink visit the Stewart Travel Homepage.

Links to the Consortium is a wise strategy, Rowely (2000) suggests that consumer search on the Internet can be split into two main categories: directed search and browsing

In a directed search consumers will have in their possession some specific characteristic such as a brand name or key word or phrase, e.g. Stewart Travel, which they will enter into a search engine such as MSN, Yahoo, AOL or Lycos. The search engine will then retrieve what it thinks are appropriate hits. Alternatively consumers may simply wish to browse the net opting to surf between websites via hyperlinks. For example, many music interest sites have hyperlinks in place to amazon.com, the largest music retailer on the web.

In most cases it is realistic that consumer search will lie somewhere in between the two extremes of directed search and browsing. For example consumers may start with a broad area of interest, e.g. a travel destination, and refine their search strategy and information needs during the search process, e.g. identifying a specific airline to take them to their desired destination. Alternatively the consumer may indeed begin with a specific targeted objective which can be entered into a search engine, but via exposure to different information they may decide to visit alternative sites that were not previously considered. In effect, then, the more links which Stewart Travel can generate the more likely it is that this will promote brand awareness and ultimately brand consideration leading to choice.

Conclusion

It is evident that Internet trade offers many business opportunities in the travel and tourism market. Forecasts for Internet trade are very encouraging in this sector. However, the reality at present is somewhat different, only simple point-to-point business appears to be prospering – consumers with more complex needs are predominantly not booking online.

Stewart Travel believe that the majority of consumers will utilize the Internet and their website for the purposes of information search and are reluctant to invest more capital at present. Ultimately, through the Internet and more traditional marketing channels, Stewart Travel are seeking firstly, to gain entry into consumers' consideration set, secondly, they are striving to become the preferred alternative and, thirdly, their brand must have enduring appeal to maintain consideration set membership over time.

Specifically the Internet site, then, is used to generate awareness for the business and to promote further investigation on the part of the consumer, prompting telephone enquiries or personal visits, in effect moving Stewart

Travel from the consumers' awareness set to their consideration set. Stewart Travel then use their 'personal touch' and attention to detail to ensure that they become the consumers preferred alternative from the consideration set. However, it must be stressed that the company does not discount the possibility that consumers may wish to purchase more complex products online in the future. Stewart Travel pursues a very proactive approach and is constantly monitoring developments in technology and consumer-buyer behaviour within the travel and tourism market. The company realizes that there is no 'end point' and that technology, like consumers, will evolve.

Finally, as the marketplace becomes increasingly crowded with competing brands and organizations, there may be increased reliance on phased decision-making strategies as consumers become less likely to search out more and more information. As a consequence consumers may place more reliance on tried-and-tested brand names such as Stewart Travel, thus simplifying their decision-making strategies.

Acknowledgements

The author wishes to express his gratitude to Mr William Stewart, founder and Managing Director of Stewart Travel, for providing important information about the company. Also special thanks to Alistair Geddes, Managing Director of Travel Transform (www.traveltransform.com) for his useful insights into e-commerce within the travel and tourism sector and industry contacts. I would also like to express my thanks to Fiona Carswell of SAC who provided important data and background material which helped to shape this case study.

Bibliography

Aaker, J. L. and Fournier, S. (1995) 'A brand as a character, a partner and a person: three perspectives on the question of brand personality', *Advances in Consumer Research* 22, 391–5.

Bronnenberg, B. I. and Vanhonacker, W. R. (1996) 'Limited choice sets, local price response and implied measures of price competition', *Journal of Marketing Research* 23, 163–73.

Brown, J. J. and Wilt, A. R. (1992) 'Consideration set measurement', *Journal of the Academy of Marketing Science* 20 (3), 235–43.

Doyle, P. (1990) 'Building successful brands: the strategic options', *Journal of Consumer Marketing* 7 (2), 5–20.

Engel, J. F., Blackwell, R. D. and Miniard, P. W. (1993) *Consumer Behaviour.* 7th edn. Florida: Dryden.

Gensch, D. H. (1987) 'A two-stage disaggregate attribute choice model', *Marketing Science,* 6 (3), 223–31.

Kardes, F. R., Kalyanaram, G., Chandrashekaran, M. and Dornoff, R. J. (1993) 'Brand retrieval, consideration set composition, consumer choice, and pioneering advantage', *Journal of Consumer Research* 20, 62–75.

Miller, G. (1956) 'The magical number 7 plus or minus 2. Some limits on our capacity for processing information', *Psychology Review* 63 (2), 181–94.

Nedungadi, P. (1990) 'Recall and consumer consideration sets: influencing choice without altering brand evaluations', *Journal of Consumer Research* 17, 263–76.

Roberts, J. H. and Lattin, J. M. (1991) 'Development and testing a model of consideration set composition', *Journal of Marketing Management* 28, 429–40.

— (1997) 'Consideration: review of research and prospects for future insights', *Journal of Marketing Research* 34, 406–10.

Rowely, J. (2000) 'Product search in e-shopping: a review and research propositions', *Journal of Consumer Marketing* 17 (1), 1–15.

Shocker, A. D., Ben-Akiva, M., Boccara, B. and Nedungadi, P. (1991) 'Consideration set influences on consumer decision making and choice: issues, models and suggestions', *Marketing Letters* 2, 181–97.

Sirgy, J. M. (1982) 'Self-concept in consumer behaviour: a critical review', *Journal of Consumer Research* 9, 287–300.

UK home internet use up by 3 Million. URL:htto//netimperative.com/ format [22 January 2001]

239

Index

242